W9-AGU-127

PUBLIC
MANAGEMENT
SYSTEMS

PUBLIC MANAGEMENT SYSTEMS

James L. Mercer
Edwin H. Koester

amacom

A Division of
American Management Associations

Library of Congress Cataloging in Publication Data

Mercer, James L
  Public management systems.

  Includes index.
  1. Public administration.   I. Koester, Edwin H.,
joint author.   II. Title.
JF1351.M39   350   77-16392
ISBN 0-8144-5456-9

© 1978 AMACOM
A division of American Management Associations, New
York.

Second Printing

TO
Carolyn, Gail, and Ora Lee

ACKNOWLEDGMENT

IN developing a book such as this where material has been drawn from many experiences and many sources, it is difficult to properly acknowledge or thank all those persons or organizations who contributed to our efforts. However, there are several individuals and organizations that stand out as having made significant contributions to our work.

The authors express particular appreciation to the following individuals and organizations for permission to use material previously published by them: Mark Keane, Donald Borut, and Rosemary Weise of the International City Management Association; Porter W. Homer, Ronald J. Philips, and Robert Havlick of Public Technology, Inc.; William Wetmore and Robert Crawford of the National Science Foundation; Robert Funk of the Municipal Finance Officer's Association; William Foster, Gary Lopenzina, and Gary Chamberlin of The American City and County; Alan Beals of the National League of Cities; Harry Hatry and Donald Fisk of The Urban Institute; Richard Morris of IBM; Leigh Wilson and Ben Taylor of the North Carolina League of Municipalities; The American Psychological Association; The National Commission on Productivity and Quality of Working Life; Elmer B. Statts, Comptroller General of the United States; Donald McIntyre, City Manager, Pasadena, California; The International Personnel Management Association; Michael Babunakis, City of San Diego, California

Urban Observatory; Office of Management Services, State of California; Richard Hackathorn, The Wharton School, University of Pennsylvania; Urban and Regional Information Systems Association; McGraw-Hill Book Company, Inc.; Fortune; Orville Powell, City Manager, Winston-Salem, North Carolina; Robert Hopson, Public Works Director, Charlotte, North Carolina; John E. Stacey, Jr., Midwest Research Institute; U.S. National Aeronautics and Space Administration; Thomas W. Bradshaw, Jr., Secretary of Transportation, State of North Carolina; Public Building Service, U.S. General Services Administration; U.S. Department of Defense; Sandy Johnson, Gordon Milliken and Edward J. Morrison, Denver Research Institute; Michael Lorz and Kazuhiko Kawamura, Battelle Memorial Institute; Bernie Hillenbrand, National Association of Counties; The Dartnell Corporation; Ben Axel, Sylvax Chemical Corporation; U.S. Department of Housing and Urban Development; The Twenty-Seven Urban Technology System Technology Agents; Edward Wright, City of San Diego, California; Richard Dietz and Gerald Miller, Technology Action Center, City of San Diego, California; U.S. Environmental Protection Agency; William H. Carper, City Manager (retired), Raleigh, North Carolina; Sandy and Robert Bauer, Rensis Likert Associates; Muncipal South; Myron Weiner, University of Connecticut; Business Horizons; Dewitt Braud and Donna Irvin, State of Louisiana; Law and Order Magazine; and the League of California Cities.

Particular appreciation is expressed to Dr. William Block, Chairman, Department of Politics, North Carolina State University, and his faculty for providing a forum to test some of the ideas presented in this book. Most sincere appreciation and thanks are also expressed to Dr. Rensis Likert, Chairman of the Board of Rensis Likert Associates and retired Director of the Institute for Social Research at the University of Michigan for his encouragement and very helpful suggestions.

Acknowledgments are also due to Grace Donehower, Bob Coe, Pop Kelly, and many others who helped us along the way.

James L. Mercer
Edwin H. Koester

CONTENTS

1

Introduction

THIS book is the outgrowth of numerous discussions the authors have had with practitioners, educators, association managers, and students in various public sector organizations. These discussions have shown a clear need for a book that describes the development and implementation of widely applicable operational management systems and procedures in a variety of public sector organizations. The purpose of this book, then, is to provide practicing public administrators with an operational management systems handbook. In addition, it can also be used by professors and students of public administration as classroom or outside reading material, research material, and case study material. This will help better prepare students for practical applications once they are employed in the public sector.

Many of the management systems and procedures in use by well-managed private sector organizations, particularly those in the aerospace and defense industries, have not been transferred or diffused to public sector organizations, particularly state and local governments. There appear to be many reasons for this, not the least of which is the absence of the profit motive in the public sector. Other reasons concern the fact that many private sector systems are proprietary in nature, and it is therefore difficult to obtain enough detail about them to permit transfer. Also, until recently, public sector managers have not been in a position to implement innovative approaches without incurring public criticism. Accordingly, the adding of sophisticated staff familiar with new technology has been subject to public suspicion.

Most public administrators want to perform well and do a good job, but many of them do not know how a better system can simplify routine work, provide better information for decision making, provide for alternatives through cost-benefit analysis, and, finally, provide a better and more productive approach to problem solving. Neither their training nor their experience has provided them with the proper tools. Students coming directly out of college into public sector positions do not know how to go about developing the management systems needed in their jobs. In the opinion of many practitioners, students of public administration should be taught some concepts of management systems approaches in college, possibly as a "finishing" course to their public administration terminal degree.

WHY USE MANAGEMENT SYSTEMS?

Why should there be a shift toward the utilization of more management systems and procedural approaches now? One very compelling reason exists: Most public sector organizations are supported by citizens through taxes or fees, and the ability to raise funds from these sources in ever-increasing amounts is diminishing. The average citizen is growing weary of paying more and more and still more in support of services from governmental units. Since the populace as a whole is becoming better educated and is demanding a more active role in public sector organizations through city councils, citizen advisory groups, boards of directors, and the like, people are demanding that their tax and revenue dollars be spent more wisely and more productively.

How can this be accomplished? One approach uses a more systematic handling of public sector activities through better management systems. Such systems, if properly developed and implemented, usually lead to more efficient and productive use of scarce resources and eventually to more effective provision of services to the stockholders of the community, the citizens. Better management systems also provide appointed and elected officials with the information they need to effectively manage, make policy, and make day-to-day operational decisions in today's complex public organizations.

It should also be pointed out that most management systems need not be particularly sophisticated in early applications. It has been said by many who are familiar with public sector organizations that the management systems and technologies of the 1940s can often meet their needs and solve their problems.

The purpose of this book is to try to meet some of these needs at both educational and practical levels. The book relies heavily on practical applications, particularly within local government. However, many of the management systems and procedures described in the book are certainly applicable, with slight modifications, to other public sector organizations, be they at the local, regional, state, national, association, or authority level.

WHAT THIS BOOK INCLUDES

Much of the background for the book is drawn from the authors' private sector experiences with Bell Telephone, General Dynamics Corporation, Litton Industries, Cal Tech's Jet Propulsion Laboratory, and the U.S. Navy, and from their public sector experiences in the cities of Raleigh, North Carolina, and Pasadena, California, and with Public Technology, Inc., the research and development arm of state and local governments. Parts of the book were originally published as articles and reports by one of the authors. Others were developed to be used at a graduate seminar in management systems that one of the authors taught as an integral part of the Master of Public Affairs Program at North Carolina State University. Still others stem from published and unpublished work and research performed by both authors.

Chapter 2, "Public Management Systems and the Public Interest," defines the public interest as it relates to public management systems. The role of the systems approach in identifying and prioritizing public needs is discussed. The chapter examines what the essential ingredients of an optimum public system are, what elements go into an analysis of the needs of public service organizations, and what role citizens may play in helping set priorities.

Chapter 3, "The Evaluation Process in Public Management," discusses how to evaluate public programs and shows how the public evaluation process is an integral part of effective, rational public management.

Chapter 4 is devoted to rational program management in public sector organizations. This chapter discusses the traditional functions of a manager, the concept of rational management, and its behavioral aspects. The chapter concludes with a discussion of management style.

Public budgeting systems is the topic of Chapter 5. After a brief review of the history of public budgeting, most of the major public budgeting systems are described. A strong recommendation is made for adoption of program budgeting as the most effective approach, wherever possible, in organizations of the public sector.

Chapter 6 is devoted to a case study of the rationale for and implementation of a five-year operating budgeting system in a typical local government.

Management information systems is the subject of Chapter 7. This chapter presents some policy-oriented recommendations concerning the ways in which public sector organizations should utilize technology for the management of information.

The purpose of Chapter 8 is to provide a basis for implementing management systems in a typical public sector organization. Emphasis is on techniques for developing and implementing written procedural systems. A spin-off benefit that usually results from this approach is a careful analysis of operational methods and procedures that in turn results in more efficient and effective day-to-day operations.

Chapter 9 describes in detail an approach to programming and controlling capital improvements in a public sector organization. It also describes several possible visual display management control rooms for controlling and tracking physical and financial progress of various capital-improvement projects. Chapter 10 describes a systematic approach to the financing of capital improvements through bond funding. This chapter was developed from "Vote for Your Future: The Anatomy of a Successful Capital Improvements Bond Campaign," by Thomas W. Bradshaw, Jr. and James L. Mercer, in *Nation's Cities,* August 1972.

Chapter 11 discusses construction management and offers suggestions to systematically improve public contracts through incentives. Much of the material in this chapter draws on a report prepared by Public Technology, Inc., for the Office of Special Studies and Programs, Washington, D.C., "Using Construction Management for Public and Institutional Facilities," February 1976.

Chapter 12 is devoted to a discussion of word processing systems, the latest automated approach to typing and processing internal and external communications.

Chapter 13 discusses several management systems for improving day-to-day public sector operations, and Chapter 14 discusses a systematic approach to the development and conduct of a local government orientation program for citizens.

Chapter 15 describes several techniques for gaining internal acceptance of management systems, and Chapter 16 is devoted to a discussion of management systems approaches that increase the efficiency and effectiveness of delivering future public services. This last chapter also describes the concept of the Urban Technology System sponsored by the National Science Foundation and its possible spin-off benefits to public sector organizations.

2

Public Management Systems and the Public Interest

IDEALLY, all public service activities operate solely for the public, or in the "public interest." How many times have we heard this platitude uttered by the makers of public policy? However, have those policy makers developed a tight, structured, workable definition for the "public interest"? Very few definitions exist, and those that do are scarcely in agreement. Yet the very reason for the existence of government in our society is to provide security and services in the public interest.

This dilemma should come as no surprise to the student of government. What is one man's security is a restriction on another man's freedom; what is a service to one is a waste to another. Even a perfectly functioning, rational, totally objective public official would be confronted with the impossibility of acting in every citizen's "interest," 100 percent.

To further complicate the situation, public officials, not unlike the rest of us, are motivated, at least in part, by their own self-interests. It is unrealistic to expect public officials to be entirely altruistic.

COMPETING or CONFLICTING INTERESTS and NEEDS

It may be said the people have certain interests and needs or wants that they expect, sometimes demand, their governmental organizations to fulfill. These may be classified as needs perceived by the public. Often differing needs compete for limited, sometimes scarce, resources. Occasionally, the interests of one group do not coincide with the interests of another group. For example, Southern California is generally arid. Its citizens need water for health and other reasons. Northern California usually has an excess of water. The solution to Southern California's problem is to dam the northern rivers, build an aqueduct system, and pipe excess water from the north to the south. In this example, the north gives resources (dollars, land, etc.) with no direct obvious benefit to itself.

Another group of needs may not be perceived by the public. Dangers to the environment or to health often are not known by the general public. In those instances where experts or specialists define a danger, public officials expend public resources to protect that public or segment thereof. Toward the end of this chapter, we discuss "needs analysis" in some depth.

What is required by units of government is a mechanism or process by which priorities may be assigned to defined needs in order of their importance to the public. This recognition sets the stage for the introduction of the systems approach to managing public affairs in the public interest.

The UNIVERSE of SYSTEMS

Webster defines system as "A set or arrangement of things so related or connected as to form a unity or organic whole." In practical dynamic terms, we may state a working definition as *The interaction of a set of forces that produces a distinguishable result.* There are many different kinds of systems. Examples are:

Natural systems—weather, solar, river, digestive.
Technological systems—computer, flight, missile, automotive.
Social systems—education, health care, economic, political.
Logical systems—language, number, management.

Systems are hierarchical: Each is made up of smaller systems, and each forms a part of a larger system. Conceptually, systems are infinite, but because most of us behave and think in finite terms, we assign a beginning and an end to the particular system that we are concerned with at a particular time.

PUBLIC MANAGEMENT SYSTEMS

Public management systems are comprised of sets of public management actions that interact to form distinguishable effects on the community or populace they serve. These are always "open" systems since corrections to these systems must be effected by decisions made outside the systems, almost invariably human decisions. For instance, results are often interpreted differently by various public interest groups, thereby making meaningful measurement of results difficult. Unique human decisions are often made to "correct" the system so that results can satisfy competing or conflicting interests. A hypothetical—but highly unlikely— example of such an "open" system follows:

In the City of Delight, the incidence of residential burglary over the past year had increased 200 percent. The police department (a public organization responsible for management of certain public safety systems) instituted a "system" for reducing the number of burglaries. This was called the Burglary Abatement Detail (BAD). A specially selected group of police officers were assigned to interrogate all "suspicious-looking" citizens in the residential areas with the highest burglary rates. The "system results" were: (1) greatly reduced number of burglaries and (2) greatly increased number of citizen complaints of police harassment. Several system "corrections" were called for by citizens' groups. One correction was the issuance of citizens' identity cards, which, when visibly displayed on the person, reduced the chance of unnecessary inter-rogation.

In this example, the system results were not accurately predicted, and given the results, corrective decisions were made outside the BAD system—an "open" system.

Public management systems are "open" for one or more of the following reasons:

■ System objectives often are not clear or are not complete. This means that system results can be interpreted differently by affected groups of citizens.

- Often it is difficult to agree on meaningful measures of system results.
- System corrections cannot usually be determined very much in advance.

Unfavorable results require individual interpretation outside the system and, often, a unique correction or set of corrections. If the system variables are complex and insufficient time and effort have been spent analyzing them and their ramifications, results are even more unpredictable.

SYSTEMS ANALYSIS and PUBLIC SYSTEMS

Systems analysis is the process of determining the problems associated with a system and its components with the ultimate objective of improving the entire system.

The optimum public system is one in which the number of decisions made outside the system to correct it and to achieve desired results are absolutely minimal. This leads to certain basic observations and conclusions regarding what is necessary to achieve an "optimum" public system. We can best present these conclusions in five steps:

1. The public needs ("interests") must be known and documented on a continuing basis. Because public needs change repeatedly, the needs-assessment process must be dynamic and continuous. Conflicting interests must be known, and the best "compromise" interest must be determined. On a given issue of concern, there are nearly always conflicting public viewpoints about how to resolve that issue. The job of the public policy makers is to ascertain the "optimum" interest—that is, what represents the largest number of individual interests with minimum negative effect on minority interests.

2. Objectives must be developed that, when achieved, can satisfy given needs or interests.* Each objective does, or should, contain within it a hypothetical assumption regarding outcome.

---

*An *objective,* as defined in this book, is a specific, quantitative statement that describes what is to be achieved, by what resources, and within what time frame. A *goal* is defined as a broad, general statement that reflects the end result or condition that, when attained, satisfies a major public need.

Example: The stated objective is to increase the number of police cars on patrol in the City of Delight from 20 to 30, thereby achieving a reduction in the incidence of crimes against persons. Hypothetically stated, if time on patrol is increased, the incidence of crime will decrease.

It can readily be seen that other very different actions can be taken to accomplish the same goal—a reduction in the incidence of crime. At this stage, however, consider as many different actions that hypothetically achieve the desired result as possible.

3. Evaluate the possible alternative courses of action. This should include an investigation of feasibility, risks (or possible negative side effects), and cost (the complete and total cost) of each alternative. Then, the "best" course(s) of action (plan of action) should be selected for implementation.

4. Develop a complete set of measures of performance for each objective, and implement a process for making and using these measures to help evaluate results.

5. Evaluate results during the implementation of the plan of action. Make changes to the plan of action and document changes that result.

There are many different ways to describe the workings of a good public system. However it is done, the description must anticipate how actions external to the system affect it and how they will be dealt with. In the typical example that follows, these considerations have been integrated.

1.   Identification of a Need

In a densely populated region of a large urban county in a western state, the fetal and infant death rates in 1971 were found to be alarmingly high in comparison with county, state, and national rates for the same period. The following demographic data were submitted for 1971: the reported childbearing-age population (females, age 15–45) was 160,000 of a total population of 770,000; 42.3 percent of the population was between the ages of 15 and 24; the median age was 27 years, $2\frac{1}{2}$ years younger than that reported for the county as a whole; median family income was $7,754 as against $10,970 for the county; and ethnic composition was 58 percent white, 37 percent black, 5 percent other.

One clear need was a reduction in the fetal and infant death rates to bring them down to at least the national average.

But let us look at this "need" in relation to the "public interest." By and large, the majority of the total county population was not affected by nor concerned about this need. The region's plight was brought to the attention of the supervisor representing the region (one of five public policy makers on an elected board for the county). This supervisor had an analysis made of the impact of the target region's high mortality rates on the county as a whole. This analysis looked at direct and indirect effects.

From this needs analysis emerged an overall picture of the target region's general poor health status, of which the high mortality rates were only one element. Indirect effects, such as low educational achievement, high unemployment, high crime rates, and high incidence of acute health problems requiring expensive, in-hospital care, also existed, to mention only a few.

After widely publicizing the results of this needs analysis, what was an *unperceived need* from the standpoint of the county as a whole became a generally *perceived need*.

A policy decision was made by the five-member board of supervisors to fund a systems design effort, which would create a plan of maternal and infant health care for the target region to reduce the fetal and infant mortality and morbidity rates.

2. Program Goal and Objectives

Having analyzed and defined the need, the agreed-upon goal for the maternal and infant health care system was formally stated:

GOAL: *Reduce fetal and infant mortality and morbidity rates to the national average within five years.*

To arrive at an initial set of working objectives, representatives from various consumer groups, medical specialties and disciplines, administrative specialties (such as budget and accounting), and program management were assembled. This group conducted a brainstorming session to develop an extensive list of possible means to accomplish the goal. No idea was rejected or belittled during this session because it was known that often very worthwhile and pragmatic new approaches evolve from seemingly absurd ideas. At this time, the purpose of the group was to compile a "shopping list" of possible approaches. (Anonymity regarding suggested approaches can, and should, be maintained by providing group members with 3 in. × 5 in. blank index cards so that each idea or approach can be written on a separate card. Such anonymity

reduces group social pressure and allows for more expansive thinking and creative suggestions.)

Next, a team of three "experts" (representing consumers, health
care providers, and program managers/administrators) ordered and
grouped ideas by categories and subcategories. These were then
resubmitted to the entire group for discussions. Each idea was
then rejected, with reasons recorded, or approved. The members
of the group then ranked the approved ideas within several different
criteria, for example, cost to implement, time to implement, and
public acceptability.

The group results were then assigned to a program analysis
team, which further refined the ideas based on program constraints
(available funds, available workforce, evaluation potential). All the
foregoing activity resulted in a set of measurable objectives and
plans of action for meeting those objectives within the five-year
plan.

3. Assigning Priorities to Activities

Some activities or tasks can better accomplish a goal than others;
some activities require more resources in both manpower and dollars
than others; and the measurable end results of some activities
are more difficult to document than others. It is therefore essential
that activities be rated along at least these three dimensions:

Importance to accomplishment of end results or goal.
Cost of implementation in manpower and dollars.
Ease of measurement of activity results.

It sometimes happens that a supervisor "rates" an activity by
making a unilateral decision, or at the other extreme, a democratic
vote is taken. But such "rating" is no more than the expression
of personal preference. On the other hand, the committee or panel
approach to forecasting or estimating ratings introduces influences
or irrelevant material that obscure or distort the most pertinent
facts because the most vocal members tend to dominate. One
promising process for predicting and comparing activity outcomes
is the Delphi Technique.*

*Major credit for developing the Delphi Technique is given to Olaf Helmer
and Norman Dalkey of the Rand Corporation in 1968-1969.

The Delphi technique attempts to improve the panel or committee approach in arriving at a forecast or estimate by subjecting the views of individual experts to each other's criticism in ways that avoid face-to-face confrontation and provide anonymity of opinions and of arguments advanced in defense of these opinions.* In one version, direct debate is replaced by the interchange of information and opinion through a carefully designed sequence of questionnaires. The participants are asked not only to give their opinions but the reasons for these opinions, and, at each successive interrogation, they are given new and refined information, in the form of opinion feedback, which is derived by a computed consensus from the earlier parts of the program. The process continues until further progress toward a consensus appears to be negligible. The conflicting views are then documented.

To clarify the principles of the technique let us consider an example, one that illustrates the procedure that would be followed in seeking an answer to a fairly narrow question . . ..

Example: Choosing a Number by Delphi. Consider the common situation of having to arrive at an answer to the question of how large a particular number N should be. (For example, N might be the estimated cost of a measure, or a value representing its overall benefit.) We would then proceed as follows: First, we would ask each expert independently to give an estimate of N, and then arrange the responses in order of magnitude, and determine the quartiles, Q_1, M, Q_3, so that the four intervals formed on the N-line by these three points each contained one quarter of the estimates. If we had eleven participants, the N-line might look like this:

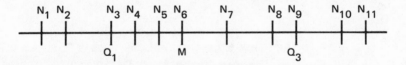

Second, we would communicate the values of Q_1, M, Q_3 to each respondent, ask him to reconsider his previous estimate, and, if his estimate (old or revised) lies outside the interquartile range (Q_1, Q_3), to state briefly the reasons why, in his opinion, the answer should be lower (or higher) than the 75 percent majority opinion expressed in the first round. Third, we would communicate

*E. S. Quade and W. I. Boucher (Eds.), *Systems Analysis and Policy Planning: Applications in Defense* (New York: American Elsevier Publishing Company, Inc., 1968), pp. 334–335.

the results of this second round (which as a rule will be less dispersed than the first) to the respondents in summary form, including the new quartiles and median. In addition, we would document the reasons that the experts gave in Round 2 for raising or lowering the values. (As collated and edited, these reasons would, of course, preserve the anonymity of the respondents.) We would then ask the experts to consider the new estimates and the arguments offered for them, giving them the weight they think they deserve and, in light of this new information, to revise their previous estimates. Again, if the revised estimates fell outside the second round's interquartile range, we would ask the respondent to state briefly why he found unconvincing the argument that might have drawn his estimate toward the median. Finally, in a fourth round, we would submit both the quartiles of the third distribution of responses and the counterarguments elicited in Round 3 to the respondents, and encourage them to make one last revision of their estimates. The median of these Round 4 responses could then be taken as representing the group position as to what N should be.

In comparison with other processes, several important observations may be made regarding the Delphi Technique:

- Face-to-face discussions are not as efficient as more formalized communication.
- Estimates are improved and made more accurate with each iteration.
- Accuracy improves when estimates of range as well as the single points are requested and supplied.

As imperfect as the Delphi Technique may be, it promises to provide a way to investigate many problems with a high social and political content. Because it can estimate the consequences of alternative actions, thus substituting for more conventional models, Delphi potentially introduces a more structured systems approach into a range of problem solving where it is difficult to formulate precise models.

4. Reporting Results

The next step in developing the optimum public system involves the development of a feedback mechanism. This is often called a progress reporting system, the intent of which is to provide all information necessary for fiscal control and management control of the program(s) involved in a given public system.

The performance report should display, either quarterly or, where appropriate, monthly, significant information that relates to each functional activity or program making up the total system. At least the following information should be listed:

- Major performance objectives.
- Performance measures.
- Performance targets for month, fiscal year to date, present fiscal year, and past fiscal year.
- Statements relating to efficiency, effectiveness, and productivity of work performed.
- Statements of conclusions, that is, suggestions for change and explanations of reported information where necessary.

5. Evaluation

The data contained in the progress reporting system are essential to overall program evaluation. After developing each report, the next step is to analyze the reported outcomes in terms of evaluations of the activities of the program. Obviously, one of the results of the analysis will be a comparison of the results versus the intended accomplishment of objectives.

Where target objectives are not being met, recommendations are then made for change or improvement, which may include actually changing the objectives.

The final step in the evaluation process, then, is the development of change plans and their implementation.

PUBLIC SERVICE NEEDS ANALYSIS

Earlier in this chapter we briefly discussed public needs and how they are perceived by the public. To expand that point: There are eight types of public service needs. Table 2-1 illustrates these. Let us look at examples of each of these needs:

1. Perceived/wanted/needed—*Police protection services*—People definitely see a need for police protection. They want this protection, and the need is real, since the crime rate is high.

2. Perceived/wanted/not needed—*Backyard pickup of trash*—

Table 2-1. Public service needs.

Public Perception of Need	Wanted / Not Wanted	Needed / Not Needed
Perceived	Wanted	Needed
Perceived	Wanted	Not needed
Perceived	Not wanted	Needed
Perceived	Not wanted	Not needed
Not perceived	Wanted	Needed
Not perceived	Wanted	Not needed
Not perceived	Not wanted	Needed
Not perceived	Not wanted	Not needed

The citizens perceive a need to have their trash picked up in their backyards. They want this special service, but from a health and environmental standpoint, there is no real identified need.

3. Perceived/not wanted/needed—*Busing to achieve racial integration*—The public agrees that there is a need to achieve racial integration in the schools. They do not want busing, although federal law requires racial integration of the schools. (In this example, the courts have "ruled" that a need exists.)

4. Perceived/not wanted/not needed—*Transferring water from Northern to Southern California*—Northern Californians understand that Southern Californians need more water. Northern California citizens do not want their rivers dammed nor do they want to spend their tax dollars to satisfy Southern California's needs. Northern California really has no interest (need) in the transfer of water.

5. Not perceived/wanted/needed—*Air pollution control*—Citizens, in general, are initially unaware that a health threat exists from air pollution. They participate in the air pollution control program by limiting automobile driving (indicative of want). It has been established by the federal administration that this program is really needed to prevent serious health and ecological effects.

6. Not perceived/wanted/not needed—*Municipal zoo*—Citizens do not perceive that there is a municipal need for a zoo. However, they like the idea and want a zoo in their city. There is no real need for a zoo. Many public projects or services fall into this category, for example, public golf courses, botanical gardens, cultural projects. They usually are set up to pay their own way, that is, as nonprofit entities.

7. Not perceived/not wanted/needed—*Inner city rehabilitation*—The vast majority of the citizens never visit, and are totally uninterested in, that portion of their city referred to as the "inner

city." They do not want to expend public funds on rehabilitation. The public policy makers recognize the severe economic implications (need) to the city as a whole if the inner city is not rehabilitated.

8. Not perceived/not wanted/not needed—*Any number of special interest "pet" projects*—The general population does not perceive, want, or actually need the project. Unfortunately, too many public activities fall into this category.

The manager or chief administrator of nearly every "full service" city or community will find public activities that exist to satisfy needs in each of these eight categories. He will often be forced to establish an activity or service that has been legislated by state or federal bodies even though his own "public" is overwhelmingly opposed to that activity. This dilemma makes the task of prioritizing each and every activity in terms of the common reference—the public interest—all the more difficult.

Notwithstanding this difficulty, all activities, functions, and projects must be so ordered and valued, or the public manager will be unable to exercise the basic functions of rational management.

ESTABLISHING PUBLIC NEEDS

In order to establish and prioritize public needs, mechanisms for identifying public attitudes and opinions must be employed. Once this identification is made, other issues must be dealt with, such as legal requirements. Laws may dictate governmental activities that run counter to what the public may want.

After an initial list of priorities has been completed, the administration must resolve conflicts and gain public support for, or at least its understanding of, the ordering of the activities by importance.

In order to achieve effective citizen participation, there are two techniques to (1) identify attitudes and opinions, (2) disseminate information, (3) resolve conflict, and (4) develop support and minimize opposition. They are:

Citizens' Advisory Committee. Citizens are convened to represent the ideas and attitudes of various groups or of the community as a whole. Several methods are available to arrive at the composition of these committees, but whichever method is used, the composition should be representative.

Short Conferences. This technique typically involves intensive meetings organized around a detailed agenda of problems, issues, and alternatives, with the objective of obtaining a complete analysis from a balanced group of community representatives.

Although there are many other techniques for eliciting citizen participation (e.g., the *charette,* * citizen surveys, ombudsman, public hearings), only the two techniques discussed accomplish all four of the objectives mentioned above.

Citizen participation activities are time consuming and absolutely essential to the principles involved in rationally managing in the public interest.

* A charette is a team effort conducted by professionals during a crisis, set up to devise a plan. Work sessions continue day and night until the goals are reached. The process aims at involving those who are most likely to be affected by the results of the planning effort.

3

The Evaluation Process
in Public Management

EVALUATION may be defined as fixing or determining a value. It may also be defined as determining the significance or worth of something, usually by careful appraisal and study.

The evaluation process comprises a flowing, systematic series of acts that all human beings perform almost constantly. It is both conscious and unconscious behavior; yet it always contains three basic elements:

Identifying a goal.
Deciding on an action that is estimated to achieve the goal.
Comparing the results of the action with what was expected (determining the value of the action).

Evaluation is often defined within the narrow context of the third element. From a programmatic viewpoint, value can be determined only in relation to goal attainment. In other words, without a goal and an act there can be no evaluation.

Most readers may protest that the above observations are

"intuitively obvious." Yet in the area of public administration, the worth of activity estimated to satisfy the public interest is seldom accurately determined. Before proceeding, this puzzling state of affairs must be examined, because no amount of pontification will produce "evaluation" unless the barriers to its accomplishment are understood and eliminated.

HUMAN NATURE and the SEARCH for "SPECIALNESS"

We cannot understand how to manage human resources unless we understand human motivation. That, in turn, will help us understand the evaluation process and how people behave when they are involved in it.

Motivation has been most vigorously studied by psychologists. One of these, Abraham H. Maslow, developed a five-tiered hierarchy of needs, which has found wide acceptance. His hierarchy works up from the bottom:

Level 5: Self-fulfillment needs.
Level 4: Psychological needs—ego status, prestige, feeling of "specialness."
Level 3: Social needs—belonging and acceptance as a group member.
Level 2: Security needs—physical and economic security, money.
Level 1: Physiological needs—shelter, food, water, self-preservation.

Maslow maintains that, when unfilled, the needs at the bottom of the hierarchy (1 and 2) are stronger motivators than those at the top. Also, once a need is fairly well satisfied, it decreases in importance. For our purposes, because we are primarily concerned with the needs of managers (they create the climate in which evaluation is conducted), we can safely assume that physiological, security, and social needs have been reasonably well satisfied. Given this, then, the fulfillment of psychological needs is of major importance to those most influential in making, or preventing, "evaluation" from becoming a reality.

Psychological needs are rarely expressed in our culture. It is socially unacceptable to say, "I'm trying to fulfill my need to feel important," or "I want more prestige," or "I've got to feel more *special.*" Yet this is precisely what most of us, in and out of public systems, are feeling and seeking.

In order to satisfy a need to feel special, a public manager may set out to prove that he is better for the job (more special) than anyone else in the organization. Because he's trying to prove how great he is, he derives no personal satisfaction from establishing a process by which others can successfully do his job. What does he do? Because he knows that it is to his advantage, he gives lip service to evaluation, but in reality, he passively, and sometimes actively, resists establishing a process of evaluation. He does this by saying that evaluation makes sense, *but:*

It's too expensive. We can't afford to implement it right now.
Many of the results of our activities can't be measured directly or precisely.
Measuring the results of our activities may prove embarrassing.
My job is to cut costs, not establish new and expensive procedures.
The council doesn't want precisely measured data. If they have too much information, they may have to make politically suicidal decisions.

In spite of such rationalizations, the public is demanding, and rightly so, that those entrusted with responsibility for managing public affairs be openly and precisely accountable for their activities. The evaluation process discussed herein provides the framework for that accountability.

THE EVALUATION PROCESS

Once the needs have been identified, the goals to satisfy them established, and a plan of action to reach those goals set in motion, the evaluation process can be started. It can be broken down into the following basic steps:

- Establish measurable objectives for each goal. (It is hypothesized that if the objectives are met the goal will be fulfilled. Evaluation tests this hypothesis.)
- List performance criteria that define exactly what satisfactorily accomplishes each objective.
- Develop measures of performance for each objective.
- Develop and agree on an initial work plan for accomplishing each objective. Include the means by which measures of performance will be made (data collection).

- Make measurements (collect data) as the work plan is implemented.
- Determine which data analyses will evaluate the results. Report performance evaluation results. (This must include a comparison between actual outcomes and those hypothesized if objectives are met.)
- Suggest and implement changes or improvements, where indicated, in approach or objectives in order to better satisfy goals (meet needs).

As can be seen, the process is dynamic and circular. That is, as measures are obtained and comparisons made, needed changes are implemented, and the process begins anew or continues.

Because certain steps seem more bothersome than others, we will discuss some in depth in the next section.

Measuring Performance

Once a work plan has been established and implemented, we need to answer two questions:

1. Is the work plan being implemented according to its design? This is often referred to as compliance auditing (or monitoring).
2. Is the work plan accomplishing its desired results?

Sufficient measures must be obtained to answer these questions adequately. The second question is further subdivided into measures of efficiency and effectiveness: How efficiently is the work plan being accomplished? How effectively are the results accomplishing the objectives?

A third type of necessary measurement is referred to as local environmental conditions, which include unforeseen occurrences or conditions that affect, either favorably or adversely, the results of the work plan.

Let us look at a simple illustration of the kinds of measurement discussed:

Work Plan

It was agreed that walking, not bicycling, was the safest method of locomotion. A steady pace of 3 miles an hour should allow for

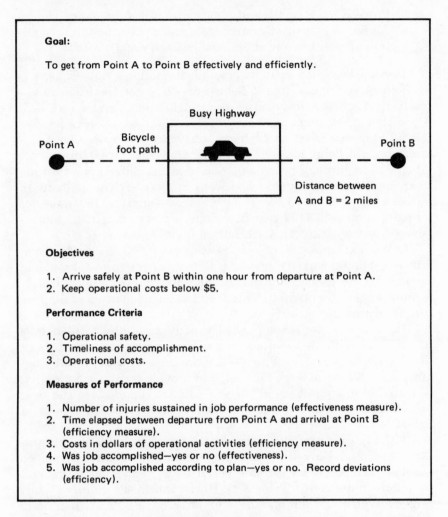

Goal:

To get from Point A to Point B effectively and efficiently.

Busy Highway

Point A

Bicycle
foot path

Point B

Distance between
A and B = 2 miles

Objectives

1. Arrive safely at Point B within one hour from departure at Point A.
2. Keep operational costs below $5.

Performance Criteria

1. Operational safety.
2. Timeliness of accomplishment.
3. Operational costs.

Measures of Performance

1. Number of injuries sustained in job performance (effectiveness measure).
2. Time elapsed between departure from Point A and arrival at Point B (efficiency measure).
3. Costs in dollars of operational activities (efficiency measure).
4. Was job accomplished—yes or no (effectiveness).
5. Was job accomplished according to plan—yes or no. Record deviations (efficiency).

sufficient time to cross the busy highway safely with total time elapsed for job accomplishment well within the hour allotted for this task.

1. Leave Point A walking. At departure, record time, general health status, condition of clothing and shoes, and amount of cash on hand.
2. Walk at a pace of 3 miles per hour to highway.
3. Stop at highway. Look both ways for approaching vehicles.
4. Cross highway when safe to do so.

5. Proceed to destination at a pace of 3 miles per hour.
6. Arrive at Point B. Record time, general health status, condition of clothing and shoes, and cash on hand.

The approach plan actually proceeded as follows: Subject departed Point A walking. (Time of departure—2:15 P.M. Health Status—perfect, no aches, pains, bruises, or scratches noted and so recorded. Condition of clothing and shoes—recorded as new. Cash on hand—$5.50. Subject arrives at highway, uneventfully crosses, and proceeds toward Point B. Subject encounters large, threatening bear. Must detour through brush and mud to avoid. Suffers one clothing tear, and shoes get muddy and wet.) Subject arrives at Point B. (Time of arrival—4:10 P.M. Health Status—anxious, but no aches or pains recorded. Notes tear in clothing—cost to repair, $3; muddy shoes—cost to clean, $1. Cash left on hand—$1.50.)

In our example, the objectives were met and the goal accomplished, but an anxiety measure (effectiveness) probably should be added to our measures of performance in order to more accurately evaluate operational safety. This would be included when evaluating the return trip.

The job was not accomplished exactly according to plan, and this, along with the reasons, must be recorded. In this case, a local environmental condition—the presence of a bear—was not anticipated. Future work plans should provide for this eventuality. For instance, subject could carry a noisemaker to scare the bear off, thus preventing the detour and probably reducing costs of operation.

Although our example is simple, the different kinds of measures are illustrated. Harry P. Hatry and Donald M. Fisk have developed a set of examples of measures of performance that is more pertinent to public systems (see Table 3-1). Hatry and Fisk's quality factors are equivalent to our measures of effectiveness, and their local condition factors are equivalent to our measures of local environmental conditions.

We prefer dividing performance measures into effectiveness and efficiency in order to distinguish between effective but inefficient operations and between efficient but ineffective operations.

Performance Reporting

Adequate and timely reports of performance provide the manager with the information he needs to monitor and control the progress of all activities for which he is responsible. This step in the evaluation process represents the feedback link between the results of activities and the objectives.

Cost is always a critical measure of performance. In view of this, all functions, activities, and programs must be accounted for in terms of cost. Although financial reports generate cost information for public service organizations, these reports have traditionally included only how public funds are being spent; they do not connect the results of activities to their total costs. However, this is precisely the information that is critically needed to evaluate total performance.

In Chapter 5 we discuss public budgeting systems. The conclusions reached in that chapter, however, relate to our concepts of evaluation. Simply stated, budgets must be directly related to the desired results, that is, "results" budgeting. Furthermore, financial reports must clearly show the costs associated with each result. This necessarily demands that a results-oriented cost accounting system be designed to provide the information needed for budgeting and financial reporting.

In 1972, the Comptroller General of the United States published "Standards for Audit of Governmental Organizations, Programs, Activities and Functions."* For the first time in our history, federal auditing guidelines require that program effectiveness be included in the external audit process. In the excerpt below, italics have been added to highlight significant items of interest to the reader.

> In earlier and simpler times in our Nation's history, when the responsibilities of each level of government could be clearly divided, each level could work somewhat independently. Today, profound changes in our social, political, and economic order have brought steadily mounting demands for new and better public services in a variety and on a scale unprecedented in our history. Response to these demands requires a process of policymaking, financing, and administration which involves the cooperation of Federal, State, and Local governments in solving public problems. Thus the Federal system of government today rests on an elaborate structure of interlocking relationships among all levels of government—between the executive and legislative branches of each, between the Federal and the State Governments, and between

*This document was signed by Elmer B. Statts, Comptroller General of the United States, June 1972.

Table 3-1. Illustrative set of workload measures, quality factors, and local condition factors, that should be considered in productivity measurement.

Selected Service Functions*	Illustrative "Workload" Measures†	Illustrative Quality Factors (i.e., Measures of Citizen Impact) that Should Be Considered in Interpreting Productivity	Illustrative Local Condition Factors that Should Be Considered in Interpreting Productivity‡
Solid waste collection.	Tons of solid waste collected.	Visual appearance of "curb" or "back-door" collection. Fire/health hazard conditions from solid waste accumulation. Service delays.	Frequency of collection. Private vs. public collection. Local weather conditions. Composition of the solid waste (including the residential-commercial-industrial mix; type of waste, etc.).
Liquid waste treatment (sewage).	Gallons of sewage treated.	Quality level of effluent (e.g., BOD removed and retained after treatment). Water quality level resulting where dumped.	Initial quality of waterway into which the sewage effluent is released. Community liquid waste generation characteristics.
Law enforcement (police).	Number of surveillance hours. Number of calls. Number of crimes investigated.	Reduction in crime and victimization rates. Crime clearance rates, preferably including court disposition. Response time. Citizen feeling of security.	Percent of low-income families in population. Public attitude toward certain crimes.
Law enforcement (courts).	Number of cases resolved.	Number of convictions/number of plea-bargain reduced sentences. Correctness of disposition. Delay time until resolution.	Number and types of cases.
Health and hospital.	Number of patient-days.	Reduced number and severity of illnesses. Conditions of patients after treatment. Duration of treatment and "pleasantness" of care. Accessibility of low-income groups to care.	Availability and price of health care. Basic community health conditions.

Service function*	Workload measure†	Effectiveness/quality measure	Conditioning factors‡
Water treatment.	Gallons of water treated.	Water quality indices such as for hardness and taste. Amount of impurities removed.	Basic quality of water supply source.
Recreation.	Acres of recreational activities. Attendance figures.	Participation rates. Accessibility to recreational opportunities. Variety of opportunities available. Crowdedness indices. Citizens' perceptions of adequacy of recreational opportunities.	Amount of recreation provided by the private sector. Number of individuals without access to automobiles; the available public transit system. Topographical and climatic characteristics. Time available to citizens for recreation activities.
Street maintenance.	Square yards of repairs made.	Smoothness/bumpiness of streets; travel time; community disruption, amount and duration; dust and noise during repairs.	Density of traffic. Density of population along roadway. Locations of residences, shopping areas, recreational opportunities, etc.
Fire control.	Fire calls. Number of inspections.	Fire damage. Injuries and lives lost.	Local weather conditions. Type of buildings. Density of population.
Primary and secondary education.	Pupil-days. Number of pupils.	Achievement test scores and grade levels. Continuation/dropout rates.	Socioeconomic characteristics of pupils and neighborhood. Basic intelligence of pupils. Number of pupils.

*Numerous subfunctions each with its own submeasures can also be identified. However, care should be taken to avoid going into excessive, useless detail.

†Dividing these by total dollar cost or by total workdays yields workload-based productivity measures.

‡Such local conditions as population size and local price levels are relevant to all service functions.

SOURCE: Harry P. Hatry and Donald M. Fisk, *Improving Productivity and Productivity Measurement in Local Governments*, The National Commission on Productivity, 1971, pp. xvi–xvii. More extensive lists of workload measures and quality factors (often called measures of effectiveness or evaluation criteria) can be found in Hatry and Fisk's report.

both and the local communities—for the conduct of programs designed to improve the quality of American life.

Accompanying this increased complexity in the relationship among the various levels of government has been an increased demand for information about government programs. *Public officials, legislators, and the general public want to know whether governmental funds are being handled properly and in compliance with existing laws and whether governmental programs are being conducted efficiently, effectively, and economically.* They also want to have this information provided, or at least concurred in, by someone who is not an advocate of the program but is independent and objective.

This demand for information has widened the scope of governmental auditing so that such auditing *no longer is a function concerned primarily with financial operations. Instead, governmental auditing now is also concerned with whether governmental organizations are achieving the purposes for which programs are authorized and funds are made available, are doing so economically and efficiently,* and are complying with applicable laws and regulations.

The GAO [General Accounting Office] statement contains a body of audit standards that are intended for application to audits of all government organizations, programs, activities, and functions—whether they are performed by auditors employed by Federal, State or local Governments; independent public accountants; or others qualified to perform parts of the audit work contemplated under these standards. These standards are also intended to apply to both internal audits and audits of contractors, grantees, and other external organizations performed by or for a governmental entity. These audit standards relate to the scope and quality of audit effort and to the characteristics of a professional and meaningful audit report.

The American Institute of Certified Public Accountants (AICPA) has adopted standards and procedures that are applicable to audits performed to express opinions on the fairness with which financial statements present the financial position and results of operations.* These standards are generally accepted for such audits and have been incorporated into the GAO statement.

A fundamental tenet of a democratic society holds that governments and agencies entrusted with public resources and the authority for applying them have a responsibility to render a full accounting of their activities. This accountability is inherent in

---

*Ed.—The basic standards are included in "Statements on Auditing Procedure No. 33," issued by the Committee on Auditing Procedure of the American Institute of Certified Public Accountants.

the governmental process and is not always specifically identified by legislative provision. This governmental accountability should identify not only the objects for which the public resources have been devoted but also the manner and effect of their application.

This concept of accountability is woven into the basic premises supporting the GAO standards. *These standards provide for a scope of audit that includes not only financial and compliance auditing but also auditing for economy, efficiency, and achievement of desired results.*

Definitions of the three elements of such an audit follow.

1. *Financial and compliance*—determines (a) whether financial operations are properly conducted, (b) whether the financial reports of an audited entity are presented fairly, and (c) whether the entity has complied with applicable laws and regulations.
2. *Economy and efficiency*—determines whether the entity is managing or utilizing its resources (personnel, property, space, and so forth) in an economical and efficient manner and the causes of any inefficiencies or uneconomical practices, including inadequacies in management information systems, administrative procedures, or organizational structure.
3. *Program results—determine whether the desired results or benefits are being achieved, whether the objectives established by the legislature or other authorizing body are being met, and whether the agency has considered alternatives which might yield desired results at a lower cost.*

The GAO audit standards are intended to do more than merely codify current practices. Purposely future-oriented, these standards include concepts and areas of auditing that, although evolving, are vital to government accountability. These standards have therefore been structured so that each of the three elements can, if necessary, be performed separately.

It should be recognized, however, that a concurrent audit of all three parts is probably the most economical approach, although often this may not be practical or necessary. For most government programs or activities, however, the public interest will not be satisfied unless all three elements are performed.

In government memoranda to independent public accountants or other audit organizations, the instructions should specifically identify which of the three elements of the audit are to be conducted. Such agreements ensure that all concerned parties understand the scope of the audit.

Although we recognize that few government agencies are presently geared to provide the level of accountability called for here, we maintain that this is precisely what is needed to manage rationally in the public interest.

A MODEL PERFORMANCE PROGRESS REPORTING SYSTEM

While one of the authors was engaged in the City of Pasadena, California, as a management analyst, a performance progress reporting system was proposed. Three exhibits from that proposal are included here to illustrate one performance reporting system. Figure 3-1 shows the goals of the city manager's office and the objectives estimated to accomplish the first goal. The goals and objectives were taken from existing city documents. No attempt was made to refine the objectives in order to make them more readily measurable. Rather, Figure 3-2 reports all significant measures of performance that are deemed necessary to fully evaluate success in achieving the stated objectives. Figure 3-3 represents a format for a monthly fiscal report. This format is deficient, however, because it does not relate operating costs to results. Moreover, the cost accounting system that was necessary for that level of detail was not appropriate when the proposal was developed.

Measures of Performance

Examples of more common measures of performance are the tons of trash collected per week, the numbers of crimes investigated, and the percent of low-income families in a given population. One troublesome measure is the determination of public attitudes about delivered services. Here we suggest using a semantic differential scale.

The semantic differential scale provides statements of meaning at opposite ends of an arbitrarily designed numerical scale. For example, if we wanted to assess public opinion about how clean the streets are kept, we could establish a scale of 1 to 5, with 1 representing "very dirty streets"; 5 representing "very clean streets"; and 2, 3, and 4 representing various carefully defined in-between conditions. By surveying a representative group of citizens (sample), an opinion measure can be obtained. Caution should be exercised to avoid assuming a level of precision to the numbers that is not justified by this technique, which best measures

Figure 3-1. City of Pasadena monthly report.

Department: City Manager	Month: September
Activity: Management Analysis	Fiscal Year: 1975

Goal(s) and Objective(s)*:

Goal 1: To evaluate city operations for the purpose of identifying the need for, and implementing methods of, increasing operational effectiveness (increase productivity).

  Objectives: 1. Identify functions/activities/products that show the most promise for effecting increased productivity and cost avoidance. (Target: Total per annum greater than $500,000.)

  2. Perform analysis on identified project and recommend changes, or perform analysis on assigned project and recommend changes.

  3. Implement changes such that the effect on the clientele and political environment is minimized and that benefits are maximized.

Goal 2: To coordinate the Interdepartmental Task Force.

  Objectives:

Goal 3: To prepare and promulgate administrative policies and procedures.

  Objectives:

Each goal is followed by an objective pertinent to that goal. The dates the objectives were established and satisfied should also be included.

Figure 3-2. Monthly performance report.

Department:	City Manager
Activity:	Management Analysis
Month:	September
Fiscal Year:	1975

Performance Objective: Identify functions/activities/projects that show most promise for effecting increased productivity and cost avoidance. (Target: Total per annum greater than $500,000.)

Performance Measure			1st Quarter			2nd Quarter			3rd Quarter			4th Quarter		
			July	Aug.	Sept.	Oct.	Nov.	Dec.	Jan.	Feb.	Mar.	Apr.	May	June
Number of functions/activities/projects reviewed.	Monthly	Target			10									
		Actual			0									
		% Target												
	Year to Date	Target												
		Actual												
Past FY Target ____ Present FY Target ____		% Target												
Number of functions/activities/projects identified that show most promise for cost avoidance/productivity improvement. (Indicator score: 35.)	Monthly	Target			100									
		Actual												
		% Target												
	Year to Date	Target												
		Actual												
Past FY Target ____ Present FY Target ____		% Target												
Cost of identifying functions/activities/projects.	Monthly	Target												
		Actual												
		% Target												
	Year to Date	Target												
		Actual												
Past FY Target ____ Present FY Target ____		% Target												

Comments:

Department:	City Manager
Activity:	Management Analysis
Month:	September
Fiscal Year:	1975

Performance Objective: Perform analysis on identified project and recommend changes, or perform analysis on assigned project and recommend changes.

Performance Measure			1st Quarter			2nd Quarter			3rd Quarter			4th Quarter		
			July	Aug.	Sept.	Oct.	Nov.	Dec.	Jan.	Feb.	Mar.	Apr.	May	June
Difference between estimated date of completion and actual date of completion (± days)	Monthly	Target			0									
		Actual												
		% Target												
	Year to Date	Target												
		Actual												
Past FY Target	Present FY Target	% Target												
Number of positive aspects of project not analyzed but subsequently deemed relevant.	Monthly	Target			N/A									
		Actual												
		% Target												
	Year to Date	Target												
		Actual												
Past FY Target	Present FY Target	% Target												
Number of negative aspects of project not analyzed but subsequently deemed relevant.	Monthly	Target			N/A									
		Actual												
		% Target												
	Year to Date	Target												
		Actual												
Past FY Target	Present FY Target	% Target												

Comments:

Figure 3-2 Continued

Department:	City Manager
Activity:	Management Analysis
Month:	September
Fiscal Year:	1975

Performance Objective: Continued

Performance Measure			1st Quarter			2nd Quarter			3rd Quarter			4th Quarter		
			July	Aug.	Sept.	Oct.	Nov.	Dec.	Jan.	Feb.	Mar.	Apr.	May	June
Number of positive aspects of recommendations not included but subsequently deemed relevant.	Monthly	Target			N/A									
		Actual												
		% Target												
	Year to Date	Target												
		Actual												
		% Target												
Past FY Target	Present FY Target													
Number of negative aspects of recommendation not included but subsequently deemed relevant.	Monthly	Target			N/A									
		Actual												
		% Target												
	Year to Date	Target												
		Actual												
		% Target												
Past FY Target	Present FY Target													
Objectivity rated on a scale of 1–10 (10 being highly objective, and 1 being highly subjective).	Monthly	Target			10									
		Actual												
		% Target												
	Year to Date	Target												
		Actual												
		% Target												
Past FY Target	Present FY Target													

Comments:

Department:	City Manager
Activity:	Management Analysis
Month:	September
Fiscal Year:	1975

Performance Objective: Continued

Performance Measure			1st Quarter			2nd Quarter			3rd Quarter			4th Quarter		
			July	Aug.	Sept.	Oct.	Nov.	Dec.	Jan.	Feb.	Mar.	Apr.	May	June
Number of subject matters not included in analysis but subsequently deemed relevant (total positive and negative aspects of project).	Monthly	Target			N/A									
		Actual												
		% Target												
	Year to Date	Target												
		Actual												
		% Target												
Past FY Target	Present FY Target													
Number of alternatives not included in recommendation but subsequently suggested for consideration.	Monthly	Target			N/A									
		Actual												
		% Target												
	Year to Date	Target												
		Actual												
		% Target												
Past FY Target	Present FY Target													
Completeness rated on a scale of 1–10 (1 being very incomplete, and 10 being very complete).	Monthly	Target			10									
		Actual												
		% Target												
	Year to Date	Target												
		Actual												
		% Target												
Past FY Target	Present FY Target													

Comments:

Figure 3-2 Continued

Department:	City Manager
Activity:	Management Analysis
Month:	September
Fiscal Year:	1975

Performance Objective: Implement changes such that the effect on the clientele and political environment is minimized and the benefits are maximized.

Performance Measure			July	Aug.	Sept.	Oct.	Nov.	Dec.	Jan.	Feb.	Mar.	Apr.	May	June
			1st Quarter			2nd Quarter			3rd Quarter			4th Quarter		
Impact on the affected personnel not anticipated and planned for, (and) subsequently deemed as having a relevant impact.	Monthly	Target			0									
		Actual												
		% Target												
	Year to Date	Target												
		Actual												
		% Target												
Past FY Target / Present FY Target														
Effects on the political environment not anticipated and planned for, subsequently deemed as having a relevant impact.	Monthly	Target			0									
		Actual												
		% Target												
	Year to Date	Target												
		Actual												
		% Target												
Past FY Target / Present FY Target														
Difference between actual and estimated cost avoidance.	Monthly	Target			10%									
		Actual												
		% Target												
	Year to Date	Target												
		Actual												
		% Target												
Past FY Target / Present FY Target														

Comments:

Department: City Manager
Activity: Management Analysis
Month: September
Fiscal Year: 1975

Performance Measure			1st Quarter			2nd Quarter			3rd Quarter			4th Quarter		
			July	Aug.	Sept.	Oct.	Nov.	Dec.	Jan.	Feb.	Mar.	Apr.	May	June
Difference between actual and estimated increase in effectiveness (displayed here either as an aggregate effectiveness measure of difference or as the difference between actual and estimated effectiveness for each performance measure).	Monthly	Target			10%									
		Actual												
		% Target												
	Year to Date	Target												
		Actual												
		% Target												
Past FY Target	Present FY Target													
Difference between actual and estimated cost of implementation.	Monthly	Target			10%									
		Actual												
		% Target												
	Year to Date	Target												
		Actual												
		% Target												
Past FY Target	Present FY Target													
	Monthly	Target												
		Actual												
		% Target												
	Year to Date	Target												
		Actual												
		% Target												
Past FY Target	Present FY Target													
	Monthly	Target												
		Actual												
		% Target												
	Year to Date	Target												
		Actual												
		% Target												
Past FY Target	Present FY Target													

Comments:

Figure 3-3. Monthly fiscal report.

Department: _____ Month: _____ Fiscal Year: _____

Activity/ Project/ Function	Revenue Source	Monthly Information									Year-to-Date Information									Yearly Information		
		Revenue			Budgeted		Expenditures		Diff.		Revenue			Budgeted		Expenditures		Diff.		Projected Revenue	Budgeted	
		Project	Actual	Diff.	$	MY	$	MY	$	MY	Project	Actual	Diff.	$	MY	$	MY	$	MY		$	MY
Management analysis																						
Public information																						
Administration																						
☐ Department total:																						

Comments:

extreme attitudes, changes in attitude, or changes in the way services are delivered.

Another troublesome area is that of measuring the results of "prevention" activities, because those correlations that are possible may be meaningless or misleading. For example, we might add three patrol units in a neighborhood to reduce the incidence of burglary, and after several months, we find that the incidence has indeed decreased. What we cannot say with certainty is that the three additional patrol units caused this decrease. Other significant local events must be measured before causality can be established. An extreme example of such erroneous conclusions is that of the antirabies program in Hawaii. For decades, Hawaii has quarantined for several months all dogs entering the state to prevent the spread of rabies to the mongoose population. Hawaii has never had a reported case of rabies in the indigenous animal population, and authorities quickly attribute this to the effectiveness of their quarantine program. A significant measure omitted from the analysis, however, was how many quarantined dogs developed rabies. The true effectiveness of this prevention activity is therefore left in doubt until this and other factors are considered.

In order to measure the performance of "prevention" activities, a baseline measure must be obtained against which to evaluate subsequent measures, for example, the burglary rate is down 5 percent from the baseline datum.

Careful analyses of data can lead to valid statements regarding the effectiveness of prevention activities. Here, more than in any other aspect of evaluation, sound judgment is needed.

INTERNAL vs. EXTERNAL EVALUATION

The evaluation process, which is essential to the successful and rational management of any human activity, is an internal, ongoing process within an organization.

External evaluation, on the other hand, evaluates the internal evaluation process. One aspect, for example, determines if the financial practices of the public organization comply with the intent and letter of the law. The "Standards for Audit of Governmental Organizations, Programs, Activities and Functions," referred to earlier, provides some guidelines for performing external audit (evaluation). All public managers should obtain a copy of this document from the General Accounting Office, Washington, D.C. 20548.

External evaluation is also valuable in that it provides a more independent and objective evaluation of operations than is possible with an internal evaluation.

4

Rational
Program Management

IN Chapter 2, we described an optimum public system. In a larger context, the public systems manager is responsible for managing a varied and diverse set of public programs. This job is made all the more difficult, because our country's urban areas, where the preponderance of nonfederal public management takes place, are experiencing an active period of growth, expansion, and technological change.

Furthermore, our nation's urban governments are no longer able to confine their activities and concerns to the traditional caretaker functions, that is, public safety, public health, public works, utilities, parks, libraries, and land-use planning and regulation. In addition to trying to satisfy these physical needs, governments must now focus on the public's social and economic needs, exemplified by such national campaigns as the war on poverty, the civil rights movement, and the model cities program.

To make matters worse, in attempting to fill these expanded needs, our nation's cities are experiencing financial crises. Taxpayers are heavily burdened, and their protests are just beginning to have an impact on local government planning. The public systems manager, therefore, finds himself involved in managing change— changing programs, financial situations, and needs. In this setting, it is all the more important that program planning, organization, and management be conducted in a dynamic and rational manner. This chapter will explore methods for accomplishing these tasks.

Traditionally, management has been divided into five basic functions: planning, decision making, organizing, directing, and controlling.

Planning consists of two basic phases. Phase one establishes the goals for each program. These goals should reflect the results that satisfy public needs. Phase two produces plans of action for conducting each and every program.

In a dynamic, well-managed organization, planning is a continuous process because opportunities are continually sought to improve the efficiency and effectiveness with which services are delivered.

Decision making used to be considered (and still is by many) the most important function of a manager. We wish to present another viewpoint regarding "decision making," however; we believe that the "best" manager is the one who has a minimum number of decisions to make. Why is this the case?

In Chapter 2, we implied that the ideal public system was a "closed" one, that is, one in which no decisions have to be made outside the system. If this closed system is designed and managed properly, few "decisions" will need to be made because problems have obvious solutions.

Admittedly, this is an ideal situation, but the manager who plans, organizes, controls, and directs efficiently should have few real decisions to make. This viewpoint is at the heart of the "rational" philosophy of management.

Organizing develops the formal structure that coordinates and integrates the resources that are available to carry out the program's work plans. For most public service activities, we recommend an organizational structure that is based on the actual "program." Lines of responsibility and accountability are readily defined, and necessary channels of communication, both vertical (line relations) and horizontal (among programs), evolve naturally.

Directing develops and maintains an organizational environment that encourages the accomplishment of the desired results. We discuss this in some detail later in this chapter.

Controlling ensures that plans of action are carried out as designed (conformance).

Now that we have briefly described the five basic functions of management, let us take a better look at "management" itself.

Management may be simply defined as working through people to accomplish specific goals.

Why "manage" at all? Every conscious, rational human activity is goal-directed; we tend to view aimless behavior as abnormal and goal-directed behavior as healthy. In attempting to reach goals, we engage in a series of acts that we feel will lead to goal attainment. As we engage in these activities, we test results in order to judge if our feelings were correct. Where results are deemed undesirable, we change or improve our activities, again hoping the new actions will more effectively accomplish our aims. We "manage" our actions to accomplish goals.

Management involves identifying goals and objectives, selecting initial activities that are judged to attain these goals, doing the activities, measuring the results, and, if necessary, changing the activities. These are the essential elements of rational management.

Unfortunately, most managers do not *appear* to manage rationally. Public management increasingly is charged with lack of responsiveness to the public interest, inefficiency in carrying out its activities, and failing to accomplish any meaningful goal. In order to understand public management, we must explore these charges and the reasons behind them.

IDENTIFICATION of GOALS and OBJECTIVES

If we look at a typical city, we see a frenzy of activities—police cars patrolling or responding to calls; fire engines racing to fires; potholes being patched; garbage being collected and relocated; committees meeting; trees being trimmed; librarians stacking books; streets being cleaned; and on and on and on. There is plenty of "doing." But do the "doers" clearly understand why they are "doing"? Unfortunately, in most cases the answer is probably no.

The following is a real situation that occurred between one of the authors and a public health nurse in one of our medium-size cities:

Cast of Characters
Author acting as Management Analyst, referred to as *MA*
Public Health Nurse, referred to as *PHN*

Scene: Public Health Nurse's office on third floor of city hall. Appoint-

ment between MA and PHN had been scheduled two weeks before.
Stated reason for meeting was to explore ways the MA, working out
of the city manager's office, might help the nursing section of the
Public Health Department more efficiently or more effectively accomplish its work objectives.

MA: Hi, Julie (fictitious name). I'm Howard Koester. How are you
      this morning?
PHN: Hi, Howard. Busy, busy, busy.
MA: Well, that's one of the areas we might explore. Do you have
      any suggestions for reducing the day-to-day workload and for
      getting the job done as well as or better than before?
PHN: Gee! That's easy! Hire four more nurses!
MA: Ha, ha. Well, as you are well aware, the overall budget for
      the Health Department this year is up 20 percent from last
      year, as are the rest of the city's departmental budgets. The
      city manager has been directed to hold the line on next year's
      budget or face a taxpayers' revolt. I'm afraid that you and
      I would have to develop some pretty powerful justification for
      adding more staff, but let's not exclude that option just yet.
      What activities are taking the most time?
PHN: Nursing home visits and filling out all these reports.
MA: What objectives or results do you work toward with the nursing
      home visit program?
PHN: Mostly we provide general basic health assessment and follow
      up and some patient health care education to those who call
      in with a health problem or come into one of our clinics, such
      as the prenatal clinic.
MA: Let's talk in somewhat specific terms now, mostly for my
      education. The prenatal program—what are the objectives of
      that program?
PHN: To provide the best prenatal care for the pregnant women of
      our city who are unable to pay for a private physician's services.
      And by so doing have healthy babies born to healthy mothers
      in a healthy environment.
MA: That's quite a tall order. But how does the indigent mother-to-be
      know about our prenatal program?
PHN: Through our outreach program.
MA: What is that?
PHN: Well, periodically we mail out flyers describing our prenatal
      services to a sample of addresses in the poorer sections of town.
      We also place spot announcements about services in the local
      papers.
MA: How often do you send flyers out? And how many?

> **PHN:** Every three months we send out 2,000 flyers.
>
> **MA:** And how effective have these mailings been in getting the word out?
>
> **PHN:** Gosh! Pretty good, I guess! Our prenatal clinics are all over-booked, and we have a patient waiting time for an initial prenatal clinic appointment of four weeks.
>
> **MA:** In how many of the initial prenatal clinic appointments had the patient heard of the prenatal program from the flyer or as a result of the outreach program, in general?
>
> **PHN:** Gee, I don't know for sure. We don't ask the patients how they heard about the program during in-take screening. There are too many questions for the patient to answer now.
>
> **MA:** I see. How long does it take you, Julie, to prepare a mailing?
>
> **PHN:** At least two working days every three months. It's a real drag to get that random sample, address all those flyers, and get them in the mail.
>
> **MA:** Do many of the flyers that you send out get returned because of a wrong address or for some other reason?
>
> **PHN:** Quite a few. You know there's quite a turnover in the population of the poorer sections of the city.
>
> **MA:** Thanks, Julie. This has been most helpful. Let's discuss another issue that may be of concern to you.

In this example (and it is typical), the Department of Health rightly felt that an outreach program was needed to get patients into the health care system. The department decided that mailings and spot news media announcements were good activities that helped meet that goal, and they instituted such activities. Period.

What went wrong here? The goal of the outreach program, that is, informing patients in need about the service, was not specific or measurable. The only activity that was measured was how many flyers were mailed and how much nursing time it took to accomplish this. The intuitive hypothesis—"If the flyers are mailed, the patients will get the word"—has not been tested for validity.

What happened here is a typical example of a management error. On the basis of a "feeling," an activity was implemented before the objectives were clearly constructed. To compound this mistake, no measurements were made to even verify the "feelings."

The lesson here is clear. Specific and measurable objectives must be constructed before activities designed to meet these objectives are planned and implemented. Furthermore, when met, objectives must satisfy an identified need.

SELECTION of ACTIVITIES

Once clear, specific, and measurable objectives are agreed upon, select those initial activities that will accomplish those objectives. We suggest that the procedure discussed in Chapter 2 be followed in arriving at initial activities. Some other procedures are, among other things, using a single "expert" or using a standing planning commission.

Regardless of which procedure is used, each agreed-upon, initial activity must state or imply a clear hypothesis, to wit: "If this activity is conducted, the measurable result will be . . . (stated objective.)"

Drawing from our scenario above, a specific objective might have been: "Inform at least 2,000 women in their childbearing years, who do not have the ability to pay for private care, about the prenatal services provided by the Public Health Department." One activity then hypothesized to help accomplish this objective could be: "Mail out informative flyers to 2,000 randomly selected addresses in the poorer sections of town every three months."

As we shall discuss, however, the hypothesis must be tested before we can determine if this activity effectively accomplishes the objective.

ENGAGING in ACTIVITY—"DOING"

As was pointed out, public sector organizations engage in a lot of activity. As rational managers, we want to determine if these activities are being conducted as planned and designed. This amounts to checking for compliance or conformance, documenting nonconformance, and making necessary adjustments to the plan.

In the activity described in our scenario, we would check compliance by asking the following:

Are the flyers "informative"?
Were the 2,000 mailing addresses selected in a random manner?
Were the 2,000 mailing addresses located in the poorer sections of town?
Were all the flyers put in the mail on time, that is, at three-month intervals?

The cost-conscious manager then determines if the activity is performed as efficiently as possible. This is usually accomplished by periodically conducting operations review and analysis studies. Several different techniques used in these studies are discussed briefly here. Although an in-depth discussion of these techniques is not within the scope of this chapter, we will briefly describe what they comprise.

1. Work flow documentation techniques consist of flow charting and procedure listing. Flow charting provides a visual picture of how a general activity proceeds through time. The flow of work is depicted horizontally across a chart from left to right, one line for each regulated type of work. Vertical relationships on the chart normally indicate time or simultaneous action. Procedure listing, an alternative to flow charting, itemizes the steps that are required in a work operation.

2. Work measurement techniques document and estimate work-loads. Two informal approaches, both with obvious shortcomings, are subjective estimates by work supervisors and historical averaging of work output per man-hour of work. More formal techniques include time logging, time ladders, work sampling, time studies, standard data, and multiple activity analysis.

With time logging, employees who are considered "standard performers" keep records of the number of minutes they spend on each operation they do and the number of "units" of work produced. From these data, unit times are established. The time-log approach is particularly useful when a job or activity is composed of a wide variety of operations.

An extension of the time log, the time ladder technique uses strings of time in minute increments, preprinted vertically in successive columns for hours throughout the day. Each type of work is assigned a code symbol. Codes are entered, and a line (ladder step) is drawn through the minute interval when the type of work changes. A new work code is entered and remains effective until the next change, when another line is drawn. The time ladder is particularly useful to document activities where a few people work on many complex duties over a long period of time.

When other work measurement techniques are too time consuming or expensive, the work sampling technique is effective. It is used to best advantage when measuring the work activities of a relatively large group of people in a large work area. It is particularly well suited for studying nonrepetitive work, such as maintenance, warehousing, or certain office operations.

This technique employs "observers," who make rounds through

the work areas under study. The activities of each person assigned to the area are briefly noted by the observer. The data collected are then summarized by work-type categories, and each activity category is expressed as a percent of the day. These percentages indicate the work done on the average, the idle time, and the type and magnitude of all delays. This technique differs from "time-and-motion" studies because it does not employ a stopwatch and the observations are not continuous.

The time study technique involves an analyst who records the number of units of work that standard performers produce in a specified period of time. The results are presented in standard unit times for various operations. This method is particularly helpful when the work cycle is short and when the frequency of steps within any given operation varies considerably.

Where clerical operations are involved, the standard data method is often used. In this technique, analysts determine the elements of the job and build total time from micromotion studies that cover a wide variety of small segments of clerical operations. This method gives consistent results, that is, two analysts timing the same job should arrive at almost precisely the same standards. It is costly, however, especially when clerical operations are not highly repetitive and work content is variable.

With general office operations, the multiple activity analysis is employed. In this approach, multiple activity charts are prepared, which, when computed, present a time picture for various activities. Each activity an employee or machine does is shown as a vertical bar, and the bar length indicates the time it usually takes to perform that element of work. The completed charts are particularly helpful in finding how work can be divided among members of a group, how the time for certain elements can be reduced, how work elements can be rearranged to reduce the overall time required to complete a job element, and how equipment time can be used more effectively.

3. Work distribution analysis techniques are employed to optimize use of personnel. Four tools are employed: (1) the task list; (2) the activity list; (3) the work distribution chart; and (4) the organization chart.

The task list, compiled by the employee, provides a systematic record of the tasks performed. Tasks are normally listed in sequence and by the amount of time devoted to them. This list determines the estimated time and the output relationship of each task to all tasks performed by a particular employee.

The activity list summarizes the activities of a program or an organizational unit, such as a department, being analyzed. The list is then used to define the program, or departmental activities, and to aid in the grouping of individual tasks contributing to these activities.

The third tool, the work distribution chart, relates the work performed by each employee to the activities of that unit (as recorded on the activity list). This chart answers many questions about the organization of work. For example, are the most important activities taking the most time, are work tasks grouped logically and equitably, is the work being done consistent with employees' assignments, and are the activities of the unit fragmented or cohesive?

In addition, the work distribution analysis can be used as the basis for reviewing job descriptions and for preparing a "real" functional organization chart.

Lastly, the organization chart, a device that most of us take for granted, shows many things to all levels of management, such as:

Span of control. Span of control is loosely defined as the number of persons or activities under one person's supervision. More important than the absolute number, however, is the amount of time that the manager takes in effectively supervising these persons or activities. That time demand is dependent on certain factors: (1) the physical area under supervision—the more widely dispersed the people or activities, the more difficult the supervisory task; (2) the extent that operational responsibility has become decentralized; and (3) the impact of planning and decisions on the budget.

Hierarchical considerations. The number of tiers between a manager and the lowest designated skill level under his supervision is critical because each tier adds another link in the communications channel. The loss in true communications between tiers is estimated to be at least 25 percent. Moreover, because this loss is worsened by "garble," the number of tiers should be kept at a minimum. Simple arithmetic tells us that four tiers produce totally unreliable communications unless managers spend a considerable amount of time forestalling this eventuality.

Human interaction. The organization chart also indicates the amount of human interaction that is both necessary and possible. The more people who report directly to a particular supervisor, the more interactions and the greater the number of "people problems."

4. Work simplification and methods improvement techniques are frequently the most productive steps in improving the efficiency

of functions and operations. An experienced and imaginative analyst can successfully simplify work by reviewing operations before any work measurement is performed.

Work simplification is a common-sense, step-by-step analysis that improves the methods by which the work is accomplished. It consists of eliminating or streamlining those aspects of a job that are deemed inefficient. Ideally, the analyst will concentrate on low-cost, short-range improvements that can be made immediately. Opportunities for long-range, major improvements can be identified for further evaluation after work has been measured.

With work simplification, we want to reduce or improve:

Processing time
Total time required to perform assigned functions
Time required to train new employees
Work accuracy (or work "error")
Amount of supervisory time required for detail work or error correction

The operations that have the greatest potential for work simplification and methods improvement are those that exhibit delays, bottlenecks, frequent errors, chronic overtime, missed deadlines, and so forth.

A Word of Caution

Almost all employees view management's efforts to improve efficiency as some type of threat. At the very least, employees may have to "change" the way they have been doing things; at the worst, jobs can be eliminated.

As a result, employees are often hostile or uncooperative when their jobs are under review and analysis. Later in this chapter, we shall discuss at length ways to reduce this hostility; however, it should be noted here that unless these attitudes are fully understood—and dealt with—by management, attempts to improve efficiency may lead to reduced efficiency because of increased employee insecurity, low morale, higher employee turnover, and, in extreme cases, work sabotages.

MEASURING the RESULTS of ACTIVITIES

The heart of rational management is *measurement*. Without it, we have, at best, only a "feel," or seat-of-the-pants, sense of

the results of "doing"; at the worst, we have activities that produce
results that run totally counter to the desired objectives. The most
negative result of management's failure to measure the outcome
of activity is probably the uncertainty concerning that outcome
and the attendant inability to justify, condemn, or change (logically)
that activity.

In chapter 3, we discussed measuring performance. We suggested
and gave examples of three different types of measures—efficiency,
effectiveness, and environmental. Another term—"productivity
measure"—is often used by managers and seen in the literature.
Because confusion often arises over the meaning of such terms
as "productivity," "efficiency," and "effectiveness," we feel it is
beneficial to clarify the jargon.

In February 1974, The Urban Institute and the International
City Management Association published a report, "Measuring the
Effectiveness of Basic Municipal Services." In chapter I, *Background, Scope, and Approach,* Section C, a number of terms were
defined so well that we have included them here.*

Placing Measures of Effectiveness in Context

It is useful to distinguish three types of performance measurement:

1. *Measures of Effectiveness.* They measure the extent to which
the goals and objectives of the service are being met. They should
attempt to measure such aspects as:

— The degree to which the intended purposes of the services
are being met.
— The degree to which unintended, adverse impacts of the service
on the community occur.
— The adequacy of the quantity of the service provided relative
to the community's needs, desires, and willingness to pay.
— The speed and courtesy displayed in responding to citizen
requests.
— Citizen perceptions of the satisfactoriness of the service (even
though these may not be in agreement with "factual" observations).

In sum, they should measure whatever is involved in answering
the question, "How well is this service doing what it should do
for the citizens and the community?"

*Initial Report, The Urban Institute and the International City Management
Association, Washington, D.C., February 1974.

2. *Efficiency Measures.* These measures attempt to relate the amount of a service output produced to the amount of input required to produce it, e.g., number of tons collected per man-hour. They indicate how efficiently the service is being provided. Governments often use the inverse form: the amount of input could be units of workload performed, or potentially, units of effectiveness achieved. Efficiency measures complement measures of effectiveness, since an "ineffective" service can be provided efficiently and an "effective" service can be provided inefficiently.

The term *productivity measure* is often used to refer to an efficiency measure in the form of output per unit of input. However, we believe that the term *productivity* should be used to encompass both effectiveness and efficiency concerns examined jointly. (This usage is in keeping with its broader meaning of "productive" as encouraged by the National Commission on Productivity.)

3. *Measures of Workload Performed.* These measure the amount of work done. They serve various operational purposes and can be used to justify expenditures and to determine budget requirements. But such measures (e.g., tons of waste collected, millions of gallons of water processed, or number of square yards of road repaired) indicate little about the effectiveness or proxies for effectiveness measures. We strongly recommend against this practice for assessing effectiveness.

In the foregoing quotation, "measures of workload performed" are in reality one part of the efficiency equation, that is, efficiency = output/input—and that is *output.*

Another section of the report deals with how to select appropriate, meaningful measures.

Sources of Objectives and Measures of Effectiveness

These sources might be used by local governments in identifying candidates:
a. Statements of goals and objectives and measures currently in use by local governments such as displayed in program budgets.
b. Those used or suggested by professionals in each service, based on numerous discussions with agency personnel and with representatives of national professional organizations.
c. Analysis of citizens' complaints to local governments.
d. Citizens' concerns as expressed in a small number of newspapers.
e. Professional literature.
f. Suggestions by reviewers of project draft reports.

Criteria for Selection of Measures and Data Collection Procedures

In selecting measures of effectiveness and data collection procedures, these criteria might be used by local governments in
selecting their own measures:

1. *Appropriateness and Validity.* Does the measure relate to the
   government objective for that service and does it really measure
   the degree to which a citizen's need or desire is being met?
2. *Uniqueness.* Does it measure some effectiveness characteristic
   that no other measure encompasses?
3. *Completeness.* Does the list cover all or at least most objectives?
4. *Comprehensibility.* Is the measure understandable?
5. *Controllability.* Is the condition measured at least partially the
   government's responsibility? Does the government have some
   control over it? (This has particular importance in the selection,
   interpretation and use of measures.)
6. *Cost.* Are cost and manpower requirements for data collection
   reasonable? This will depend partly on the government's funding
   situation and its interest in a particular measure. To keep
   data collection economically feasible, measures and procedures
   are suggested for use that are the same, or as similar as possible
   to those currently in use.
7. *Accuracy and Reliability.* Can sufficiently accurate and reliable
   information be obtained? This is a problem not only with
   procedures that use samples, such as citizen surveys, but with
   many government statistics, such as crime rates.

The report recommends *against* excluding a measure solely
because there does not appear to be any current problem associated
with the characteristic to be measured. It is important that all
important service characteristics be covered by the total measurement system, so that the citizens and their government may be
sure that the possibility of problems has been periodically checked.
Regular measurement may find the existence of a wholly unsus-
pected problem. If not, then the set of measures will include relevant
measures on which current performance is good, and thus properly
credit good performance.*

Program Planning and Budgeting

For some governments, program planning and budgeting will be
the principal uses of effectiveness measurement. It can show where

*The uses of effectiveness data are outlined in the 1974 Urban Institute report.
The material in this section is drawn from that report.

the government and its services are or are not meeting objectives. As information is collected over time, it will indicate whether progress is being made and to what extent.

Exhibit A illustrates a format for summarizing effectiveness measurement data. It illustrates the presentation of data on population groups within the community (major neighborhoods in this case) and on time trends.

Higher management may want to see only a few key measures for each service area on a regular basis, while the full spectrum of measures would be useful to agency heads. However, in view of the potential importance of each measure, it would be appropriate to do some reporting by exception, in which information would be reported when a preselected threshold was exceeded.

This information should help government officials identify priorities for allocating resources by indicating problem areas and areas of particular citizen concern (for measures where citizen surveys are used). Where this reflects service effectiveness levels delivered to major population groups, the government obtains a perspective on the balance of service delivery among the various clientele groups.

Service effectiveness data *by itself* will not generally indicate why a condition is poor or what to do about it. However, analysis of that data can help identify what may be wrong and why. For example, citizen ratings of such services as recreation, libraries, and transit may suggest ways in which service is falling short—one city found that many people failed to use public recreation facilities simply because they were unaware of their existence. This has led the city to consider programs for increasing awareness.

For budgeting, effectiveness information should be helpful not only in the preparation phase, but also in making the budget more understandable to the council and the general public.

Management Operations

Effectiveness data can be used to supplement other types of data in managing operations. To be useful for operational purposes effectiveness data needs to be collected more frequently than for annual program planning or budgeting. Some effectiveness measures already are reported frequently, such as crime, fire, and traffic accident data. Much other data can also be collected and reported more frequently if the local government is willing to pay the cost.

There are two ways such data can be used. First, it can be channeled

Exhibit A. Illustrative summary format for presentation of selected effectiveness measurement data: recreation services.

Measures of Effectiveness	Neighborhood (Current Year)									Whole City Current Year	City Previous Year
	I	II	III	IV	V	VI	VII	VIII	IX		
Percent of persons who participated less than 5 times during the year in major government-sponsored activities.	15%	25%	25%	70%	10%	60%	5%	70%	80%	40%	50%
That portion of #1 whose reasons for non-participation were at least partially affectable by government action.	(7%)	(20%)	(10%)	(40%)	(2%)	(40%)	(4%)	(50%)	(60%)	(25%)	(30%)
Percent of persons *not* within 15 minutes' walking time of a neighborhood park or playground.	6%	8%	10%	8%	7%	21%	3%	16%	22%	11%	14%
Total number of severe injuries.	4	0	2	3	1	3	1	4	7	25	32
Percent of persons rating overall recreation opportunities as either "fair" or "poor."	10%	7%	5%	18%	14%	30%	5%	12%	25%	12%	12%

into weekly or monthly resource allocation decisions. For example, the street cleanliness rating information could be used to help establish monthly, or even weekly, assignments of street cleaning crews.

The second use of more frequent data is to identify quickly problems needing early or immediate attention. For example, if daily water supply tests for harmful chemicals indicate a dangerous level, this is acted on when discovered, not at the next reporting interval. Or, if the crime rate is reported weekly or monthly, a sharp increase in home burglaries could be detected quickly and the police could take immediate action. Even citizen surveys can be spread throughout the year to provide more frequent (but, because of the smaller sub-samples, somewhat less precise) information on operational aspects such as the courtesy of public employees.

Data classified by service districts can provide agency management information on relative performance of district teams and indicate where changes might be desirable.

When data is provided for periods of less than a year, care should be taken to identify and allow for seasonal differences.

Program Evaluation and Analysis

"Program evaluation" attempts to determine the impact of current programs and includes the attempt to screen out impacts of "external factors." "Program analysis" examines alternative courses of proposed government actions.

Effectiveness data is vital to both evaluation and analysis. Programs should be assessed in terms of the changes they can produce in service effectiveness. Evaluation measures the changes that have occurred; analysis predicts changes in effectiveness.

Regular effectiveness measurement does not replace the need for program evaluation or analysis. Rather, it is a necessary step in carrying out such evaluation and analysis.

Systematic program evaluation and analysis is not a major activity in local government today, but interest appears to be growing. A recent development is the Government Accounting Office's recently established performance auditing standards that encourage the auditing of program results as well as government efficiency and fiscal compliance. [This is discussed more fully in Chapter 3.]

The effectiveness measures used by a local government for regular measurement should serve as a good starting point for evaluation and analyses by suggesting candidates for evaluation criteria in those studies. Also regularly collected data may be of direct use in the studies. However, for many programs evaluations and analyses, special data collection will be needed to fit the particular timing and scope of the particular study.

Establishing Performance Targets

One way of measuring that effectiveness measures make a difference in local government operations is to establish effectiveness targets. This gives employees goals to work for and may encourage innovations. Exhibit B illustrates a reporting format for summarizing progress against targets.

Only a few governments, most notably New York City, have established performance targets and a regular reporting system. Many governments have established workload targets, such as the number of park benches to be maintained in a given period, but these tell little about progress in effectiveness or quality. In fact, used alone, they can be perverse, by encouraging agencies to increase their workload (and hence their budget) by creating work or, at least, by discouraging a reduction of workload.

In setting targets, it is important not to rely on mandatory standards of performance when the means to achieve those standards are not known. If targets are used punitively, all the problems involved in interpreting the data become potential grounds for unjust punishment. Personnel who will have responsibility for meeting targets should help select them.

Establishing Employee Incentive Programs

One increasingly popular use of targets is in incentive programs for both managerial and nonmanagerial personnel and using both monetary and nonmonetary awards. Such incentive programs, if not based on comprehensive measurements, can be perverse, encouraging employees to emphasize certain service aspects at the expense of others. As meaningful and comprehensive effectiveness measures become available, better incentive programs become increasingly possible.

Few government employee incentive programs are yet linked to performance. However, in 1973, some potentially ground-breaking experiments were initiated. Cost sharing or wage-related experiments are being tried in Detroit and Flint, Michigan, and in Orange City, California. Detroit and Flint have a cost-sharing formula for sanitation workers based on both efficiency and quality. The Orange City experiment relates future police salary increases to crime rates. As more comprehensive measures become available and more experience is gained, potential perversities in the

Exhibit B. Illustrative format for reporting actual vs. targeted performance: solid waste collection.

Performance Measurement[a]	Actual Value Prev. Yr. (FY '73)	Target Current Year (FY '74)	Status of Targets as of ⸺ Target[c]	1974 Quarterly Performance[d] 1st	2nd	3rd	4th
Percent of blocks whose appearance is rated unsatisfactory (fairly dirty or very dirty—2.5 or worse on visual rating scale).[b]	18%	13%	Target	16%	14%	12%	10%
Average block cleanliness rating.	2.2	1.8	Actual	—	—	—	—
			Target	2.1	1.9	1.7	1.6
Number of fires involving uncollected solid waste.	17	12	Actual	—	—	—	—
			Target	3	4	3	2
Percent of households reporting having seen one or more rats during period of 1 year.	15%	8%	Target	Citizen survey to be undertaken once in 3rd quarter.		8%	—
Percent of households reporting 1 or more missed collections during 1 year.	17%	12%	Actual				
			Target	Citizen survey to be undertaken once in 3rd quarter.		12%	—
Percent of households rating overall neighborhood cleanliness as "usually dirty" or "very dirty."	23%	18%	Actual				
			Target			18%	—
			Actual				

[a] Room for agency comments on its performance on each measurement would also be desirable.

[b] Ideally, estimates of the amount of (statistical) uncertainty should be provided when they are available.

[c] Quarterly targets should be set to reflect seasonal variations.

[d] A government may also want to display the cumulative results as of the end of each quarter.

incentives should be reduced. But governments, their employees, and the public will have to accept less than perfect accuracy in the performance measures. They will also need to accept the fact that improved performance may not always be due solely to the action of the rewarded government employees.

To maintain public credibility and the accuracy of collected data, periodic audits of the effectiveness (and efficiency) measurement will probably be needed.

Performance Contracting

When a government contracts for a service (whether with another governmental body or with a private organization), some measures may be useful in controlling the quality of the contractor's performance. For example, if a government contracts for solid waste collection, at least some of the measures for solid waste collection should be included in the contract to set minimum quality levels (such as a particular street cleanliness rating) or even to provide performance incentives such as specified bonuses for attaining higher quality levels.

Improving Citizen Feedback for Government Decision Making

The type of measurement described in the Urban Institute-ICMA report can stimulate more and better citizen feedback in two ways.

First, some measures require systematic surveying of citizens. With proper procedures, the information obtained can be considerably more representative of the community than mere citizen complaint data (which is highly self-selective), or the personal observations of individual managers or officials, or periodic contacts by officials with a selective part of the population.

Second, availability of such information should promote more meaningful dialogue between citizens and their government. The ordinary citizen has only a limited understanding of technical issues such as workloads. Information on service effectiveness and quality will be more interesting and understandable to him.

Not all public officials will welcome such increased involvement, particularly of the second type. Increased citizen interest could involve more problems and more demands. However, many governments already face increasing pressure from special interest groups and communications media. Systematic, objective believable information should prove useful to government officials in responding to citizen concerns.

Justifying Wage and Salary Increases

Data on changes in effectiveness (as well as efficiency data, cost-of-living information, etc.) can provide a basis for determining and justifying annual wage and salary increases. This important use of effectiveness measurement data has the problem discussed earlier that government employees seldom have complete responsibility for, and control over, changes in the measured values. Nevertheless, effectiveness data seems likely, on balance, to provide relevant information for help in the determination of wage and salary changes, and this usage seems likely to grow in the future.

Interpretation of Effectiveness Data

To use effectiveness data, measured levels of effectiveness will inevitably need to be compared with reference levels to determine if a measured condition is good or bad. Some local governments will want to set targets against which actual performance can be compared. Some ways to establish these reference levels or targets and some problems in using them are as follows:

(a) *Performance can be compared with that of performance in previous years.* Such information will not become available until a measure has been used for more than a year. When data on more than one previous year is available, the government may want to establish targets based on projected trends over these past years. Such targets need to be modified, however, if external factors affecting the measure have changed. If comparisons are made for periods less than a year, seasonality factors will need to be considered.

(b) *In some cases, the performance of other governments will be available for comparison.* Such comparisons, of course, are valid only if the same measurements are used. For example, data are available nationally on both reported and unreported crime rates and on arrest and fire rates. But there is little data permitting comparisons on most of the proposed effectiveness measures. As more local governments undertake such measurement, more information will become available. But comparisons will have to be made carefully because of the many differences between jurisdictions.

(c) *Comparisons among service districts or population groups within a jurisdiction may be used.* This may become a major basis for setting targets. For example, one city recently used street cleanliness ratings to set targets to improve the cleanliness of the dirtier areas by stages to more nearly the level of the cleaner areas of the city. Governments could use service districts (sanitation, park, or police districts) that perform well as targets for poorer performance districts. But since differences in performance may reflect inherent differences among the districts (or population groups) rather than differences in the effectiveness of the city service, different targets for different population groups or service districts may be justified.

(d) *Targets might be based on estimates of how much change in effectiveness the government can achieve.* This may be the best approach but requires in depth analysis and even then is likely to be feasible only in very selective circumstances.

These approaches can be used individually or in combination. But managers and staff should use sound judgment in adopting any of them.

Another important interpretation problem is to determine *why* a measured condition has changed and *what government action,* if any, is desirable. Some of the measurement data may provide some clues (such as differences in the measures for different geographical areas of the community). Governments using effectiveness measurement certainly will want to examine changes in measurement results carefully so as to identify the causes and suggest appropriate actions. It is important that local governments use their measurement experience as it develops to improve their understanding of what is achievable and how and at what cost.

CHANGING ACTIVITIES

When activities have been measured and it is learned that the projected, hypothesized, or hoped-for results are not being achieved, then *change* should be implemented.

Change may affect the plan of action, establish new and different objectives, or refine or alter the manner and nature of the measurement itself. Effective management, which by its very nature is dynamic, is characterized by automatic "system correction."

Because change is seen as necessary, desirable, and inevitable and because it should be rational, managers could facilitate control of change by *documenting* it as it occurs or as it is imposed. This is often referred to as "change control," "configuration control," or "change management." We suggest that a management journal be used to document change. This journal can vary in format depending on the activities being managed or supervised and the level of supervision in the organization, but it should contain entries that state the time/date of an event that is suspected of creating a change, the nature of the event, and the suspected effect. Periodic summary statements can make the journal inestimably valuable when reviewing program operations.

BEHAVIORAL ASPECTS of RATIONAL MANAGEMENT

Public management is concerned with the behavior of people. Of all the resources available to the public manager, people are the largest, most expensive group (comprising about 85 percent or more of a typical local government operating budget). It is essential that the effective manager understand how people behave, at least in a general sense.

In Chapter 3, we described Maslow's hierarchy of needs and how such needs affect motivation, that is, human behavior is goal-directed toward need satisfaction. What people expect and want from their jobs is of prime importance in terms of motivating them to perform work effectively and efficiently. Further, most workers, including managers, in public sector organizations are fulfilling needs on three levels of Maslow's hierarchy—security, social, and psychological needs levels. Only security needs are basically satisfied by salaries and wages.

Because most public employees receive wages that satisfy reasonable security needs, employees are really working to satisfy social and psychological needs. This flies in the face of the old concept that people are "motivated" by money.

Frederick Herzberg* dealt with the motivational factor in a way that is very practical for the public manager. He defines two different aspects of the motivational problem: hygiene factors, which prevent dissatisfaction, and motivational factors, which lead to more positive attitudes and higher motivation.

Hygiene factors include wages, fringe benefits, physical working conditions, and the administration's general style or policy. Herzberg states that dissatisfaction will disappear when these factors are adequately taken care of; however, *no positive attitudes and motivation result.* In other words, hygiene factors do not motivate workers to increase their levels of productivity.

Motivational factors include recognition, a sense of accomplishment, opportunities for advancement and personal growth, a sense of individual importance, new experiences, and challenging work

*Frederick Herzberg, "The Motivation-Hygiene Concept and Problems of Manpower," *Personnel Administration*, January-February 1964, pp. 3–7.

situations. These factors act to develop positive job attitudes, thereby increasing productivity.

To sum up, employees are dissatisfied when hygiene needs are not met; however, they are not motivated to improve productivity when they are met. To motivate workers, social, psychological, and self-fulfillment needs should be considered.

In order for an employee to be positively motivated to increase or improve his productivity, he must know that a given behavior will result in a favorable state of affairs (reward). Management must therefore communicate to the employee in understandable and consistent terms that certain behavior will result in specific rewards.

Although the student of management has been bombarded with different concepts and theories relating to management style and the effect of style on the outcomes of managed activities, let's look at "management style" from a simple, common-sense approach. Before doing so, however, a framework of assumptions is needed:

Assumption. There are jobs that need doing.
Assumption. Managers want the work done efficiently and effectively.
Assumption. A general feeling of goodwill throughout the organization is desirable.
Assumption. Jobs are not created merely to provide employment opportunities.

Given the above assumptions, let us imagine that we have a meaningful job that needs doing in the most efficient and effective manner possible. In terms of style, management can take two extreme positions. One position entails using negative reinforcement—that is, threats and punishment to achieve worker performance and desired job results; the other entails using positive reinforcement—that is, rewards and other positive incentives. Although both positions *can* result in job or task fulfillment, what are the side effects?

Students of animal behavior have long observed that the use of negative reinforcement in training sessions produces rigid, accurate, mechanical, and fearful or angry performance; whereas positive reinforcement produces spontaneous, joyful, and sometimes creative and less accurate performance. Rigid, errorless, and inflexible performances are absolutely mandatory in a few public activities. Public safety activities have these requirements. We certainly don't want those charged with guarding the public treasury to become "too creative" or inaccurate. For the vast array of public activities, however, such rigid performance is not only not needed, it is undesirable, especially if we want to improve productivity.

If we wish to exemplify the style of management that achieves maximum organizational productivity, the successful manager would:

- Delegate rather than "do."
- Interact with employees on a one-to-one basis.
- Avoid "scaring" or intimidating employees.
- "Overcommunicate" rather than "undercommunicate."
- Encourage open communications at all levels. Abhor secrecy.
- Encourage and positively reinforce rational management at all levels of the organization.
- Encourage desired performance by "setting an example."
- *Listen* to all employees.
- Require a rigid organizational structure only when it is absolutely necessary from a legal standpoint or from an efficiency/effectiveness standpoint. Rigid structure produces rigid behavior.
- Follow the Golden Rule, that is, "Do unto others as you would have them do unto you."

MANAGEMENT BY OBJECTIVES

No discussion of management style would be complete without including management by objectives (MBO). MBO is not new; yet there are relatively few success stories about it in the private or public sector. It seems important to discuss the reasons behind the failures. Six are singled out here for discussion.

1. MBO is often thought of as another faddish procedure imposed on the organization by top management. In too many cases this is true. Although lip service is paid to MBO by all levels of management, the basic style of management remains unchanged.

MBO is a management style. The objective is "improved performance" through more effective communications. The hypotheses underlying this style are, first, objectives have a greater chance of being attained if they are clearly defined and understood and, second, progress should be measured against the organization's agreed-upon goals.

Management style must change from one of "intuition"* to one of measured accomplishment.

2. MBO is often used to appraise personnel: people who meet their objectives get raises and promotions. This results in "game playing" by those writing the objectives so that their own images are enhanced. It is unlikely that performance will improve under these conditions. MBO will improve performance if it is used to:

   a. Develop greater commitment and motivation of employees by including them in the development of work goals and objectives.
   b. Encourage a broader base for decision making.
   c. Provide better direction and control of organization operations through performance reporting.

Objectives should come from a consensus among different levels of management and between management and working personnel.

Encourage development of objectives in the organization from the bottom up.

3. Because objectives are often too easily achieved, they should be written so that people have to stretch to achieve them. Success reinforces a person's ability to succeed, but only if he knows that success was not certain. No failures indicate that people are being too cautious. A failure rate of 10 to 20 percent probably should be expected, and failure certainly should not be interpreted as prima facie evidence of poor performance. Objectives should be achieved because of the combined efforts of management and those managed.

The most important role of management is to provide an environment that encourages accomplishment of objectives.

4. Agreed-upon objectives are too seldom reviewed. After the manager and his subordinate agree on the most important aspects of the latter's job in terms of objectives, performance in meeting those objectives is never discussed.

In many ways, the review is the most crucial part of MBO. It is here that, among other benefits, employees are recognized

---

*Defined by "management" as what is "best" (by intuition rather than measurement of results of activity).

for their accomplishments, gain fresh insights about their jobs, improve interpersonal relationships with their superiors, and become motivated to seek still higher goals.

Performance reviews must be conducted regularly and take priority in the managers' work schedules.

5. Reviews are often conducted in a threatening manner or hostile environment.

When reviewing progress, the manager should show his concern for the importance of meeting objectives. The reasons for not meeting objectives should be explored in a positive manner, and adjustments made in either the objectives or the steps that are taken to meet them. At the same time, the manager must be concerned about the subordinate being reviewed. The superior should take the role of a helper.

The focus of the review should be on the present and the future, not on past mistakes, which should be analyzed and turned into guidelines for future successes.

Reviews should be positive and helpful.

6. Before they can be truly committed to the philosophy underlying MBO, top managers must believe in certain principles:

a. *Self-Control.* Employees are capable of controlling themselves and the important aspects of their jobs without close supervision.

b. *Knowledge.* The person doing the job is in the best position to assess the realities of that job. With knowledge of organizational goals and with the guidance of his superior in setting objectives, a person has the knowledge to plan actions and make effective decisions.

c. *Record of Progress.* A system is needed to record progress and accomplishments. Merely holding a job in the organization is not enough. A person's credentials should be established by more than his having spent so many years in a position. Management wants to know (and the person in the job wants to know) what he has done—in other words, his track record.

d. *Two-Way Communication.* A firm understanding between a superior and a subordinate regarding what the latter is attempting to accomplish lays a foundation for cooperation,

coordination, and effective interpersonal relations. It gives
the subordinate autonomy to pursue his objectives, and it
creates a climate of open communications.

*Top management must be truly committed to a new management
style.*

5

Public
Budgeting Systems

BY definition, budgeting is the process by which resources are allocated to accomplish a specified task or tasks. Although the concept of budgeting is very old, it is only during the last two centuries that budgetary systems have formally appeared in organized governments.

In the young United States, the new federal government quickly gave Congress direct control over appropriations of public monies, primarily in reaction to the excessive power of the monarchical governments of that time.

Until the Bureau of the Budget was established in 1921, Congress maintained almost exclusive control over federal appropriations. Prior to 1921, a standard method of accounting did not exist. Each federal department submitted requests for funds to Congress, often at different times during the year. These requests were usually made on the basis of unsupported and general estimates. In the early 1900s, public dissatisfaction with increased government spending and numerous exposés of corruption and incompetence led to a nationwide reform movement.

Fiscal control budgeting, which grew out of the reform movement, was used to exercise administrative control over spending. Uniform accounting procedures were established, purchasing and personnel controls were centralized, and auditing methods were initiated.

During the 1920s and 1930s, the *line-item budget* evolved, and it flourishes to this day. It should be emphasized that until the late 1930s the budgetary process focused on controlling expenditures, not on planning or program development. The line-item budget listed expenditures under broad headings, for example, engineering support, clerical support, number of pieces of equipment purchased.

During World War II, the Bureau of the Budget gained more authority over coordinating operations and improving the general management of the governnent. As a result of Hoover Commission recommendations, the National Security Act Amendments of 1949 and the Budget and Accounting Procedures Act of 1950 required the federal government to use the performance budget. Primarily concerned with after-the-fact auditing of programs and activities, the performance budget was not interested in how well revenues were allocated. Program descriptions were based on the activities being performed rather than on resources required to perform those activities effectively. Program control was shifted from fiscal officials to general managers.

Performance budgeting did not catch hold, probably because the 1950s did not encourage change and, more importantly, because this type of budgeting dealt with how efficiently an activity was conducted, not with whether the activity was worthwhile in the first place. As a result, government officials and administrators returned to the line-item budget.

LINE-ITEM BUDGETING

The line-item, or object-account, budget enumerates estimated expenditures by type and quantity for a specified period of time, usually one year (the fiscal year). Personnel are listed by type of position, such as clerk typist, engineer, and inspector; that is, the budget is divided into sections according to organizational units, department, division, section; and types of expenditures are listed by category.

As we stated earlier, the primary purpose of the line-item budget is *control*—control of expenditures to ensure that public monies are spent for the purpose intended and to monitor and protect fiscal resources. Because of this "controlling" nature, the line-item budget encourages management to balance the budget and to review regularly how the financial affairs of the organization are proceeding. The line-item budget contains several inherent disadvantages:

1. It does not lend itself to long-range planning.
2. It does not encourage examining whether or not activities are producing desirable results. The budget cannot be related to measurable objectives.
3. New appropriations are made on the basis of the previous year's budget.
4. It encourages competition for available funds among units of the organization.
5. Any duplication of effort is hard to detect and document.
6. It encourages "management-by-crisis," because there is a tendency to concentrate only on the most pressing demands, thereby avoiding activities whose fiscal effects cannot be seen immediately.

In summary, the line-item budget provides for short-range fiscal control with built-in rigidity. Although it inhibits rational management of public activities and programs, it is nonetheless the budget process that is prevalent in government.

In previous chapters, we have emphasized the necessity for evaluating the outcomes or results of activities. Measurement is an essential component of evaluation. The "cost" of activity is a prime measure. Let's review the steps in the evaluation process:

Establish goals deemed necessary to satisfy needs.

Establish measurable objectives for each goal, that is, if objectives are met, goal attainment will be fulfilled. (Evaluation tests this hypothesis.)

List performance criteria necessary to define satisfactory accomplishment of each objective.

Develop measures of performance for each objective.

Develop an initial plan of action for accomplishing each objective. Include the means by which measures of performance will be made (data collection).

Make measurements (collect data) as plan of action is implemented.

Determine data analyses to evaluate efficiency.

Report performance evaluation results. (Must include a comparison of actual outcomes to those hypothesized to result if objectives are met.)

Suggest and implement changes, improvements, and so forth, in operation or objectives to better satisfy goals (meet needs).

If we look at these steps, we can see that, almost without exception, "operational cost" will be a performance criterion for every objective. Because the line-item budget does not present cost data in a manner that is usable for program or activity evaluation, program budgeting was designed to meet the requirements of rational management concepts.

PROGRAM BUDGETING

Although first suggested at the turn of the twentieth century, program budgeting was not used until Robert McNamara introduced it in the Defense Department in 1961. As a result of its success there, in 1965 President Lyndon Johnson ordered all federal departments to adopt program budgeting. It was referred to as the Planning-Programming-Budgeting System (PPBS).

Although PPBS worked well under McNamara's leadership, it did not succeed with the rest of the federal government, and its use was abandoned in 1971. The most significant reason for this failure was that PPBS was held out as a panacea for all federal government problems. Since instant solutions were not available, PPBS was regarded as a failure.

As the 1970s ground on, the costs of government at all levels skyrocketed, the public's distrust of government grew, and the public began to demand that government "be accountable" for what it was doing and spending.

First, what was needed to respond to the public? We needed a budgeting system that would improve the chances that tax dollars would be allocated in such a way that the system could achieve its stated goals and objectives in satisfying public "needs." Second, a system was needed that inhibited "seat-of-the-pants" (intuitive) allocation methods or those that allocated funds according to past budgets. Some public managers began to realize that program budgeting provided these factors. Program budgeting allocates public funds to specified programs whose activities are hypothesized to satisfy specific public needs.

Let's look at an example. Most medium- or large-size cities have separate police, fire, and building (or public works) departments. Most of the activities of police and fire departments and some of the activities of the building department are concerned with public safety. With program budgeting, we first identify a public need. For our example, we will define a public need thusly: "The public wants and needs activities that promote public safety." We can translate this need into a program goal statement: "The goal of the city's Public Safety Program is to promote public safety throughout the city." (Remember, goals can be general, "motherhood" statements of purpose or intent.) But now we must become specific and list program objectives that are measurable and attend to specific needs. Some public safety objectives might be:

Reduce the incidence of residential burglaries in the city from 3,000 to 2,000 per year in this program year.
Reduce the value of unrecovered stolen property from $2 million to $1.5 million per year in this program year.

Although in reality we would list many more objectives, for illustrative purposes let's stop with the two listed. At this point, we suggest activities that are hypothesized to accomplish the objectives. They might include:

Adding three 24-hour patrol units to the existing patrol force.
Conducting public courses in burglary abatement.
Organizing citizen burglary abatement watches.

Which if any of these activities we select is dependent on cost. However, it should be apparent that even before objectives are developed, activities selected, or dollars allocated, public needs must be prioritized in terms of their *importance to the public* ("public interest"). As we have stated, program budgeting allocates public funds to specified programs whose activities are hypothesized to satisfy public needs. It should be apparent that any public manager who intends to rationally manage programs in the public interest will insist that program budgeting is the only satisfactory approach. Later in this chapter, we will discuss some of the criticisms of program budgeting.

Elements of Program Budgeting

The program budget comprises several basic elements,* each of which will be discussed separately:

1. *Program*—A program is comprised of all those interdependent, closely related services or activities that, operating together, are expected to fulfill a major public need (goal). It should be limited in scope, have overlap with other programs only minimally, be outcome-oriented, and have measurable program results. Examples are: fire suppression program, crime prevention program, recreation program, building safety program. All activities within individual programs are functionally related, and each activity is hypothesized to meet, or help meet, a specific, measurable objective. Activities, acting together, tend toward goal attainment.

2. *Goal(s)*—A goal is a broad, general statement that reflects an end state or condition that, when attained, satisfies a major public need. For example: "The goal of the crime prevention program is to conduct activities in the community that result in a significant reduction in the incidence of crime and create a community feeling of 'personal safety' when living, working, and playing in the community." As can be seen, although goals are broad and idealistic, progress toward their attainment can be measured. The incidence of crime is measurable as are citizens' feelings about their personal safety.

3. *Need*—Before objectives can be formulated and plans of action developed, a public need must be identified. A need is a statement of the problem that the program is designed to alleviate, phrased in such a way that it is possible to measure and state results of activities in terms of need fulfillment. For example: "Because of the high current burglary rate in the city (compared to ten years ago), there is a need to significantly reduce that burglary rate." A need must be real for a program to be justified. If a program does not fulfill an identified need, it should be abandoned.

4. *Objective(s)*—Objectives are specific and quantitative statements that describe what is to be achieved, by what resources, and within what time frame. Objectives must be realistic, attainable,

*Some of the descriptive material presented here was drawn from Michael Babunakis, "Recasting the Budgetary Process," Urban Observatory, City of San Diego, California, 1974.

and contribute to the attainment of a goal(s). For example, in satisfying the above need, it is hypothesized: "Establish four burglary abatement details, two-man shifts in the four high crime areas of the community by September 1, 19—, in order to effect a reduction in the incidence of burglary in the community."

The proper definition and drafting of objectives are critical aspects of the program budget, because they influence a program's activities and ultimately its success or failure. Objectives should not be formulated with the sole purpose of justifying ongoing activities. Rather, they must be stated in terms of satisfaction of public needs. In other words, objectives should guide the type and direction of activities engaged in.

5. *Program element*—A program element is a subdivision of a program with its own set of specific objectives. For instance: Within the fire prevention program, we might have "the building inspection program element," "the citizens' fire prevention education program element," and "the brush fire abatement program element." Satisfactory accomplishment of the objectives of each of these elements helps satisfy the objectives of the overall fire prevention program.

6. *Authority*—Authority is that section of the legal code that allows or requires the existence of a program or program element. It may be local, state, or federal.

7. *General program description*—The general program description briefly explains the activities of the program or program element. It provides the lay person with a basic understanding of what the program is all about. Anyone examining the budget document will know what activities are planned and what changes (if any) are planned for the new program year.

8. *Program resources required (or expended)*—This provides a description of manpower and other resources required or expended by a program. It lists expenditures by the various activities that comprise a program or program element.

9. *Measures of performance*—Measures of performance should establish the degree by which objectives are met. They are divided into: (a) measures of effectiveness; (b) measures of efficiency; and (c) measures of workload performed. (See Chapter 4, "Rational Program Management," for a description of each of these measures.)

Generally, the most troublesome of the elements are the objectives and the measures of performance. The principal problem with drafting objectives relates to the specificity that is required for an objective to be measurable. First attempts often result in objectives like the following: "Operate the motor pool in an efficient and effective manner," "Provide adequate recreational activities for the community," "Maintain the parks so that they are aesthetically pleasing," "Operate the city swimming pool in a safe manner."

Each of these objectives is deficient, because the terms that are used, such as "efficient," "effective," "adequate," "aesthetically pleasing," "safe manner," are nonspecific in terms of measurement. Each term must be further defined before the objective can be described as measurable. Better objectives might be: "In the operation of the motor pool, maintain a sufficient inventory of vehicles so that a vehicle is available upon request at any time during working hours for 90 percent of the working days in the year" (effectiveness measurements can be made). "In the operation of the motor pool, maintain a sufficient inventory of vehicles so that no more than 20 percent of the total inventory is not in use at any one time during working hours" (efficiency measurement is possible). "Operate 8 tennis courts, 4 hours per evening, 5 weekdays per week" (effectiveness measure).

In each of the "better" objectives above, a need was carefully determined before a sensible objective was stated. Objectives are usually vague when needs are inadequately assessed.

The more accurately the need is assessed, the easier it is to arrive at measures of performance that relate to whether or not objectives are being met.

In general, the greater the precision employed in determining needs and selecting objectives that satisfy those needs, the easier it is to meet public accountability demands. All government activities must, either directly or indirectly, accomplish measurable objectives that, when met, satisfy a public need. Activities that do not meet these criteria are suspect and should be carefully investigated for legitimacy.

Implementing Program Budgeting

Most public organizations still use line-item budgeting. Because the changeover from line-item to program budgeting is time consuming and adds extra work, experience indicates that a transitional period of at least three and preferably five years be allotted before program budgeting is fully in use. Moreover, the right kinds and numbers of personnel and fiscal resources must be committed throughout the entire implementation period.

Controversy has arisen over whether or not both budgeting systems should be used during the changeover period. We strongly recommend against using both budgeting systems for any period of time: the duplication of effort, added to the trauma associated with such a major "change," usually leads to tremendous resistance to the program budgeting system. Once the program budget format is developed and adopted, line-item budgeting should be discontinued.

Two issues are critical to successfully implementing a program budget: (1) top management commitment and (2) the manner in which change is managed. Discussion of these issues follows.

Top Management Commitment

We strongly believe that unless the chief executive of the public organization fully comprehends and *champions* the management concepts of program budgeting, the effort required to implement the process will be a waste of time. The top manager must firmly believe that all the public organization's activities must relate to, and be accountable in, the satisfaction of public needs.

Students and practitioners of public administation often give lip service to this principle, hastening to add, however, that "political realities" and "nontangibles" make it impractical in the real world. This is simply not valid. In a free society, governments are created by the public to provide in an organized manner public services that satisfy public needs. Any other reason given for "government" is neither moral nor legitimate.

Government officials are therefore morally and ethically bound to manage public organizations in a rational fashion, that is, goals are selected and prioritized on the basis of public need and activities are evaluated for effectiveness and efficiency in meeting the public need. Officials who are not committed to this rational approach are working for some reason other than "the public interest."

Managing "Change"

Even if the best plan and the greatest commitment for program budgeting were present, the implementation involves considerable change for all the employees. Almost universally, people resist change—even when that change is perfectly rational—because change generates feelings of insecurity.

All of us have a considerable investment in our jobs in terms of time, energy, and experience. When a new rule, procedure, or process is introduced, it can be viewed as a threat to that investment. Moreover, the older and more experienced we are, the greater our investment and the greater our resistance to change.

Furthermore, if the reasons for change are not clearly and fully communicated, feelings of ambiguity can result. Even when communication is clear, there will still be uncertainty and suspicion regarding the change.

Resistance to change can result in aggravated absenteeism, lateness, grievances, employee turnover, low morale, or decreased productivity. Because the consequences are serious, certain actions should be taken to minimize resistance:

1. Do everything possible to reduce the perceived threat to the employees' investment.
2. Provide as much information as possible about the reasons for and the details of the change, including predictions of likely effects on individuals, groups, or the organization as a whole.
3. Communicate through group discussions as much as possible. When employees have an "investment" in the mechanisms for change, resistance will be reduced.
4. Involve key members of the informal organization in all phases of the changeover.
5. Develop ways to reinforce, positively and publicly, employees' efforts in adopting the new system.

Information Management in the Program Budgeting Process

One major benefit from program budgeting is the amount and availability of information that can be used for more effectively managing the organization. On the other hand, however, supervisors, managers, and politicians may be unexpectedly burdened with more day-to-day information, *which they must deal with*, than they have received before. The long-term effect is nearly always beneficial, because the organization is forced to operate more efficiently and openly. This usually results in reorganization along program lines, increased lateral communications among programs, decentralized decision making, more participative management, and more open or public operations in general.

In a practical sense, the organization that is responsible for handling or processing data will experience a significant increase in its workload because of the data requirements of the program budgeting process. Because new data-gathering systems must be developed to evaluate programs more effectively, it is important to include data-processing personnel in the initial and ongoing implementation of the program budget.

Because this increase in workload is inevitable, every effort should be made to collect only meaningful and useful data. A balance must be struck between too few and too many data: too few data are obviously not meaningful; too many frustrate those collecting data and confuse those examining the budget. There is a tendency to acquire more data than can be sensibly handled; this tendency should be recognized and resisted.

ZERO-BASE BUDGETING

During the last few years, zero-base budgeting has been advocated. Zero-base budgeting requires that every expenditure be justified every year as if it were a new expenditure that has to be rationalized. Organizational units or programs are required to justify not only increased levels of spending but the continuance of current spending levels as well. In very large organizations, this may be too costly, time consuming, and impractical.

Although program budgeting does not necessarily imply zero-base budgeting, it does provide the data necessary for the analysis required by zero-base budgeting.

6

The Five-Year Operating Budget

THE short-run key to sound public sector program and financial planning is the five-year operating budget.* The five-year budget provides public administrators and policy makers with a very effective tool for matching program needs with revenue sources in time to identify new revenues, if needed and justified. Given the era of federal revenue sharing, it is particularly important to consider the development of a five-year budget. This chapter describes the development and implementation of a five-year operating budget in the City of Raleigh, North Carolina, with an estimated population of 150,000 in 1977. Many of the attributes of this system are applicable to other public sector organizations.

Why was the five-year budgeting program developed in Raleigh? In December 1969, a management study of Raleigh's operations, prepared by an outside consulting firm, listed three weaknesses of the city's existing budget preparation process:

---

*James L. Mercer, "The Five-Year Operating Budget," *Governmental Finance*, Vol. 2, No. 1, Chicago, Ill.: Municipal Finance Officers Association, February 1973.

1. In preparing his budget, the department head began, not with what he accomplished with his resources during the previous year, but simply with how much he spent.
2. The department head's budget estimate for the coming year was first presented in terms of expenditures, rather than of projects and activities to meet objectives.
3. An estimate for only one year in advance did not account for ongoing programs and new capital improvements that will require future operating funds.

In an effort to correct these weaknesses, the consultants recommended that the city conduct a budget and fiscal control study, one of the products of which was a budget manual for the city. This manual was to include a standardized format for budget preparation by each city department head, including objectives and descriptions of activities to meet those objectives. The system and format were to include provisions for projecting the operating budget request for a five-year period, by year, rather than for a single year. These projections were to include operating estimates for capital improvement projects that would become "on-line" during that period. This was to be the first step in a four- to five-year program of budget system improvements.

It was further recommended that the city contract for outside assistance in designing these budgeting systems. This assistance was to include developing the budget manual, the forms to be used in formulating and preparing the budget, a method of effectively communicating the budget to all interested parties, and performance criteria for all departments. The entire program was to be assigned a very high priority and was to be the major responsibility of a new assistant city manager for programming and budgeting, a position that was also recommended by the consulting firm.

The new assistant city manager for programming and budgeting was employed in July 1970, and during the first year, he worked almost exclusively on the capital improvements program and the annual operating budget. During the summer of 1971, with the assistance of the outside consultants, the first *Five-Year Operating Budget Instruction Manual* was prepared and issued to city department heads. However, because of a tremendous city effort that went into a successful 1971 capital improvements bond issue, the five-year operating budget had to take a low priority until 1972. The operating budget was prepared without the assistance of the outside consultants, whose contract had expired. Therefore, the *Five-Year Capital Improvements and Five-Year Operating Budget Instruction Manual* was the first real effort on the part of the City of Raleigh to prepare and adopt a five-year operating budget.

The five-year capital improvements and the five-year operating budgets were both included in the same instruction manual because they necessarily go hand in hand. Most capital improvements, when they become operational, increase the operating budget because of the addition of personnel, equipment, or materials.

THE PURPOSE

The primary aim of a five-year operating budget is to translate the planning goals and objectives of each city department and division into cost estimates of the various services to be provided during the next five-year period. These planning estimates identify a city's program needs and serve as guidelines for resources that must be available for the orderly growth of a city's services. Today's knowledge of tomorrow's operations is vital to the successful implementation of a city's programs.

Five-year budgeting attempts to answer some of the following questions:

1. What will existing programs cost five years from now?
2. Will the existing sources of revenue provide a desirable level of service in the years to come?
3. Given a five-year growth rate, what new programs will be needed in the next five years? Will the revenue sources be adequate to cover these needs?
4. How can the various functions and programs be made more efficient and effective in the next five years in order to balance revenues with expenditure needs?

A good five-year budget requires department heads to plan their functions and programs several years in advance. They must analyze their program impacts, costs, justifications, and priorities. By doing this, the operational and financial planning processes are strengthened at the functional organizational level, where they most need strengthening.

ESTIMATING AND PROJECTING FIVE-YEAR OPERATING REVENUES

Before reviewing the methods used by Raleigh for projecting five-year revenues, it is helpful to outline the city's major sources of revenue (see Table 6-1).

Table 6-1. Major sources of revenue—City of Raleigh.

Revenue Source	Estimate for FY 1973
Property tax and payments in lieu	$10,214,308
License fees and permits	909,650
State and county refunds	3,847,952
Penalties—arrest fees	186,000
Rents—miscellaneous income	444,552
Parking meter receipts	122,000
Water revenues	4,506,000
Assessment payments	257,000
Interest earnings	575,000
Interfund transfers	1,195,122
Total:	$22,257,584
Less: Interfund transfers	.−1,195,122
Net estimated revenue:	$21,062,462
Add: Continuing operating reserve for all funds	$4,100,799
Net revenue and operating reserves:	$25,163,261

In Raleigh, the following revenue-forecasting method is used:

1. Wherever possible, historical data for the past ten years are maintained on each item of revenue.
2. The year-to-year growth factor is computed and a ten-year average is obtained.
3. In developing an average growth factor, considerable practical experience is applied. Atypical years, which show unusual declines or increases, are eliminated. Some of the factors that determine atypical years are:
   a. Large annexations causing significant increases in assessed property values.
   b. Significant economic fluctuations, that is, depressions, recessions, decreases in population due to plant shutdowns, and so forth.

4. In addition, any known extrarevenue sources must be added. Such items include:

   a. Known or expected rate of tax increases.
   b. Known or expected large annexations.
   c. Expected increases in economic activity.
   d. Expected unusual population growths.

5. An excellent guide is the annual revenue publication of the North Carolina League of Municipalities. This publication gives the league's opinions as to what may be expected in various categories of state-distributed funds for the upcoming year. (Other states may have similar data available.)

6. The average yearly growth rate that is finally determined for each category of revenue is then applied and a five-year projection is obtained. This is then closely watched each year to determine how closely the actual revenue is to the revenue originally projected.

Throughout the revenue-projection process, the watchword is "conservatism." If revenues are projected too optimistically, false hopes and expectations will be generated and disappointment will result, usually at the governing board or city council level. On the other hand, if estimates are too conservative, essential programs and services may be curtailed. The real challenge is to walk a tightrope between optimism and conservatism, staying slightly on the conservative side.

ESTIMATING AND PROJECTING EXPENDITURES

Each operating department and division projects expenditures in three different categories:

Basic budget expenditures
Service maintenance budget expenditures
Service improvement budget expenditures

For example, let us look at Raleigh's basic solid waste collection program, which currently provides for six routes, with collections made two times each week. The basic program consists of six sanitation vehicles and six crews. If the same program is to be continued at the same level next year, then the cost of these items would be placed in the basic budget. Cost increases attributable to inflation or equipment replacements would also be included in the basic budget items.

If the city has grown because of, say, annexations and if the existing service level is to cover this additional area, then one new sanitation truck and one new crew will be needed. These additions would be included in the service maintenance budget.

Suppose, instead, that we wanted to provide for four collections a week, thereby doubling the current level of service. In order to do this, 12 sanitation trucks and 12 crews would be required. The extra trucks and crews would be included in the service improvement budget.

In projecting expenditure levels, city department heads must be provided with guidelines as a part of their instructions. The following basic assumptions must be established when the five-year budget is first being prepared:

- A standard rate of population growth for each year. (The planning department can usually provide this.)
- Effective dates when city services are to be provided to areas annexed.
- A standard yearly salary growth figure.
- Cost-of-living adjustment and inflationary factor information.
- Assumptions relative to economic fluctuations.
- Standard cost information relative to furniture, fixtures, equipment, standard services, and so forth.

In projecting five-year operating expenditures, Raleigh uses the current year's operating budget as the base year. Instructions state that estimates for projected expenditures should include those operating expenses necessary to carry out departmental plans and objectives at the current established level of service. If new programs are projected or existing programs and service levels are expanded, they must be fully justified and documented on the budget forms. As mentioned earlier, projected operating expenses also must include those personnel, materials, supplies, contractual services, and equipment expenses necessary to carry out the proposed five-year capital improvements program.

Under normal circumstances, the budget calendar for the five-year capital improvements program should coincide, insofar as possible, with the five-year operating budget calendar. This is necessary in order to facilitate the coordination of both program estimates.

7

Management
Information Systems

IN order to manage effectively, the public systems manager must be supplied with a continuous stream of information. The varied types of information, their availability, and the manner in which they are used require that the manager develop a system for dealing with this flow of information.

GENERAL CONCEPTS

Information comes from data, which are logical representations of measurements, observations, and computations. Logical is here defined as orderly, intelligible, objective, and capable of forming accurate relationships based on principles and rules of reason.

Although the information made available by an information system is always in the form of data, as defined here, not all data are information, that is, capable of being assigned a useful meaning. An information system is a "white elephant" if the data it supplies are not useful to the recipient.

These concepts, although basic, are too often ignored by designers and implementers of information systems. The user often is not involved either in the initial design or in the implementation of an information system, which is invariably a fatal error in developing a useful management information system.

Other important concepts relate to data processing and data management. Information is produced through data processing, which structures, collects, records, communicates, manipulates, interrelates, stores, retrieves, and reports data. Data processing is controlled by data management, which is the planning, design, direction, and control of data-processing systems.

Data management is summarized below, emphasizing the role information plays in the process:

1. Work data are derived as by-products of work performed and related environmental conditions.
2. Work data are then sorted, classified, summarized, and structured into information products.
3. These products are delivered to management.
4. Management analyzes the information for meaning and significance.
5. Management decides what actions, if any, should be taken, accordingly instructing workers to change or continue work processes.
6. Back to number one. (As we have pointed out earlier, the management process is dynamic and circular.)

One last, but very important, observation is offered: nowhere in our discussion have we mentioned computers, which, it must be emphasized, are not synonymous with information systems. They may sometimes be effective and efficient tools for data management, but not always. Too often designers of management information systems start with a "hardware specification," not with a management process specification. Computers are expensive, and they must be justified from an overall cost-benefit standpoint.

DEFINING INFORMATION NEEDS

From a management perspective, three different levels of information are required:

- Top management needs "over-the-horizon" intelligence, that is, trends, forecasts, simulations, probabilities.

- Middle management needs "line-of-sight" intelligence, that is, analyses, correlations, "exception" data reports.
- First-line management needs "working" intelligence, that is, counts, ratios, data retrievals.

An experienced management analyst should be responsible for developing a definition of needs and a conceptual design for a management information system. If the organization is too small to afford such a position on a full-time basis, it is essential that this person be employed at least until the complete system is implemented. Busy managers usually lack the time, objectivity, and range of viewpoint necessary for designing and implementing a totally integrated system.

Furthermore, because most public organizations tend to be organized vertically according to functional divisions of labor, for example, administration, finance, engineering, public safety, the management analyst is preferred to the systems analyst. Systems analysts often view only these divisions, or subsystems, ignoring the fact that the objectives of the total organization usually move horizontally across these divisional lines. If this shortsighted approach is taken, the resulting management information system serves the divisions of the organization, not the organization's overall program objectives. Organizational processes themselves become the goals, which leads to bureaucratic redundancy, needless complexity, and additional work.

Although few public organizations are organized by program, the management analyst must take the program viewpoint when designing the management information system. And this viewpoint, although necessary, often leads to conflict and resistance (discussed in earlier chapters). To help minimize this disruptive and counterproductive activity, the chief executive must take certain steps. He must:

- Carefully study and personally approve the conceptual design of the management information system.
- Make organizational changes along program lines or insist on program-oriented organizational arrangements needed to implement the system design.
- Hold his line and program managers responsible for system results.
- Insist that the management information system be made an integral part of operating plans and budgets.

■ Aggressively follow through to assure that system results are achieved.

Even before information needs are defined, the chief executive should send to all managers a memorandum that outlines his intention to take these steps. In addition, it is important to realize that, if the public organization already exists, as indeed it must, then a management information system also exists. It may be undocumented, crisis-oriented, inefficient, and so forth, but it exists. This realization clarifies the fact that the management analyst is not only involved in designing a conceptual system but is also involved in changing the "old" system. He must be willing to work as an agent of change.

As indicated earlier, three distinctly different types of information are needed. The first step in defining these needs is documentation of the existing information system, that is, what information is currently available; in what form is it available; how, when, and where it is communicated. The next step is to ascertain what is lacking in the current system. Two techniques are suggested, and when used skillfully together, they can effectively produce a comprehensive needs statement. The two techniques are: the user-interviewer technique and the Delphi Technique.

By applying the Delphi Technique (discussed in Chapter 2) at different levels of management, a set of system needs emerges. When these needs are compared to those derived from a series of selected user interviews, the final needs statement results.

From the management analyst's viewpoint, the final information-needs statement will probably be less than ideal. Therefore, at this time the analyst must advise the chief executive, because the conceptual design will eventually be implemented from his office.

INFORMATION SYSTEM REQUIREMENTS*

After system needs are identified, system requirements should be rigorously defined, including:

Outputs: The information or actions that the system must generate.

*This subsection was drawn from Unit 23 of the course "Fundamentals of Systems Analysis" prepared by the Office of Management Services of the State of California, Sacramento, August 1970.

Inputs: The raw data needed to produce the output required.
Processing: The step-by-step procedure needed to transform the
               raw data into the required output.

The Importance of Output

Information systems exist to produce output, which may be used
by:

Top managers for making overall decisions and setting policy.
Middle managers for day-to-day decisions as set by policy.
Operating personnel in the performance of their work.
Other information systems within the organization as input.
Other information systems outside the organization as input.

The system designer must see that this output satisfies the
needs of these users in terms of: timeliness, contents, degree of
detail, and accuracy. The system requirements should be established
in the following sequence:

Outputs it must produce
Inputs it must receive
Operations it must perform
Resources it must use

Initially, it is important to specify only those outputs, inputs,
operations, and resources that are really required. Extraneous
specifications will lessen design flexibility by reducing the number
of available options. Required specifications should be established
first and then adjusted to accommodate practical considerations.
System activities usually involve many interacting variables and
conditions, so it is difficult to develop a definitive requirement
specification on the first try. Several attempts are usually needed.

After the system designer develops descriptive requirements
for outputs, inputs, operations, and resources, he then adds volume
and time requirements. Management science techniques, such as
queuing theory, trend projection, sampling, and simulation, may
be used to increase the precision of the specifications (see Figure
7-1).

Figure 7-1. System requirements model.

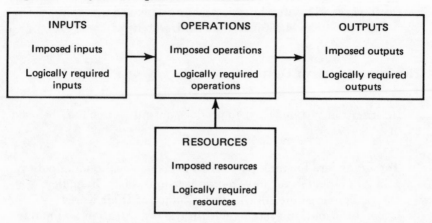

COMPUTERS and MANAGEMENT INFORMATION SYSTEMS

We earlier cautioned that computers and management information systems are not synonymous. On the other hand, the incredible advances made in the last three decades in computer technology excite all public managers with their possibilities for revolutionizing public systems management.

Richard Hackathorn, Assistant Professor of Decision Sciences, The Wharton School, University of Pennsylvania, has very ably presented the role of the computer *as it should be presented* in helping to manage public sector organizations. (We have included at the end of this chapter his extensive reference section.)

Public Sector Organizations as Information Managers. * Improvement in the capacity of public agencies to manage their affairs is a critical national concern. As governments are called on to satisfy increasing demands for services and facilities of many varieties, their capacities to fulfill these demands are being stretched to their limits. Various alternatives can be used by public sector organizations to effect improvements in their capacities to manage community affairs. Examples of these alternatives are training of government personnel, new forms of service delivery, and new procedures for planning and decision making.

---

*Richard Hackathorn, "Technologies for Information Management," paper presented at the Twelfth Annual Conference, Urban and Regional Information Systems Association, August 20–24, 1974, Montreal, Canada.

The main assumption is that these improvements depend heavily on the way in which information is managed within the public sector organization. The management of information, in turn, depends on the available technology (particularly computer and communications technology) and the policies for the utilization of this technology. The management of information in the past has been fragmented among various units responsible for collecting the data, focused on single-purpose uses of data, and bound to particular techniques for data handling. Thus, information management rarely has been denoted as a separate activity in governmental organizations.

Given that information management is crucial for meeting increasing demands for services and facilities, the question is asked: "How can public sector organizations utilize technology to manage their information effectively?"

The Concept of Information Management. The term "information management" is borrowed from the Organization for Economic Cooperation and Development (OECD) Informatics Study of Automated Information Management in Public Administration (1973). The study recommended that:

> Greater emphasis should be given to the overall system improvement of public administration rather than just to development of sophisticated data processing techniques making use of the newest technologies available. [OECD, 1973, p. 14]

In other words, information management implies a shift away from a computer-centered emphasis and toward an emphasis on the output of computers—information. Moreover, information should be considered a valuable resource to the public sector organization in the same manner as buildings and capital equipment.

As used here, the word "data" will refer to the numbers and characters appearing in computer systems or file cabinets, while the word "information" will refer to the human interpretation of the data. Information management is, therefore, the systematic handling of information as a valuable resource of management for decision making. The terms used in the following discussion are defined as follows:

System building: Techniques and procedures for building systems to accomplish information management.

Data management: Computer software for performing the actual manipulation of the data.

Geoprocessing: Techniques for handling data related to geographic areas.

Distributed computing: A trend toward decentralizing the architecture of computer equipment.

Need for Effective Information Management. New information technology, particularly computers, is considered by its promoters to have the potential of contributing significantly to three areas: decision making, service delivery, and work environment. The problems related to each of these areas are:

Decision Making

1. Scarcity of time for attending to problems and information overload.
2. Inadequate information and manipulation capability for use with otherwise useful problem-solving models.
3. Inadequate information structures for problem solving and horizon scanning.

Service Delivery

4. Inaccessibility of data even when actually stored somewhere.
5. Escalating cost of data handling and record keeping.

Work Environment

6. Poor use of people in routine information-handling tasks.
7. Invasion of privacy and government secrecy.

Public sector organizations can be considered as large information processors. The way in which their information management is organized, therefore, has a marked influence on all their activities. Since data management in public sector organizations will undoubtedly undergo major changes through the 1970s because of modern computer technology, automation of information management is no longer simply subject to well-defined economic considerations. It has become part of a political process of reforming public sector organizations.

Public sector organizations have a tremendous investment in basic record keeping. Moreover, the newer functions of these organizations, such as social, economic, and environmental development, require information from many departments and from all levels of government.

In making the major record-keeping function of government more cost-effective, the responsibility of government to act as the information managers goes beyond simple economic considerations. The data have a high utility, not only to the public sector organization, but also to various public interest groups and to the electorate in general. This utility, moreover, is highly dependent on the effectiveness of the governmental organization's information manager.

Implications of Information Management. An important implication of information management is the twofold change in the decision agenda for government policy makers: (1) increased focus on information needs and availability within the government and (2) a reversal of the usual order of making decisions concerning computing equipment.

Government policy makers are usually confronted with decisions relating to capital expenditures for computing equipment, rather than with decisions on the handling and utilization of information. Traditionally, public sector organizations first determine what computing equipment is both available and economically feasible. Next, an operating system is placed on the hardware, followed by some general set of input/output access routines. Finally, consideration is given to the kind of data-management software that can be supported by the underlying structure. This approach is called the "bottom–up" approach (see Figure 7–2). Many textbooks on modern data management develop the subject matter in a similar manner.

Figure 7-2. Information management pyramid.

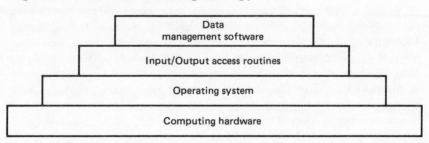

This chapter adopts the "top–down" approach, focusing on the top of the pyramid. As a result, data-management software will be explored in depth, while many aspects of computing hardware will be left to the computer manufacturers to specify. This "top-down" approach to information management is in keeping with the data-centered perspective recently advocated by Charles Bachman in his article, "The Programmer as Navigator."* As a prominent pioneer in data-base management, Bachman compares the development of this technology to the Copernican revolution, which changed humanity's view of planetary motion from an earth-centered to a sun-centered view. Similarly, data-base management is changing the way we look at data processing from a computer-centered view, in which data flow sequentially through computer programs, to a data-centered view, in which computer programs move through the data. The role of the application programmer in the data-centered view is changed to that of a navigator who guides his program through an "n-dimensional data space." Likewise, the user becomes less concerned about the mechanics of the computer system and more concerned about the content, structure, and use of the data.

Evolution of Information Management Technology. The evolution of technology for managing information is shown in Figure 7-3. The columns depict various periods of time as segmented by the type of information technology, while the rows present various characteristics of the technology. As in all figures that attempt to categorize broadly the evolution of technology, there are exceptions to, and misrepresentations of, some aspects of that technology. The usefulness of the figure, however, is in allowing the reader to grasp an overview of this evolution.

The first period shows manual methods as the primary means of performing information management. Although this column is labeled Before 1920, these methods are still viable today. Many discussions of information management assume that the field began with the advent of computers, or is to a great extent dependent on them. This assumption can be misleading. Some of the advanced techniques of modern data-management systems were practiced over a hundred years ago by file clerks. Inverted file structures that were in vogue several years ago are simply a fancy version of manual indexing files that have been an integral part of office operations for many years.

As you move toward the right in Figure 7-3, most characteristics typically increase in speed, quality, or complexity (see pages 96–97). There are several interesting exceptions to this trend.

---

*Charles W. Bachman, "The Programmer as Navigator," *Communications of the ACM,* 1973, pp. 653–658.

1. Direct user interaction with the data is eliminated with the second-generation computers and then reappears with the third-generation computers. Will the technology of the fourth generation be personal minicomputers to be used like pocket calculators?

2. The time lag in keeping the data current could be less under a manual technology for all periods but the third-generation computers.

3. The scope of individual applications is multifunctional with manual technology (i.e., more than one function performed by a single application program), while the next three periods support only single-function applications. With third-generation computers, multifunctional applications started to span organizational levels in the late third generation (i.e., multilevel).

This illustrates the need for a comprehensive viewpoint when studying the evolution of information management. For example, designers of data-base management systems would probably benefit from a careful analysis of the operations of libraries. Because of the sheer volume of text data, libraries have been forced to evolve effective heuristics in cataloging materials and are presently pioneering efforts in human/machine interfaces, such as computer-accessed microfilm. A great challenge will be met when technology is developed to obtain optimal mixtures of manual and computer technologies.

Recommendations for Policy Makers

Public sector organizations must formulate intelligent and comprehensive policies toward information management, as opposed to policies solely concerned with the management of data-processing equipment. As a prerequisite, public sector organizations should have at least one person who is thoroughly knowledgeable about the important aspects of information management, particularly in the areas of data-base management, system building, distributed computing, and geoprocessing.

Unfortunately, the rapidly changing nature of information technology makes sound policy advice difficult to formulate, because new alternatives arise before old ones can be assessed. Confusion in terminology, lack of compatibility in computer hardware and software, and lack of data standards make the utilization of technology for information management a difficult problem for public sector organizations. Therefore, the following recommen-

Figure 7-3. Evolution of information management technology.

Characteristics	Manual (Before 1920)	Unit Record Equipment (1920–1040)	First-Generation Computer (1940–1950)	Second-Generation Computer (1950–1964)	Third-Generation Computer (1964–1968)	Late Third-Generation Computer (1968–Present)
Active components	People	Relays, switches	Vacuum tubes	Transistors	Integrated circuits	Integrated circuits
Time/operation	1 min–1 hr	1 msec–1 sec*	0.1–1 msec	1–10 μsec	0.1–1 μsec	0.1–1 μsec
Storage	File cabinets	Punch cards	Delay lines, paper tape, punch cards	Magnetic core, magnetic tape	Magnetic core, mass core, disk	Semiconductor memory, disk
Time for access	1–10 min	1 sec–1 min	1 msec	1 μsec	0.1–1 μsec	0.1 μsec
Programming language	Administrative regulations	Plug wire board	Binary code, symbolic code	High-level language, subroutines recursion	Same as second, plus data structures	Same as third + extensible languages, concurrently
User interaction	Yes; completely	Yes; completely	Yes; hands-on	No	Yes; interactive languages	Yes; interactive languages
Supporting services	None	Arithmetic, sorting	Arithmetic	Floating-point arithmetic, interrupts, batch monitors	Paging, parallelism, pipelining, multiprogramming, virtual memory, file management	Same as third, plus microprogramming, data-base management

Data structures	Sequential with manual indices	Sequential	Sequential	Sequential	Sequential, tree	Network, relational
Time lag in updating data	1 hr–1 wk	1 day	1 day	1 hr–1 day	1 sec–1 min	1 sec
Analysis techniques	Process flowcharts	Forms flow	Forms flow	General flowcharts, block diagrams	Event triggering, organizational scope, computer-assisted analysis, data element dictionary	Same as third
Application development scope	Multifunction	Single function	Single function	Single function	Multifunction	Multifunction, multilevel

*msec is one-thousandth of a second; μsec is one-millionth of a second.

SOURCE: Richard Hackathorn, "Technologies for Information Management," presented at the 12th Annual Conference, Urban and Regional Information Systems Assoc., 1974, Montreal.

dations must be interpreted in terms of the unique situations of each governmental body:

Recommendation: Public sector organizations should seriously consider data-base management as a means of accomplishing information management.

The basic concepts embodied in current data management systems are inherently good. This does not mean that data-base management systems are a universal panacea for governments. Unfortunately, the research does not offer any advice on how a particular organization should go about weighing the expected benefits against the expected costs. Because of the complexity of a data-base management system, the supporting computing equipment, and the organizational environment, it is impossible to analyze the situation in any comprehensive manner.

Most research indicates that as much time and effort should go into the initial decision and subsequent preparation as goes into the actual implementation. This has been summarized as:

Proceed slowly.
Study all considerations.
Plan for the long term with many milestones in between.
Follow a phased, incremental development strategy.
Modularize the design along functional lines.
Implement batch processing before interactive processing.
Implement small applications before large ones.
Implement noncritical applications first.

Recommendation: Public sector organizations should utilize a generalized data-base management system that is commercially available, as opposed to developing such a system in-house.

There are five ways of implementing a data-base management system:

1. Use the usual data management functions (e.g., sequential, direct, or indexed sequential access methods) supplied with the operating system.
2. Add special data management functions to those of the operating system.
3. Develop specialized data-base management systems for the

particular requirements of the public sector organization.

4. Utilize an existing generalized data-base management system such as IMS/360 or TOTAL.
5. Modify or extend an existing generalized data-base management system to suit the governmental needs.

The first two alternatives are only suitable in very simple and isolated cases for public sector organizations. Essentially, all the problems of file management systems, such as the lack of data independence, are present in the first two alternatives. On the other hand, other factors, such as the limited capacity of existing computing equipment and high conversion costs, may preclude all alternatives but these.

The third alternative is infeasible for many public sector organizations, because the implementation of a data-base management system (DBMS) requires more time and money than most public organizations can reasonably expend. Informal estimates of the implementation costs run to several million dollars, requiring quite a few man-years of effort spread over several years' duration. Moreover, the cost of maintaining and upgrading the DBMS will also be expensive, as new features are desired and as manufacturers change hardware and software.

The last two alternatives are preferable for a public sector organization. An increasing array of generalized data-base management systems are available commercially, thus allowing the selection of a system that is comparatively close to the needs of a particular organization. The initial purchase or rental costs are usually quite high; however, the vendor, not the governmental body, usually has the headaches of maintaining and upgrading the system.

Recommendation: Public sector organizations should utilize a data-base management system that attempts to meet the Conference on Data Systems Languages (CODASYL) standards.

Since the mid-1960s, an effort has been made to formulate standardized specifications for a generalized data-base management system by proceeding in a manner similar to the COBOL standardization. In 1969, the Data Base Language Task Group of the Conference on Data Systems Languages (CODASYL) made a first proposal of languages to describe and manipulate a data base using COBOL as a host language. In 1971, the CODASYL Data Base

Language Task Group published a revised draft of their proposal and established a new CODASYL standing committee—the Data Description Language Committee. This new committee recently published further specifications of a Data Description Language (DDL). Other work is proceeding in CODASYL on Data Manipulation Languages (DML) other than those based on COBOL.

After a decade of working on a common specification for a data-base management system, CODASYL is beginning to have some major impacts. In the first two years, six new data-base management systems based on the CODASYL specifications have become available commercially. The problem is that the specifications are still being formulated and have not been officially recognized by the American National Standards Committee. It is estimated that a standard will not be adopted until 1980.

Public sector organizations have long recognized the benefits from adopting policies to program computer applications in standardized computer languages, such as COBOL. For the same reason, governments should utilize data-base management systems that attempt to meet the CODASYL specifications. Although an official standard may be five years away, several software vendors have implemented the current CODASYL specifications, because they do not expect the specifications to change substantially. Even if CODASYL implementations are currently unsuited for a particular government, the CODASYL specifications can be used as a yardstick to measure the capabilities of other data-base management systems.

Recommendation: Public sector organizations should investigate the feasibility of distributed computing that utilizes the technologies of minicomputers, data communications, and data-base management.

Today's trends to virtual storage, star-structured data communications systems, and huge centralized mass storage capacities are serious blunders that should be reversed as soon as possible. An alternative system, called distributed computing, is now emerging from advances in computer architecture, data communications, and data-base management. Distributed computing does run counter to the trend toward centralized large-scale computer systems—a trend supported by many of the large computer manufacturers because of the latter's economies of scale. It is true that the larger the size of the computer or storage, the smaller the per-unit cost of computing. However, as the amount of computing resources increases, the need to share resources among users also increases, utilizing such techniques as multiprogramming and virtual memory. The overhead attached to the coordination of the sharing of computing resources may negate any economy-of-scale benefits. It is not known what factors affect the balance between such benefits and the costs of resource sharing.

The important considerations for public sector organizations are how to lessen the burden of costs of capital equipment, complexity of system building, and sophistication of software. Except for the largest governments, the burden has necessitated cooperation among government bodies. Unfortunately, there are numerous instances when this cooperation is very difficult to achieve and, once achieved, difficult to maintain.

In order to reduce the burden of sharing computing resources while retaining some of the benefits of economy of scale, governments should investigate the feasibility of distributed computing, utilizing the technologies of minicomputers, data communications, and data-base management. Particular attention should be given to formulating systemwide rules for integrating the data base and the processing of the data.

Recommendation: Public sector organizations should eventually utilize a CODASYL data-base management system for structuring and manipulating a geographic base file.

A data-base management system provides general capabilities of describing, retrieving, and updating the content of and the relationships among data items. Geographic data are simply a special type of item that represents a physical location. By utilizing a generalized data-base management system, geographic data can be easily linked to other data used by the organization. Several local governments (Des Moines, Iowa, with FFS/360 and Long Beach, California, with IMS/360) are presently using data-base management systems for geographic base files. Data structures other than the Dual Independent Map Encoding (DIME) system, designed for stand-alone operation, should also be examined to provide such additional capabilities as:

Retrieval of data indexed on street intersections.
Routing capability over multiple streets.
Locating on parcels of utility networks.
Indexing on the name of places.

Many-to-many relations between parcels and structures.
Street segments as lines or as polygons.

For the reasons cited in this chapter, the description of these data structures should eventually be based on the CODASYL specifications.

Selected Literature on Public Management Information Systems*

Aangeenbrug, R. I., "Theoretical and Practical Constraints of a Geographic Base File." In D. Moyer et al., *Land Parcel Identifiers for Information Systems.* Chicago: American Bar Foundation, 1973, pp. 1157–1176.

Abramson, N., and Kuo, F. (Eds.), *Computer-Communication Networks* (Englewood Cliffs, N.J.: Prentice-Hall, 1973).

Aron, J. D., "Information Systems in Perspective," *Computing Surveys,* 1969, pp. 213–236.

Bachman, C. W., "The Programmer as Navigator," *Communications of the ACM,* 1973, pp. 653–658.

Bender, W. et al., "Introductory Manual to Data Base Management," *Management Informatics,* 1974, pp. 87–98.

Canning, R. G. (Ed.), "Trends in Data Management, Part II," *EDP Analyzer,* 1971, pp. 1–13.

Canning, R. G. (Ed.), "The Debate on Data Base Management," *EDP Analyzer,* 1972a, pp. 1–16.

Canning, R. G. (Ed.), "The Data 'Administrator' Function," *EDP Analyzer,* 1972b, pp. 1–14.

Canning, R. G. (Ed.), "The Cautious Path to a Data Base," *EDP Analyzer,* 1973a, pp. 1–13.

Canning, R. G. (Ed.), "In Your Future: Distributed Systems?" *EDP Analyzer,* 1973b, pp. 1–13.

Canning, R. G. (Ed.), "The Current Status of Data Management," *EDP Analyzer,* 1974a, 1–14.

Canning, R. G. (Ed.), "Problem Areas in Data Management," *EDP Analyzer,* 1974b, pp. 1–13.

Charlotte USAC Consortium, *System Design Guide.* Charlotte, N.C.: Charlotte USAC Project, 1973.

Computerworld Special Report, "Charting a Course with Data Base Management Systems," *Computerworld,* 1974.

Computerworld Special Report, "Minis Answer to Counties' Needs," *Computerworld,* Vol. 8, No. 13, 1974.

Conference on Data Systems Languages (CODASYL), *CODASYL Data Base Task Group Report* (New York: Association for Computing Machinery, 1971).

Conference on Data Systems Languages (CODASYL), Data Description Committee. *CODASYL: Data Description Language; Journal of Development,* June 1973. Washington, D.C.: U.S. Government Printing Office, 1974.

Conference on Data Systems Languages (CODASYL), Systems Committee. "Introduction to Feature Analysis of Generalized Data Base Management Systems," *Communications of the ACM,* 1971, pp. 308–318.

*Richard Hackathorn, "Technologies for Information Management," paper presented at the Twelfth Annual Conference, Urban and Regional Information Systems Association, August 20–24, 1974, Montreal, Canada.

Conference on Data Systems Languages (CODASYL), Systems Committee. *Feature Analysis of Generalized Data Base Management Systems* (New York: Association for Computing Machinery, 1971).

Cooke, D. F., *Geocoding and Geographic Base Files: The First Four Generations* (San Francisco: American Institute of Planners, 1971).

Cooke, D. F., *Admatch Adventures* (Washington, D.C.: U.S. Department of Commerce, 1972).

Couger, J. D., "Evaluation of Business System Analysis Techniques," *Computing Surveys*, 1973, pp. 167–198.

Couger, J. D., and Knapp, R. W. (Eds.), *System Analysis Techniques* (New York: John Wiley and Sons, 1974).

Dodd, G. G., "Elements of Data Management Systems," *Computing Surveys*, 1969, pp. 117–133.

Everest, G. C., *Database Administrator: Organizational Role and Functions* (Minneapolis, Minn.: MISRC, Graduate School of Business Administration, 1973).

Farber, D. J., "Networks: An Introduction," *Datamation*, 1972, pp. 36–39.

Glassman, N., Quigley, R. D., and Neigut, E. G., *A Broad Perspective of the Geographic Based Information System (GBIS) in the Urban Environment* (Washington, D.C.: National Bureau of Standards, 1972).

Guide Data Base Administration Project, *The Data Base Administrator*. Unpublished manuscript (Guide International, 1972).

Hackathorn, R. D., "Managing Government Data Bases with Minicomputers," *State Government Administration*, June 1974, pp. 18–19.

Hearle, E., and Mason, R. J., *A Data Processing System for State and Local Government* (Englewood Cliffs, N.J.: Prentice-Hall, 1963).

IBM—City of New Haven, Connecticut, Joint Information Study Staff, *An Urban Management Information System: UMIS Summary Report* (New Haven, Conn.: IBM—City of New Haven, April 1969).

Koehr, G. J., Connolly, J. T., Rhymer, P. P., Gerken, G. L., and Sahr, E. V., *Data Management Systems Catalog* (Bedford, Mass.: Mitre Corporation, 1973).

Kraemer, K. L., Emery, R. C., Hackathorn, R. D., Hackathorn L. D., and Connors, J., *Systems Analysis in the USAC Cities* (Washington, D.C.: Office of Research and Technology, USAC Program Office, 1972).

Long Beach, City of; Department of Administrative Management, Data Processing Division, *Geocoding: State of the Art Report* (Long Beach, Calif.: City of Long Beach, 1970).

Long Beach USAC Consortium, *Data Base Administration Guide* (Long Beach, Calif.: Long Beach USAC Project, 1971).

Nolan, R. L, "Computer Data Bases: The Future Is Now," *Harvard Business Review*, 1973, pp. 98–114.

Organization for Economic Co-operation and Development (OECD), *Automated Information Management in Public Administration. Present Developments and Impacts* (Paris: OECD, 1973).

Phillips, R. L., "Computer Graphics in Urban and Environmental Systems," *Proceedings of the IEEE*, 1974, pp. 437–452.

Rustin, R. (Ed.), *Computer Networks* (Englewood Cliffs, N.J.: Prentice-Hall, Inc., 1972).

Senko, M. E., Altman, E. B., Astrahan, M. M., and Fehder, P. L., "Data Structures and Accessing in Data Base Systems," *IBM Systems Journal*, 1973, pp. 30–93.

Taylor, D. R. F., *Bibliography on Computer Mapping* (Monticello, Ill.: Council of Planning Librarians Exchange Bibliography, 1972).

Thomas, U., *Computerized Data Banks in Public Administration* (Paris: OECD, 1971).

Urban and Regional Information Systems Association, Geocoding—1971, *URISA Conference Proceedings* (Pomona: URISA, 1971).

8

Standard Procedures and Departmental Operating Instructions

STANDARD procedures and departmental operating instructions, when reduced to writing, provide a means of controlling various governmental operations. When formulating such procedures and instructions, government officials must analyze operations and consider more effective or efficient methods of administration.

Procedures should be viewed as total systems and plans. They should be written only when there is a need, removing or replacing them when they become obsolete. In addition, the chief administrator must thoroughly support the formulation of written procedures if they are to be accepted by employees.

With these basic guidelines in mind, a governmental unit can undertake the design, development, and implementation of written procedures. Commitment to the system should be followed by designing forms and manuals. Throughout this process, government employees should be involved and meetings held to explain how the final system will operate.

This chapter, which details how a system was formulated, provides a model for developing similar systems in other governmental units. Specific examples of typical forms, procedures, paragraph structuring, procedure organization, and numbering, as well as numerous suggestions for developing similar systems, are included.*

Emphasis is placed on techniques for developing and implementing written procedural systems in governmental units, the detailed analysis of which results in the spin-off benefits of more efficient and effective approaches.

INTRODUCTION

Are you asked the same questions over and over again by the public you serve? Such questions as: "How do I get on the welfare rolls?" "My water bill is too high! How do I get it adjusted?" Do your employees ask you such questions as: "What is the procedure for requesting a service from data processing?" "What is our procedure for requesting vacation?"

In most organizations, many policies, procedures, practices, and instructions apply indefinitely and should be reduced to writing and placed in an administrative manual.† As the functions of government become more complex and the demands for service become greater, the need for written policies and procedures becomes more acute.

Written policies and procedures can provide an established method or standard for handling given situations that frequently arise. Instead of repeatedly explaining the policy or procedure verbally, a written document would specify the policy or procedure, assuring that the standard method is followed and that most unasked questions are answered.

This chapter concentrates on the design, development, and implementation of two specific types of manuals: Standard Procedures and Departmental Operating Instructions.

*J. L. Mercer, International City Management Association, Management Information Service Report, Vol. 3, LS-7, "Standard Procedures and Departmental Operating Instructions" (ICMA, July 1971).

†International City Manager's Association, Management Information Service Report, No. 211, "Preparation and Use of Administrative Manuals" (ICMA, August 1961).

ADVANTAGES of WRITTEN PROCEDURES

The major advantage of written procedures is the way they facilitate your control over various operations in your organization. If properly utilized and postaudited for compliance, written procedures can relieve you of much detailed training and supervision. Another significant advantage is that the very process of writing procedures forces you to analyze your operations, which may lead you to a more efficient or effective method of doing things.

Checklist of When and When Not to Use Written Procedures

Use written procedures when:

- Formal instructions and guides to action are needed. This may result when your service area or organization grows, although smaller units may also require written instructions. Written procedures will, of necessity, almost be a must once a governmental unit has reached a certain size.
- Internal controls and established (standard) methods of operation are needed.
- Systems approach to managing your operations is needed.
- More efficient methods of operation are indicated.

Do not use written procedures when:

- There are indications that your controls are already too tight (that is, when more management flexibility and individual discretion are needed).
- One-time controls are needed.
- Situations are not suited to written procedures (for example, your personnel problems are better handled orally on the merits of the individual cases rather than with written procedures to cover every situation).
- Automatic problem solver is desired. (Written procedures can help, but they won't solve every problem every time.)
- Cheap method is desired. (Written procedures create paperwork, and analysis, writing, typing, reproduction, and so forth, cost money.)

GUIDELINES for PLANNING and CONTROLLING
PROCEDURES*

Procedures as Systems

When creating procedures, the designer frequently fails to regard them as systems. Procedures of any kind, whether interdepartmental or intradepartmental, usually do not consist of individual steps in series. In any given procedure, activities are interrelated in a manner closely resembling a network, and this network calls for the use of analytical processes. In planning and controlling procedures, however, a good grasp of analytical techniques is seldom utilized, because it is believed that the cost will be too great. Frequently, however, the cost resulting from poorly planned and analyzed systems can be even greater.

Procedures as Plans

In designing procedures, it is very important to make sure that they support the overall objectives and plans of the entire governmental unit. This is one reason why they should be reviewed prior to their issuance. Procedures must not only support the objectives of a specific function, but they must also support the overall goals, objectives, and plans of the entire organization.

Procedures as Control Tools

As mentioned earlier, written procedures can be tremendously effective as control tools. A word of caution is in order here, however: written procedures facilitate control only up to a certain point. They will not solve all problems all the time. Moreover, they should be checked frequently to make sure that they do not become obsolete and that they do not encourage a resistance to change. Care should also be exercised so that the same procedures are not duplicated by more than one department.

*Harold Koontz and Cyril O'Donnell, *Principles of Management: An Analysis of Managerial Functions* (New York: McGraw-Hill, 1968), pp. 672–675.

Use Written Procedures Only When Clearly Needed

Refer back to the checklist for when and when not to use written procedures. Do not go to the trouble of developing a procedure if one is not really needed. This could quickly make ineffective those procedures that are vital to your organization.

Chart and Analyze Your Operations

In order to ensure that your procedures do not conflict with, overlap, or duplicate other procedures or systems, chart out their steps. This can be done on a simple chalkboard, or if you prefer, more sophisticated flow-charting techniques can be used. Considerable analysis of operations will be necessary before a clear flow of steps can be portrayed, however. This is the place where many of the "bugs" in a proposed procedure are worked out before it is ever issued.

Develop Cost Trade-offs

Concurrent with the analysis of a proposed procedure, a cost trade-off analysis should be developed to determine if the procedure is worth what it will cost. In other words, weigh the cost of developing and implementing a particular procedure (especially if it significantly changes a current method of operation) against the savings in dollars, labor, materials, and so forth, that result from the use of the procedure or method. Quantify as many factors as you can. Intangibles also often play a very important role in this analysis.

Audit and Follow-up

As previously mentioned, postaudits are a *must* to ensure that the written procedure is being followed. Before this can be accomplished, however, a follow-up should be made shortly after the procedure has been implemented to make sure that no misunderstandings exist. To assure objectivity, this phase should be performed by someone outside the line organization.

Remove or Replace When Obsolete

Nothing is as damaging to credibility as a manual that contains even a few obsolete procedures. Continual checks should be conducted to make sure that procedures are current and that they reflect changes in operations, methods, systems, and so forth. New advances in automation, particularly in data processing, can significantly change numerous procedures almost overnight.

A MODEL SYSTEM: The RALEIGH EXAMPLE

Establishment of Need for Procedures

Raleigh, North Carolina, with an estimated 1977 population of 150,000 and an operating budget of $50+ million, offers a diversity of municipal services common to many cities throughout the United States.

In 1947, when the council-manager plan was first adopted as the form of government, Raleigh had a population of about 60,000. This population more than doubled by 1970, and this tremendous growth led to greater demand for services. The demand in turn placed a strain on the city's revenues and created a very real need for more effective and efficient methods of operating city departments.

Over the years, the city had added functions, departments, and personnel in various capacities, although the professional, supervisory, and management personnel were still being taxed in their day-to-day tasks because of the ever-growing demands for more services. Departmental personnel had no time to formulate written guidelines for action. In addition, departmental managers did not have enough time to implement a systems approach to any of their respective operations. Further, internal systems and procedures capabilities among departmental personnel were generally lacking. Very little time was devoted to training personnel in systems techniques, and for several years, a conservative city council was not receptive to hiring additional outside systems engineers.

The controls in effect in Raleigh were mostly line-item and were related to budgeting, travel, and other specific expenditures. Management directives on specific subjects were issued periodically from the city manager's office, but no program was undertaken to incorporate these directives into a comprehensive procedures manual.

Method to Proceed

How did Raleigh embark on a systematic program to design, develop, and implement standard procedures and departmental operating instruction manuals? How was the lack of systems engineers among the administrative staff overcome?

As mentioned, the tremendous growth that Raleigh underwent led to greater and greater demands for services and created a need for additional top-level professional management. This need was confirmed in December 1969 in a report prepared by a group of outside consultants hired by the city council to perform a management study of the city's operations.

These consultants recommended the addition of two assistant city managers and an intergovernmental relations coordinator to strengthen the management capabilities of the city. These recommendations were approved by the city council, and a "management-team" concept was instituted in Raleigh. This team, made up of the city manager, assistant city manager for operations, assistant city manager for programming and budgeting, and intergovernmental relations coordinator, was charged with administrating the city.

In filling the position of assistant city manager for programming and budgeting, the city manager conducted a nationwide search for a person skilled in systems and procedures; program management, planning, budgeting, and control; and electronic data processing. This search centered primarily on private industry, because the skills required were more advanced in the private sector.

Although this new assistant manager was primarily responsible for capital improvements management, programming, and budgeting and for developing an annual and five-year capital and operating budgeting system, he also was charged with developing Standard Procedure and Departmental Operating Instruction Manuals.

One of the first tasks the new assistant city manager for programming and budgeting undertook was that of writing procedures. In addition to developing needed guides to formal action, it was felt that this would be a good way for him to learn the operations of the city.

Commitment to System

How does one go about developing a system of written procedures? The first step is to get a commitment to the system by the city council and the city manager. Although this task is easier said than done, the concept is usually sold by logically enumerating and extolling the advantages of such a system. This step is a must if the system is to get off the drawing board. Without top management's commitment to the idea, the support of other key individuals, so necessary in developing a procedures system, is likely to be halfhearted, at best.

Design of Basic Forms

After a commitment is received from the city council and city manager (even a "Go ahead! I'll wait and see!" is better than none at all), the next step is the design of the basic forms. After all, if standard procedures are going to be developed, then standard forms are required for preparing, coordinating, and issuing each stage of the procedure.

In the Raleigh example, several basic forms were developed, printed, and stocked. These basic forms included zhe Standard Procedure and Departmental Operating Instruction (same format, different title); Management Policy, Functions and Responsibilities, and Bulletin formats. In addition, provisions were made for standard design of Organization Charts and Procedure Review Forms. Samples of these various forms are reproduced in Figures 8-1 and 8-2.

Arrangements were made with the office services section of the purchasing division to preprint and stock reproducible masters of each form for the convenience of each department. Form masters were requisitioned by each department in the same manner as routine office supplies. Procedures and other documents were typed on the preprinted masters, and sufficient copies were subsequently reproduced to cover distribution and file requirements.

Numbers were assigned to each form for quick reference, identification, and control. The numbering system consisted of up to five digits: the first three digits identified the department or function designating the form, and the last one or two digits, preceded by a dash, were sequence numbers for that form that separated it from other forms designated by the same function. An example of a typical form number is outlined below:

Form No. 104–3
104—identified the form as being designed by the assistant city manager for programming and budgeting (100 is administration and 4 is assistant city manager for programming and budgeting).
3—identified the form as the third form in a series (or the third form designed by this particular function).

Figure 8-1. Various procedures forms.

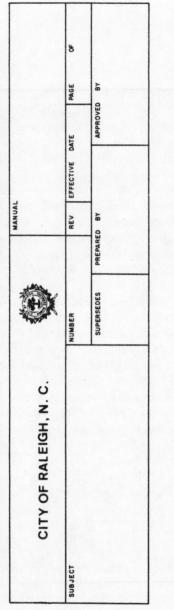

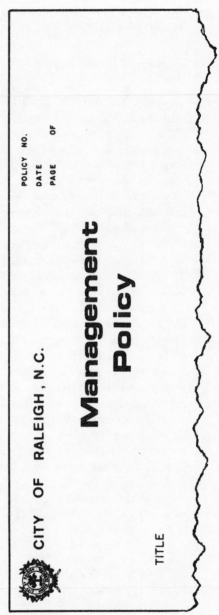

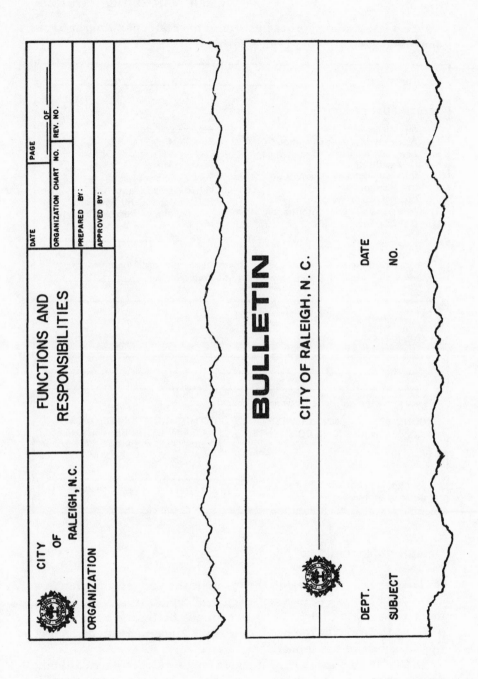

CITY OF RALEIGH, N.C.

FUNCTIONS AND RESPONSIBILITIES

DATE

PAGE _____ OF _____

ORGANIZATION CHART NO. REV. NO.

PREPARED BY:

APPROVED BY:

ORGANIZATION

BULLETIN

CITY OF RALEIGH, N. C.

DATE

NO.

DEPT.

SUBJECT

Figure 8-2. Standard procedure/departmental operating instruction/management policy review form.

SUBJECT _____

DISTRIBUTION

City Manager   Finance Director
Asst. City Manager: Operations   Fire Chief
Asst. City Manager: Programming   Parks and Recreation Director
   and Budgeting   Planning Director
Intergovernmental Relations Coordinator   Public Utilities Director
City Attorney   Public Works Director
City Clerk and Treasurer   Raleigh Community Relations
Research and Public Information Officer   Committee: Executive Secretary
Chief Engineer   Right-of-Way Agent
Chief of Police   Others_____
City Traffic Engineer

This Standard Procedure/Departmental Operating Instruction/Management Policy*
and Review Form with your comments must be returned to _____
_____ ,

Ext._____ on or before_____.

COMMENTS

_____
_____
_____

Please circle the appropriate comments below:

I CONCUR.   I CONCUR, WITH   I DO NOT CONCUR. I REQUEST
                 ABOVE COMMENTS.   THAT A MEETING BE ARRANGED
                                        TO DISCUSS THIS PROCEDURE.

                                        _____
                                                            Signature
*Circle as appropriate.

Design of Manuals

The next step is to design the manuals themselves. Ring binders are a good choice because updating and replacing procedures can be done easily. In addition, if it becomes necessary to reproduce a procedure, it can be removed from a ring binder without damaging the procedure or the binder.

In the Raleigh example, 3-inch binders were selected. Additional volumes could be added as the number of procedures increased.

Raleigh chose a green vinyl binder for Standard Procedures and a red vinyl binder for Departmental Operating Instructions. The front cover of each binder was silk-screened and the rear panel displayed the name of the manual, city identification, and city seal. (Most printers accept only a minimum order of 50 or more, so take this into consideration when deciding binder preprinting.) Each binder was also equipped with pressboard end sheets to prevent the beginning and ending procedures from being damaged.

Each manual had functional and subject separation inserts that were Mylar reinforced and had Mylar-covered preprinted tabs. The Standard Procedures Manual had 16 different preprinted inserts, and the Departmental Operating Instruction Manual had four. For the Standard Procedures Manual, the following inserts were selected:

100—Administration	800—Traffic Engineering
200—Legal	900—Planning
300—Personnel	1000—Fire
400—Public Works	1100—Police
500—Finance	1200—Parks and Recreation
600—Public Utilities	1300—Community Relations
700—Engineering	Policies
	Bulletins

For the Departmental Operating Instruction Manual, the following inserts were chosen:

Functions and Responsibilities
Procedures
General

In order to control the manuals once they were issued, the sticker form outlined in Figure 8-3 was devised. This form was preprinted with adhesive backing and was attached to the inside front covers of the manuals. Each manual was assigned a number, and the name and department of the manual holder were entered on the form. The manual number and the holder's name were then listed on the distribution sheet for all procedural documents.

Issuance of Pilot Procedures

Once the basic forms and manuals are designed and ordered from the selected printer, the next step is to implement the program.

Figure 8-3. Sticker to prevent loss of manuals.

```
+---------------------------------------------------+
|              CITY OF RALEIGH                      |
|                                                   |
|  Book No. _____   Date_____         |
|  Assigned To _____          |
|  Department _____          |
|                                                   |
|  This book must be returned to the Assistant      |
|  City Manager for Programming and Budgeting        |
|  prior to termination or transfer of assigned     |
|  holder.                                          |
+---------------------------------------------------+
```

This is done by preparing and issuing the pilot procedures that lay the groundwork for the Standard Procedures and Departmental Operating Instruction programs. These are then distributed to all departments.

In Raleigh, the first two procedures defined and delineated the Standard Procedures and Departmental Operating Instructions. Procedures such as these should be issued as the first step in any procedural program in order to facilitate further development of the system.

When these procedures are issued to all departments, a cover memorandum should be included to briefly describe the program and establish the general objectives for preparing procedures for each department.

In the Raleigh example, a bulletin was also issued to call attention to the new forms that had been developed for the Standard Procedure and Departmental Operating Instruction Manuals. This bulletin has been reproduced in Figure 8-4.

Presenting the Concept to Department Heads

Merely explaining the system in writing is not enough. If the program is to be effective, a written explanation must be accompanied by an oral presentation. At this presentation, the personnel who are to be involved with the system must be given the opportunity to make comments and ask questions. Moreover, they must be given responsive answers at the meeting or at a later date.

In the Raleigh example, department and division heads, and

Figure 8-4. Sample bulletin listing new forms.

BULLETIN

CITY OF RALEIGH, N. C.

DEPT. Assistant City Manager for   **DATE** September 17, 1970
Programming and Budgeting
SUBJECT City of Raleigh Standard Forms   **NO.** 104-1

Arrangements have been made to stock several new City of Raleigh standard forms in Purchasing - Office Services.

Supplies of the enclosed forms are being reproduced and will be made available to departments on request.

In order to obtain these forms, it will be necessary for departments to requisition them from Purchasing - Office Services in the same manner that Inter-Office Correspondence Forms are requisitioned.

The following new forms are being made available. A copy of each of these forms is enclosed in order to familarize you with them. These forms should be used in accordance with instructions in Standard Procedures 100-1 and 100-2.

    (1) 104-1 - Standard Procedure Form - (Enclosure 1).

    (2) 104-2 - Standard Procedure and Departmental Operating Instruction Continuation Sheet - (Enclosure 2).

    (3) 104-3 - Departmental Operating Instruction Form - (Enclosure 3).

    (4) 104-4 - Management Policy Form - (Enclosure 4).

    (5) 104-5 - Functions and Responsibilities Form - (Enclosure 5).

    (6) 104-6 - Bulletin Form - (Enclosure 6).

    (7) 104-7 - Standard Procedure Review Form (Revised) - (Enclosure 7).

J. L. Mercer

JLM:dsd

Enclosures

in many instances their secretaries, were involved in the oral presentation. Because the secretaries were very interested in the design of the various forms, an overhead projection transparency was developed to show the spacing and the arrangement of information on the forms. During the oral presentation, overlays and other visual aids were used extensively to provide specific information on procedure format, procedure numbering, paragraph structuring and numbering, wording, title, sections, document differentiation, and numerous other items, in addition to the actual mechanics of typing the procedure.

Sufficient time was allowed to ask and answer the many questions, for the program was greeted with resistance from many sources. Several department heads obviously wanted the advantages of the program to be proven before they would readily accept it, even though it had been wholeheartedly endorsed by the city manager and the city council. Almost without exception, however, nine months later these administrators had been persuaded that the program merited their support.

In general, additional follow-up meetings with involved personnel should be held. In these sessions, numerous questions can be answered that have arisen as a result of actual experience with the system. The give and take in these meetings is usually much better than in the initial presentation, and enthusiasm for the program should begin to show itself after two or three sessions.

It is usually a good idea to invite the city manager to speak at the first session at least in order to set the stage for the program. In addition, this notifies the department heads that the city manager *really* supports the program.

The project manager should offer assistance in explaining the system and in preparing procedures at these oral presentations.

Developing and Structuring the System

As was mentioned earlier, functional groupings of procedures are made, and assigning departments to each of these functional areas is the first step. As an example, the procedures prepared by the city clerk and treasurer are included in either the administrative, legal, or financial sections of the manual, not in a separate section. The procedures of the right-of-way agent are included in either the legal or the engineering sections of the manual, not in a separate section. In grouping procedures in the manual, stress should be placed on function or program, not on organizational structure.

In the Raleigh example, instructions were issued to all manual holders that management policies, bulletins, and other documents not functionally indexed in the manuals should be filed numerically. In other words, all citywide management policies should be filed in ascending numerical sequence behind the "Policies" tab of the Standard Procedure Manual. Likewise, all Departmental Operating Instructions should be filed in ascending numerical sequence behind the "Procedures" tab.

Each department head was asked to appoint one person in his department who would be responsible for preparing, issuing, and controlling procedures. In some instances, this person was the department head himself; however, this task should never be delegated below a division-head level. If the assignment is delegated too far down the organizational hierarchy, the job will not be done well, the procedures will not be effective and, quite possibly, the job may not be done at all.

Specific instructions for reviewing, approving, reproducing, issuing, filing, and revising each procedural document must be given so that the preparer has a clear path on which to proceed. In the Raleigh example, instructions were issued in the pilot Standard Procedure Manual and in accompanying bulletins covering these items.

In terms of review, each procedure was issued to affected individuals, using the procedure review form outlined in Figure 8-2. An action date was given and a specific person for the document to be returned to with comments was included. If the procedure had not been returned by the action date, the preparer was to call the individual being asked to comment in order to determine his position. If the procedure required significant coordination or clarification, the preparer set up a meeting of concerned parties to iron out the differing opinions. In all cases, regardless of the type of document being prepared, the members of the management team were to be on the distribution list for comments prior to issuance.

Procedures being issued for review generally did not carry a document number but had the word "Preliminary" printed in the procedure block. The city manager gave final approval of all Standard Procedures issued in Raleigh. However, this approval was given only after affected parties and other members of the management team had made a thorough review. In some instances, no significant comments needed resolving, and the procedure was simply typed on a final master format, approved, and issued. In other cases, the procedure needed to be sent out for comments after the recommended corrections had been made.

Procedures were issued in Raleigh according to a set pattern of events. The procedure was prepared, reviewed, typed in final form on a reproducible master, and finally reproduced and issued. Bulletins with accompanying distribution lists (one for Standard Procedures, one for Departmental Operating Instructions) were prepared and issued to all holders of both manuals by the assistant city manager for programming and budgeting. The Standard Procedures distribution list included all manual holders plus selected supervisory personnel not holding manuals. The Departmental Operating Instructions list included the preparer, any internal department distribution he specified, any outside department head affected by the procedure, and members of the city council and the management team.

Enough copies also were made to include in departmental files. Instructions were given to th reproduction section of the purchasing department to make a certain number of all procedural documents, unless unusual circumstances required more copies. (In Raleigh, the standard quantity was 70 copies.) Instructions were issued to each procedure preparer to send copies of these documents automatically to each person on the respective distribution lists.

Instructions for revising the documents were issued to all procedure preparers in the pilot procedures and in the appendix to SP No. 100–1, which had been issued initially.

In order to keep the program moving, constant offers of clarification and assistance were made to departmental personnel.

Departmental Subject Listing, Schedules, and Monitoring

Once the pilot procedures had been issued, the system concept presented to department heads, and the development and structure of the system explained and implemented, each department was then requested to prepare a listing of procedures to be developed. This list was initially "brainstormed" to ensure that most of the subject areas were covered and then formalized to make it specific. The list was then carefully reviewed to remove any duplications of subject listings, and this list was sent, along with schedule dates for preparation of Standard Procedures, Management Policies, Functions and Responsibilities, and so forth, to the program's central control agency.

The control agency specified a deadline for receiving these listings from each department, and once these listings were obtained, subject titles were carefully screened across departmental lines to ensure that no duplications existed. A composite listing of these procedures by functional groupings was then prepared, along with the corresponding projected issue date. (In Raleigh, a special form was designed for this purpose; see Figure 8-5.) This form also provided an index to the Standard Procedure and Departmental Operating Instruction Manuals.

The control agency constantly followed through to ensure that the departments were preparing and issuing the procedures as scheduled.

Figure 8-5. Composite list of forms.

				Organizations Affected																			
CITY OF RALEIGH, N. C. ADMINISTRATION Index of Procedural Documents				Council	City Manager	Asst. CH - Ops.	Asst. CH - P&B	Int. Gov. Rel.	City Attorney	City Clerk & Treas.	Personnel	Public Works	Finance	Public Utilities	Engineering	Traffic Engineering	Planning	Fire	Police	Parks & Recreation	Community Relations	Other
Number	Rev.	Title	Effective Date																			
100-1	0	Standard Procedure Documents	8-4-70	S	P	S	S	S	S	S	S	S	S	S	S	S	S	S	S	S	S	S
100-2	B	Departmental Operating Instructions	12-3-70	S	S	S	S	S	P	P	P	P		P	P	P	P	P	P	P	P	
100-3	0	Program Plans, Program Schedules, Networks and Associated Data; Authorization, Preparation, Approval and Control	8-6-70		S	S	P	S	S	S	S	S	S	S	S	S	S	S	S	S	S	
100-4	0	Design Reviews	10-7-70	S	S	P	P	S	S		P	S	P	P	P	P	P		P			
100-5	0	Memorandum Preparation (Research & Information Responsible)	Not Issued																			
100-6	0	Capital Improvements Program Reviews	10-27-70	S	S	S	P	S	S			S	S	S	S	S	S	S	S	S	S	
101-1	0	City of Raleigh Safety Program	8-12-70	S	S	P	S	S	S	S	S	S	S	S	S	S	S	S	S	S	S	
		Initiating Capital Improvements Projects and Processing Invoices for Payment (ACM - P&B Responsible)	Not Issued																			
		Applications for Grants (Intergovernmental Relations Coordinator Responsible)	Not Issued																			
		Communications Center Charter (ACM - Operations Responsible)	Not Issued																			

P - Organization having primary responsibility
S - Organization having support responsibility

In Raleigh, a progress review session was conducted by the assistant city manager for programming and budgeting after the program had been under way for about three months. By this time, about 400 procedures had been identified for issuance and about 35 procedures issued. At this session, each department's progress was compared to its scheduled issuance of procedures. Several departments were 100 percent delinquent. This session, an exercise in "management by embarrassment," had excellent results. Considerable impetus was given to the program, and two months later the program was virtually back on schedule.

Quarterly review sessions were planned until the program had almost completed its initial stage. After that, periodic review sessions for needed revisions were held.

Auditing and Policing the System

After the system was under way and most of the procedures had been issued, an internal audit was performed to ensure that the system was functioning as planned. This was accomplished by a person who could cut across departmental lines and who had no ties to any one particular department.

Like any good system or program, if it is to be maintained in topnotch condition, it must be policed. This means review by department and division heads and by top-level administration. When revisions are required, specific assignments must be undertaken to bring the procedures up to date. Without this step, the result of the above efforts is only a costly, attractive book gathering dust on a shelf.

Longer-Term Results

What has been the result of the Standard Procedures and Departmental Operating Instructions? At the writing of this chapter, Raleigh's system is almost eight years old.

The city administrators in Raleigh reveal that the system is going strong. In fact, a current effort is under way to audit, revise, review, and reissue many of the procedures. A second volume of the Standard Procedures has been added to contain the number of procedures that have been developed. The procedures, particularly as guides for new personnel to learn the various operations and functions, have proved invaluable. They also have proved very beneficial to citizens who want to determine how, for example, to obtain building addition permits or who just want to learn more about how their local government operates.

The Raleigh system, drawing the attention of dozens of other governmental jurisdictions across the country, also has served as a model for the development and implementation of similar systems.

9

Programming
and Controlling
Capital Improvements

PUBLIC administration of capital improvements can benefit from the modern program management techniques of private industry. This chapter describes how such techniques were applied to several governmental units in Raleigh, North Carolina. The Raleigh program, which is administered by an assistant city manager for programming and budgeting, operates from a "control room" (or "chart room") that visually displays the status of capital improvements projects. Existing project plans provided the basis for sorting projects into logical subprograms, establishing tentative priorities, and filling in missing information. After projects were ranked in priority sequence, program plans and schedules were prepared, with major events designated in each project.

All information about projects is continually charted for visual display in the control room, and periodic program review sessions are held with department heads to discuss the status of projects.

Incentives for meeting schedules are provided through an award program that honors project directors who complete projects ahead of schedule or under budget.

The program in Raleigh, which can be easily adapted for other governmental units, has been highly successful in increasing the efficiency of the programming and scheduling of the city's capital improvements.*

THE RALEIGH MODEL SYSTEM

As was mentioned in Chapter 8, a group of outside management consultants was hired in December 1969 by the Raleigh city council to study the city's organization. In the process of their study, these consultants recognized the need for better program management and better program plans and controls for the city's ever-growing capital improvements. Among other changes, the consultants recommended that the city create the position of assistant city manager for programming and budgeting. As described in Chapter 8, this new assistant city manager would be responsible for the capital improvements program, development and control of the city's budgeting systems, and development of citywide systems and procedures.

Management of the capital improvements program would include overall program management, development of a program planning and control system, and development of a capital budgeting system. This new assistant city manager was to work within a management team concept being developed for Raleigh. This team was to consist of the city manager, the assistant city manager for operations, the assistant city manager for programming and budgeting, and the assistant to the city manager for intergovernmental relations. Each assistant city manager would be given the authority to carry out his assigned duties, and the intergovernmental coordinator was to function primarily in a staff capacity to the city manager. The various city department heads would still report administratively to the city manager, but they would also report functionally to the two assistant city managers in their assigned areas of responsibility.

*J. L. Mercer, International City Management Association, Management Information Service Report, Vol. 4, No. LS-2, "Programming and Controlling Capital Improvements" (ICMA, February 1972).

Beginning the Capital Improvements Programming

In addition to initiating and developing citywide procedures and annual and five-year operating budgeting systems, the new assistant city manager for programming and budgeting was to set up a capital improvements planning and control system and a five-year capital improvements budgeting system. A capital improvements committee, already in existence, consisted of the city department heads involved in the various capital programs and was headed by the assistant city manager for operations. This committee met monthly and discussed the progress of the various projects. A progress report reflecting the status of the various projects was being published monthly by the assistant city manager for operations. This was all turned over to the new assistant city manager for programming and budgeting.

Establishing a Chart Room or Control Room

The assistant city manager for programming and budgeting established his chart room or control room for the capital improvements program in the Raleigh Municipal Building. This room served as the nerve center for the program and housed the current status of zhe projects in the capital improvements program, visually displaying progress.

Because the new control room had formerly been an office complex, the assistant city manager for programming and budgeting had a wall removed, thereby making one rectangular-shaped room approximately 12 feet by 30 feet. Several 4-feet by 8-feet sheets of one-quarter-inch-thick Plexiglas were mounted on two walls over 1-inch grid engineering graph paper. Two-inch aluminum and cork strips bordered the Plexiglas and allowed regular charts to be hung over the Plexiglas as necessary, making the walls multipurpose. A drafting table, file cabinet, and chart file were secured for the control room. Later three standard $2\frac{1}{2}$-ft by 6-ft formica-topped cafeteria-type tables and 15 cushion chairs were purchased. Framed beaver boards were mounted on the remaining long wall, and the fourth wall, which was brick and housed a window, was left as it was. Control rooms are widespread in the defense industry, although Plexiglas on the wall is not the only approach used. The Department of Housing and Urban Development's Operation Breakthrough Control Room in Washington used magnetic boards on the wall surfaces,* and other approaches, such as rear projection screens, have also been utilized.

Development of a Program Structure

The control room was now ready for the planning and development schedules. But which project should be first? Should the projects be grouped together or be separated into logical subprograms?

Previously, the city planning department had always prepared the capital improvements program, and it had published a listing of program projects in 1968. In addition, the Research Triangle Regional Planning Commission had requested the planning department to develop a capital program for its consideration. The project listings in this suggested program, coupled with the projects outlined in the capital improvements committee progress report and other internal and external memoranda and correspondence, provided a basis for the program's structure.

Without attempting to establish priorities or program structure, all projects were first laid out on a large paper chart. In this brainstormed listing, the project name was listed, followed by other project information, such as the overall program the project was housed in, the estimated start and completion dates, the current status, the source of funding, and any other available pertinent information. Once this had been accomplished, the chart was cut into individual strips, by project, and each project strip was pinned to the beaver boards in the chart room. Push pins were used to facilitate rearranging and removing projects as required. A preliminary attempt was made by the assistant city manager for programming and budgeting to group projects into the following tentative program categories or structures: streets, public utilities, public works, parks and recreation, fire service, and miscellaneous.

Once the preliminary program structures had been established, the next step was to involve the affected department heads. Separate sessions were held for each of the initial program categories, although several "think" sessions were usually required to sort projects into logical subprograms, establish tentative project priorities, and fill in missing information. In most instances, the responsible department heads were encouraged to involve their division

*A. James Reichley, "George Romney Is Running Hard at HUD," *Fortune*, December 1970, p. 100.

heads and various supervisory personnel. The planning director and other members of the management team were also involved in these sessions. Several months were required to review, rereview, add, or delete projects and to polish the entire program.

Once the department heads and administration had agreed on various program structures, the recommended programs were reviewed with the city council. This review was accomplished in several stages, because the program categories were prepared for review at different times. The council made a few specific changes, primarily in project priorities, and gave general program approval. However, the council approved each category with the understanding that each project would be considered for final approval on its own merits when the project was activated.

The outline of the final program structure developed at this stage is as follows:

Parks and Recreation Program
Public Utilities Program
    Water Program
    Sewer Program
Fire Service Program
State Highway Program
TOPICS Program (Traffic
    Operating Program to Increase Capacity and Safety)
City Street and Sidewalk Program
Miscellaneous Projects (including such items as Public Works
    Landfill Development, New City Garage Construction,
    Southside Urban Renewal Project, and Historic Sites Preservation).

In all, about 575 individual projects were identified and categorized, priorities were assigned, and general approval was received from the city council. The planning period was approximately ten years. The total program value, considering all matching funds from other governmental units, was around $150 million.

Preparing the Program Plan

With the projects ranked according to priority, program plans and schedules had to be prepared and had to meet the established objectives. First, the assistant city manager for programming and budgeting issued a Citywide Standard Procedure establishing specific scheduling steps in the overall capital improvements program entitled "Program Plans, Program Schedules, Networks, and Associated Data; Authorization, Preparation, Approval, and Control."

This Standard Procedure specified the various schedules developed for each active project in the program. Such widely accepted program planning, control, and scheduling techniques as Gantt and Milestone Planning Charts, Program Evaluation and Review Technique (PERT), and Critical Path Method (CPM) were utilized. The assistant city manager for programming and budgeting did much of the initial detailed scheduling. Early in the program, various affected department and division heads initially were trained in preparing departmental schedules and later were guided in preparing total project schedules. The most popular of the techniques among department heads was the Gantt Chart because of its ease of usage and clarity. Most of the original detailed schedules were prepared on preprinted scheduling forms such as those reproduced in Figure 9-1. Copies of each schedule were distributed to responsible internal and external organizations, including outside utility companies. They also were posted on the beaver boards in the chart room. The assistant city manager for programming and budgeting compared actual progress against what each schedule called for, with considerable input being provided by each project's department head.

Using these detailed schedules, the assistant city manager for programming and budgeting began preparing for each project a "major event" schedule (also called "key event"). As a starting point, the project control form, shown in Figure 9-2, was developed to identify the project and the program in which it was categorized. In addition, the project was described, and its latest status was listed. The schedule was prepared by selecting the major events from the previously detailed Gantt or Milestone Charts. Only the major events were entered on the Status Control Log Schedule Sheets, such as those that involved project approval by the city council, selection of architect, completion of plans, awarding of contracts, and beginning and ending construction dates. Two-digit project event designators were assigned to each major event in ascending sequence, beginning with 00. A brief description of each event was also entered. In addition, the department responsible for each event was identified along with the schedule for the event. Later, actual progress was tracked against each schedule by the assistant city manager for programming and budgeting. The Status

Control Logs were separated into the program structure categories identified earlier and were placed in ring binders with index tabs.

Once the Status Control Logs were prepared for each project in the overall Capital Improvements Program, the major event schedules were posted on the Plexiglas boards in the chart room. In anticipation of this, a date strip had been affixed to the top of the Plexiglas, and the boards had been divided into sections according to the preciously identified program structure categories.

In scheduling the individual projects in each program structure category, active projects were scheduled first, because they naturally carried high priorities in each category.

Each project was assigned a project identifier, which served as the foundation for the project major event schedule. Such identifiers as the following were used in each program category:

>   SH 3—State Highway Program,
>   Priority Project Three
>   US 10—Public Utilities Program,
>   Sewer Program, Priority
>   Project Ten
>   P 7—Parks and Recreation
>   Program, Priority
>   Project Seven
>   M 2—Miscellaneous Public
>   Works Program,
>   Priority Project Two

The project identifiers were placed on Mylar pressure-sensitive standard PERT symbols using Prestype. These symbols were attached to the Plexiglas in ascending priority sequence, with the highest priority project in each program at the bottom (see Figure 9-3).

After individual project identifiers had been placed for each program structure category, actual project scheduling was begun. Mylar standard planning and control symbols and pressure-sensitive tape was used extensively throughout the scheduling process. Figure 9-4 is the legend used in scheduling the major events for each project in Raleigh's chart room. (These standard symbols and tapes are available from most engineering supply houses that stock graphic art supplies.)

Figure 9-1. City of Raleigh detailed scheduling format.

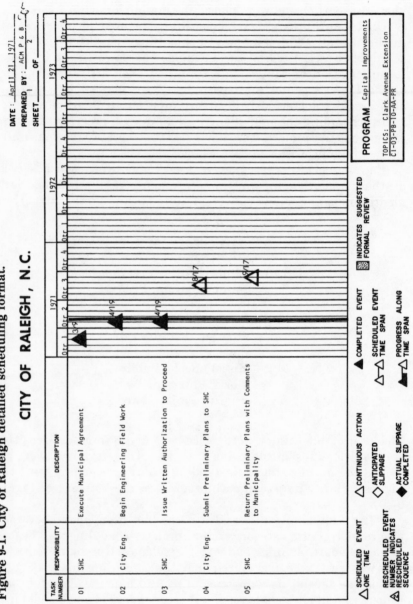

DATE: April 21, 1971
PREPARED BY: ACM P & B
SHEET __2__ OF __2__

PROGRAM Capital Improvements

TOPICS: Clark Avenue Extension
CI-03-PB-T0-AA-PR

CITY OF RALEIGH, N.C.

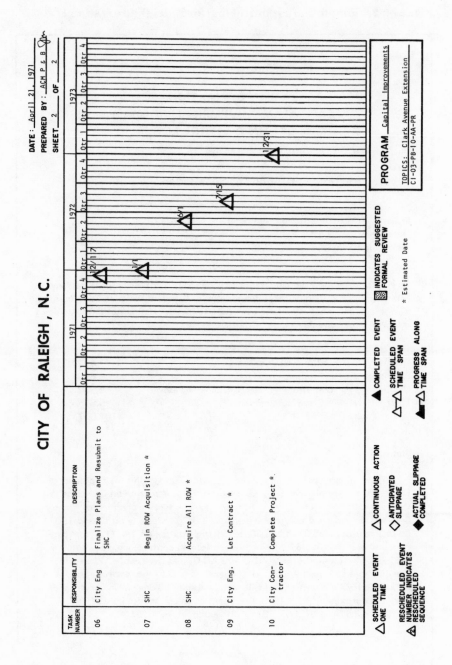

CITY OF RALEIGH, N.C.

TASK NUMBER	RESPONSIBILITY	DESCRIPTION
06	City Eng	Finalize Plans and Resubmit to SHC
07	SHC	Begin ROW Acquisition *
08	SHC	Acquire All ROW *
09	City Eng.	Let Contract *
10	City Contractor	Complete Project *

PROGRAM Capital Improvements

TOPICS: Clark Avenue Extension
CI-03-PB-10-AA-PR

SCHEDULED EVENT ONE TIME △

RESCHEDULED EVENT NUMBER INDICATES RESCHEDULED SEQUENCE

△ CONTINUOUS ACTION

◇ ANTICIPATED SLIPPAGE

◆ ACTUAL SLIPPAGE COMPLETED

▲ COMPLETED EVENT

△ SCHEDULED EVENT TIME SPAN

◣△ PROGRESS ALONG TIME SPAN

▓ INDICATES SUGGESTED FORMAL REVIEW

* Estimated Date

Figure 9-2. Sample status control log for Raleigh fire station 11.

CITY OF RALEIGH
CAPITAL IMPROVEMENTS PROGRAM
STATUS CONTROL LOG

Subprogram: Fire Prevention and Suppression

Project: F-11 — Fire Station Number 11 — Glenridge Drive
Date: February 22, 1971
Description:

Standard two-company, two-truck station, except living space has been enlarged to accommodate three district chiefs. Standard design, layout, colors, furnishings, and equipment have been used to match existing stations. Architect is McGee-Scovil and Associates. Contractors are:

General: Clemmer Construction Company	$ 77,492
Plumbing: Rural Plumbing and Heating	9,800
Heating and Air Conditioning: Mechanical Associates	8,900
Electrical: A-A-A Electrical Company	5,875
Total	$102,067

Status:

Preliminary cost estimate was $192,000. Topographic map completed 11/24/70. Utility plans completed. Water main construction on Glenridge Drive in front of site completed. Sanitary sewer extension completed. Planning Commission approved subdivision plan on 12/8/70. Property purchased 1/4/71. Council appropriated $143,103.85 to construct station on 1/4/71. Total construction cost is $102,067, plus architect's fee and contingency, for a total of $125,000. Project schedule CI-03-PB-00-AC-OF has been issued. Plans and specifications approved 2/5/71. Bids opened 2/11/71. Bids approved by Council 2/15/71. Construction will require about 180 days from construction start on approximately 2/24/71. Preconstruction conference held 2/19/71. Contract deadline is 8/24/71. Groundbreaking set for 2/23/71.

Project Event Designator	Event Description	Function Responsible	Scheduled / Actual (A)
00	Select general area	Planning Department	7/1/70 (A) / 7/1/70
01	Authorize site search	City Council	8/1/70 (A) / 8/1/70
02	Approve site	City Council	10/19/70 (A) / 10/19/70
03	Complete plans, specs, and cost estimates	Architect	2/5/71 / 2/5/71
04	Open bids	Architect	2/11/71 / 2/11/71
05	Approve bids	City Council	2/15/71 / 2/15/71
06	Groundbreaking	City Council	2/23/71
07	Begin construction	All Contractors	2/26/71
08	Complete grading	General Contractor	3/28/71
09	Set door frames and windows	General Contractor	4/18/71
10	Complete exterior masonry	General Contractor	5/30/71
11	Pour slab	General Contractor	6/15/71
12	Complete roofing	General Contractor	6/20/71
13	Complete interior masonry	General Contractor	7/4/71
14	Complete doors, millwork, and trim	General Contractor	8/1/71
15	Complete tile and finish interior	General Contractor	8/8/71
16	Finish paving, clean up, and hold final inspection	General Contractor	8/15/71
20	Contract deadline	Contractor	8/24/71
25	Station Operational	Fire Chief	9/7/71
27	Dedication	Fire Chief & Res. & Info. Ofcr.	10/2/71

Figure 9-3. Project identifiers and project priority ranking in the Raleigh city streets and sidewalks program.

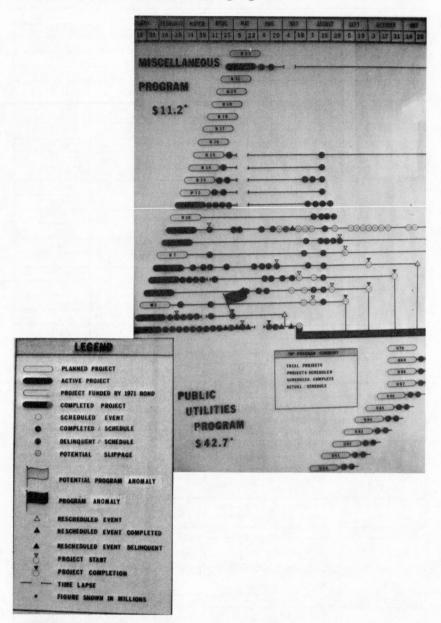

Figure 9-4. Legend used in scheduling the major events for each project in Raleigh's chart room.

Updating the Status of the Chart Room

In order to set the stage for planning, controlling, and updating the status of the Capital Improvements Program, a Standard Procedure was issued specifying who was responsible for managing each capital project.

Once major events had been scheduled on the Plexiglas boards in the chart room, the next step was to status the schedules. In the scheduling process, it was necessary to do a bit of "historic scheduling" in order to establish a total picture of the time span for the project. This helped later when time requirements were estimated for future projects.

Status information was obtained from such sources as external and internal correspondence, departmental project status reports, minutes of meetings, newspaper articles, personal contacts, and on-site observations. The most important form of status gathering, however, resulted from a biweekly Capital Improvements Program Review, which was established by a standard procedure.

Among the major contributions of this standard procedure were the periodic capital improvements program reviews and the quarterly comprehensive progress reports issued on all active capital projects. The programs under review were not known by department heads until they received their agenda, and in many respects, this had the advantage of encouraging them to keep a close surveillance on all their projects, thus improving scheduling and quality. The quarterly comprehensive report was necessary to keep the city manager and city council informed about all active projects.

All the program review sessions in Raleigh are held in the chart room. At the beginning of each review session, the assistant city manager for programming and budgeting, who serves as chairman, reviews those projects that are behind schedule in each department head's program. The technique of Management by Embarrassment* is occasionally used, because department heads who are behind schedule sometimes have no valid reason for their lack of progress. These are "closed" meetings, with no press allowed, and the pressure frequently shifts from meeting to meeting so that no one individual is continually singled out. This technique has been found to be quite effective in stressing individual responsibility in projects.

*J. L., Mercer, "Reward–Penalty Plan Delivers Capital Improvements on Time," *American City* [*and County*], June 1974.

Attendance at all program review sessions is mandatory for all department heads involved in the capital improvements program. Although formal minutes are not published, the status of each project reported at the meetings is noted and later posted on the Status Control Logs and subsequently on the schedules in the chart room. A vertical felt string is hung over the Plexiglas boards to indicate the present date on the chart room schedules. Every event behind this date line must have a status, that is, either "completed" or "incomplete," either "green" or "red." Events ahead of this date line may have a status of "Complete ahead of schedule," which is shown in "green." However, events ahead of this date line may also be shown as "yellow," indicating that the event probably will not be completed on schedule. Colored flags indicate what impact an uncompleted event will have on the final completion date for the project.

The chart room is an excellent center for the city manager and the city council to see the status of the overall program. In addition to the statused individual program schedules, summaries by subprogram and for the entire capital improvements program are displayed. Furthermore, various statistics are gathered and plotted in order to determine overall trends, which help to demonstrate problem areas, such as under- or overuse of resources. Detailed schedules for the more complicated projects also are maintained on the beaver boards, and their status is kept current.

Although the program reviews are held only biweekly, status is posted daily in the chart room from status input sheets, memoranda, personal observation, data furnished from key personnel, and so forth. The more current the status information in the chart room, the more effective the room and the system. In Raleigh, a full-time administrative assistant, who reports to the assistant city manager for programming and budgeting, was employed to keep the chart room up to date and to perform scheduling, and so forth.

The "DoMore Award"

The control process is not all "negative" or "hard nosed"; exceptional positive effort also is recognized. The "Bottomly Q. DoMore Award," which is in the form of a framed certificate (see Figure 9–5), is made to department heads or other project directors for completing a project ahead of a published schedule.

The DoMore Award is ceremoniously presented by the assistant

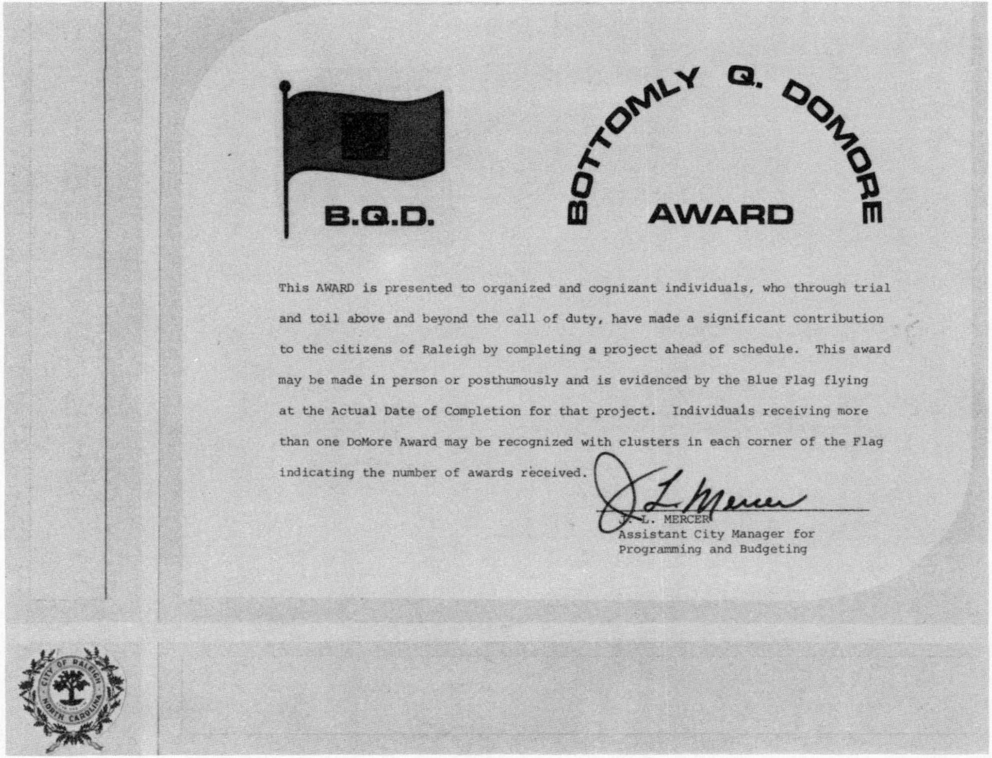

B.Q.D.

BOTTOMLY Q. DOMORE AWARD

This AWARD is presented to organized and cognizant individuals, who through trial and toil above and beyond the call of duty, have made a significant contribution to the citizens of Raleigh by completing a project ahead of schedule. This award may be made in person or posthumously and is evidenced by the Blue Flag flying at the Actual Date of Completion for that project. Individuals receiving more than one DoMore Award may be recognized with clusters in each corner of the Flag indicating the number of awards received.

J. L. MERCER
Assistant City Manager for
Programming and Budgeting

CITY OF RALEIGH · NORTH CAROLINA

Figure 9-5. Raleigh's semiserious DoMore Award certificate given for completing a project ahead of schedule.

city manager for programming and budgeting to the deserving individual at a monthly staff breakfast or at a biweekly staff meeting. Although this idea may sound whimsical, it has been very effective. The DoMore Award has been a very positive incentive to department heads to complete their projects ahead of schedule and within budget. They prefer to win a DoMore Award than to be singled out in the "management-by-embarrassment" sessions mentioned earlier.

Design Reviews

Another integral part of the program control system is the capital improvements design review committee, established to work the "bugs" out of projects before they are submitted to the city manager and city council for approval.

The permanent design review committee consists of the department heads involved in all phases of the capital program and is chaired by the assistant city manager for programming and budgeting. Temporary members are assigned according to the type of project being reviewed.

The design review committee meets at the request of a department head who is ready to submit a capital project to the city manager and the city council for approval. The design review, a "closed work session," is usually held in the chart room. The object of the review, which has been successfully met, is to remove potential project problems or anomalies prior to its submission to the approving authority.

Advantages of the System

Six months after the program planning and control system became operational, several positive results were noted:

- Five major projects were completed ahead of schedule, within budget, and with requisite quality, which was almost unheard of before.
- The next annual paving program was completed on schedule and substantially ahead of the previous paving program, which had not been subjected to the new system.
- At least thirty days were cut from the time required to construct a standard fire station, and a larger station was constructed at less cost and with requisite quality.

- Response from outside contractors and from outside telephone and utility companies to the city's needs on individual projects improved. This was primarily brought about through better project planning and better communications through published schedules provided at preconstruction conferences.
- More general status information on the capital improvements program was available, and this information was disseminated throughout the organization, to the city council, and, in some cases, to the general public.
- Improved response was received from all program participants. More efficient methods were being applied on all projects, and the proper attention was being given to the program to ensure success.
- More management and policy decision information was available to the city manager and to the city council. A status technique that proved very successful, not previously mentioned, was labeled the "Council-Adviso-Gram" (see Figure 9–6). This bulletin was forwarded to the city council and to the other internal program participants by the assistant city manager for programming and budgeting whenever a noteworthy program was accomplished. This helped provide the necessary policy making and executive attention to the program to ensure success.
- Because of the comprehensive identification and scheduling of the overall capital program, better fiscal control was established, paving the way for implementation of a five-year capital improvements budgeting system.
- One year after the program was implemented, at least ten capital projects had been completed on or ahead of schedule and within budget.

OTHER SYSTEMS

This chapter has thus far been devoed to a detailed discussion of one model for programming and controlling capital improvement projects. However, other systems have been developed that are worthy of discussion.

Project Control System: Winston-Salem, N.C.

After studying the Raleigh system as well as other project control systems, the city of Winston-Salem, N.C., developed a project control

Figure 9-6. An example of Raleigh's Council-Adviso-Gram.

BULLETIN

CITY OF RALEIGH, N. C.

DEPT. Assistant City Manager for   **DATE** May 26, 1971
Programming and Budgeting
SUBJECT Capital Improvements Program   **NO.** 10

COUNCIL - ADVISO - GRAM

It is a real pleasure to advise you that several of our Capital Improvements Projects have recently been completed ahead of the contract completion date. These projects, the contractors and their respective dates are as follows:

Project	Contractor	Contract Completion	Actual Completion
Millbrook Road Widening and Sidewalks - Six Forks Road to Falls of the Neuse Road	Rea Construction Company	5-18-71	5-12-71
Old Wake Forest Road - Widening - curbs, gutters and sidewalks in front of Mordecai House	Gelder & Associates, Inc.	7-1-71	5-20-71
Roberts Park Center	Clemmer Construction Company	8-12-71	5-24-71

In addition, the paving of Old Wake Forest Road - Person Street - Blount Street Connector will be completed May 26, 1971. Landscaping and seeding should be completed by June 2, 1971. The contract completion date is July 1, 1971. The Morgan - New Bern Connector, which is also part of this same contract, is projected for completion the first week in July, 1971. The contractor for this project, C. C. Mangum, Inc., was held up since February 18, 1971, awaiting the closure of New Bern Avenue. Work resumed on this project May 19, 1971.

The contractors involved in the above projects, and particularly our Chief Engineer, deserve a great deal of credit for beating the contract completion dates.

It looks like our programming is beginning to pay off!

J. L. Mercer

JLM:dsd

manual to address both capital and operational project management requirements.* This manual described the purpose and method for

---

*Orville Powell, "City of Winston-Salem Project Control Manual," unpublished report, January 1972. Mr. Powell is city manager of Winston-Salem, N.C.

project control and established a method for status reporting and project review.

Introduction and Purpose of Project Control

The purpose of Winston-Salem's project control system was to make sure that actual performance equaled planned performance. Historically, cities have perceived their role in terms of recurring and routine operations; therefore, many believed that project control was unnecessary. Increasingly, however, cities find that their responsibilities have grown into such areas as large-scale urban renewal, model cities projects, and complex inner city highway construction. These and other programs require, among other things, coordination and integration of resources from traditionally diverse areas. In addition, Winston-Salem wanted to emphasize the end products of such programs and their effectiveness relative to stated objectives.

The Winston-Salem manual provides practical guidance for successfully applying the tools and concepts of project management to city operations.

Examples of typical projects are:

Physical
The building of a solid waste disposal facility.
The construction of a new sewer system.
An urban renewal project.
The construction of a new sanitary landfill.
Administrative
An annexation study.
The development of a management information system.
A PPBS feasibility study.

Method of Project Control. The tools available for controlling resources to achieve project objectives are varied. Each defined project must be examined as a special situation in which it is necessary to determine the degree of complexity involved in control, the amount of resources needed, and the importance of the project. However, by borrowing elements from several of the methods available, most projects can be handled by one set of guidelines.

The methods incorporated into these guidelines are: Gantt and Milestone Planning Charts, Program Evaluation and Review Technique, and Critical Path Method, discussed in greater detail later in this chapter.

Under the Winston-Salem system, the involved department heads submit two reports each month to the assistant city manager for operations (see Figure 9–7). In order to compile these reports accurately, the department head develops a daily reporting system of information for his line supervisors. Without such daily information, the monthly and bimonthly reports will be largely estimates that tend to be slanted in favor of the supervisor. Although this also is a problem with daily reports, exaggerations are much easier to spot on a daily basis. The format of these daily reports should be as simple as possible, but at least should list the equipment, materials, and amount of manpower used (see Figure 9–8 for a typical daily work report).

Report 1 (Figure 9–7) is to be completed and sent to the assistant city manager for operations by the 15th of each month. If that falls on a weekend, the report is due the following Monday.

Report 2 (Figure 9–8) is to be completed and sent to the assistant city manager for operations by the last day of the month. If that falls on a weekend, the report is due on the preceding Friday.

The contents of these reports serve as the agenda for a meeting of department heads on the first Monday of each month. Information derived from these reports also is used to update a project board that shows the status of each current project that costs more than $50,000. This project control board is made of Plexiglas and is mounted on one end of a rectangular conference room adjacent to the city manager's office. Press lettering, similar to that used in Raleigh, is used to list projects and status on the Plexiglas.

In addition to the project control board, each project has its own loose-leaf notebook. This notebook includes the monthly and bimonthly reports; the critical path analysis; a description reflecting the costs, time schedules, and so forth; and a copy of the summary reports sent to the city manager.

Project Control Techniques

Program Evaluation and Review Technique. The basic elements of PERT networks are events and activities. An event represents a distinguishable point in time that coincides with the beginning or ending of a specific activity (for example, "blueprint completed"). An activity represents a network of time-consuming effort or work necessary to proceed from one event to another (for example, "prepare blueprint"). The primary tool of PERT is a network or flow chart of events joined by activity lines that depict interdependencies and interrelationships. The network provides a technique

Figure 9-7. Project report form.

Date:

Project Number:

Project Name:

Person Reporting:

Period Covered: _____ to _____

I.   **Project Performance**

      Percent complete: _____

      Scheduled percent complete: _____

      Current slippage (days or weeks): _____

      Scheduled completion date:

      Anticipated and/or Adjusted completion date: _____

      Anticipated slippage (total days or weeks): _____

II.   **Workforce Utilization**

      Scheduled manpower usage to date (work days): _____

      Workforce expended to date (work days): _____

      Workforce variance (work days): _____

III.   **Project Costs**

      Scheduled expenditure to date: _____

      Actual cost to date: _____

      Variance: _____

IV.   **Discussion of Project Progress**

      Discuss variances between actual and scheduled performance and costs.

      Highlight areas needing administrative attention.

      Show graphic displays of actual vs. planned performance, cost, and workforce.

V.   **Actions Taken to Rectify Project Deficiencies**

      List specific actions taken or to be taken. Those which require approval

      of higher authority should be specifically identified.

Figure 9-8. Daily work report.

Date:
Project Number:
Project Name:

Number of people on job _____

Number of work hours worked _____

Equipment Used   Equipment Time
1.
2.
3.
4.
N

Materials Used   Amount
1.
2.
3.
4.
N

Work Accomplished (Specific)
1.
2.
3.
N

Problems Encountered
1.
2.
3.
N

for analyzing time requirements, establishing schedules, and continually measuring variations from the schedule.

Critical Path Method. The CPM is an arrow-design network that develops from detailed, job-oriented bar charts. The critical path represents the path of activity completion that will involve the most time in reaching the end event. The proper application of this method to a well-constructed network will provide information on the following:

1. How delay in one activity will contribute to delay in reaching the end event, unless the time loss is compensated for in some other part of the remaining sequence of work.
2. Activities that are most critical for meeting objectives.
3. Activities that will be most responsive to management changes and efforts to improve performance.

After the critical path is established, it is possible to derive "float paths," which show how much certain activities can be delayed without affecting the critical path of the project, thereby allowing the manager to use his resources for maximum economy. For example, he will know which tasks are important enough to justify overtime to prevent delay or when to pay a premium for earlier delivery of materials.

The Gantt and Milestone Planning Charts. The Gantt chart consists of a scale divided into units of time (days, weeks, months) across the top and project elements (each representing the beginning, duration, and end of some aspect of the total job to be done) down the side.

The Milestone chart lists the significant project events in chronological order, forming a diagonal from left to right on the chart.

Winston-Salem Project Review and Evaluation System

Each capital improvement project that costs more than $25,000 is included in the system. Each project is given a reporting number based on the following:

Streets	100
Sanitation	200
Water and Sewer	300
Traffic	400
Buildings and Grounds	500
Public Works	600

Table 9-1. Winston-Salem evaluations of events.

Event*	Duration	Activity Description	Early Start	Early Finish	Late Start	Late Finish	Total Float
001–a	10	Draw plans	Jan. 3	Jan. 14	Jan. 3	Jan. 14	0
001–b	5	Review plans	Jan. 17	Jan. 21	Jan. 17	Jan. 21	0
001–c	10	Seek approval	Jan. 21	Feb. 4	Jan. 21	Feb. 4	0
001–d	5	Grade	Feb. 7	Feb. 11	Feb. 14	Feb. 18	5
001–e	10	Let bids for paving	Feb. 7	Feb. 18	Feb. 7	Feb. 18	0
001–f	10	Pave	Feb. 21	Mar. 3	Feb. 21	Mar. 3	0

*Refers to a particular point in time, either the beginning or completion of some phase. The number (001) is the project number. The letter (a, b, c) is the event symbol.

Table 9–1 is the Winston-Salem prototype for listing the many individual events that make up a project. Duration refers to the estimated number of days to complete a particular event, activity description to a description of activities necessary to complete the event, and early start to the earliest time at which the activity could be expected to start.

The Winston-Salem project control system was put into operation early in 1972. The city administration and the departmental personnel involved found the system to be very effective in providing much needed management information about project status. The project has proved its worth and continues to be operational today. The status is maintained by an administrative assistant to the Winston-Salem city manager.

Capital Improvement Projects
Planning and Review Center, Charlotte, N.C.

After studying the Raleigh model and several other program control centers, the City of Charlotte, N.C., developed and implemented a Capital Improvement Projects Planning and Review Center. The center was developed under the direction of Robert S. Hopson, director of public works of Charlotte and formerly public works director of Richmond, Virginia. In Charlotte, most city departments that are involved in capital improvements are under the control of the public works director. That is not necessarily true in other cities and is not the case in Raleigh.

In the Charlotte system, a visual display was developed to indicate the current progress of various capital improvement projects.* The system also provides information on the project's physical location and status of funding. Considerable care is devoted to make the system understandable without prior knowledge of the system and the various techniques employed.

The task was assigned to the engineering division of the public works department. The result, a Capital Improvement Projects Planning and Review Center, lists information for capital projects currently funded at greater than $50,000.

The center is located in a conference room in the city hall. It contains an 8-by-30-foot Plexiglas project board and a map of the city that cross-references each project to the project board. A cork panel is used to display details and photographs. The center is equipped with a conference table that can be used for group meetings and status briefings. In addition to the information displayed, a monthly capital improvement program status report is prepared, giving detailed information about each project.

The Plexiglas project board is divided into five basic program areas that relate to some of the standard services provided by the city government. These are:

Community development.
Environmental health and protection.
Leisure-time opportunities.
Protection of persons and property.
Transportation.

Colored tape and press lettering, similar to that used in the Raleigh model, list information on the project board. Each area of city service is further subdivided into the division or organization responsible for it. The projects administered by each organizational unit are listed below their respective areas of responsibility. The following information on each project is displayed on the Plexiglas board:

A. Project Title
B. Funding Source
   General Fund (basically property taxes)
   Water and Sewer Fund
   Airport Revenue

*Robert S. Hopson, "Capital Improvement Projects Planning and Review Center," Charlotte, N.C. Unpublished report, 1975.

Bond Fund
Federal Funds
State Funds
Model Cities Supplemental Funds
C. Amount Funded from Each Source
D. Activity (phase of activity project is in)
Engineering
Land Acquisition
Federal Application
Bids Received
Construction
Project Life
E. Percentage Completion of Each Activity
F. Elapsed Time for Each Activity

The capital improvement projects monthly status report, mentioned earlier, contains the status of all capital projects. The report is updated monthly by a staff member in the public works department, known as the capital improvement projects coordinator. Status information is gathered from various city departments, council minutes, project files, and capital budget status reports. Copies of the report are distributed to the mayor, city council, city manager, budget officer, and each of the reporting departments. The report also serves as the basis for updating the project boards in the center.

As mentioned earlier, major projects are located on the project map of the city. Each project is cross-referenced by color to its respective program and area of service and by letter and number to the administering department or organizational unit.

Charlotte city officials believe that the following benefits are derived from their Capital Improvement Projects Planning and Review Center:

- It serves as a reference source of project goals and community progress.
- It provides a total view of the scope and location of city projects.
- It facilitates effective capital improvement projects briefings for the staff, management, the city council, visitors, the press, and civic groups.
- It provides a planning tool for city council and city staff.

Kansas City International Airport Management Information Center

A very sophisticated Management Information Center, or control room, was developed for the construction phases of the mammoth Kansas City International (KCI) Airport. A Kennedy Space Center-type control room was created for Kansas City by Midwest Research Institute. Its concepts are based on National Aeronautics and Space Administration (NASA) technology, and it represents an effective application of that technology by a unit of local government. Many of its concepts were originally used in the Apollo space program.

When KCI reached the construction phase, it became clear that a special approach was required to manage and control the approximately $200 million project. Several steps to accomplish this were undertaken by city officials:*

- Organization of a KCI management team.
- Establishment of a separate on-site construction management group.
- Implementation of a computer-assisted system of schedule and cost control.
- Steps to improve communications, including the creation of the KCI Management Information Center.

The center, located in city hall, functions as both a meeting and a briefing room and provides the management team with information required for good decision making.

Features of the Center. The center's design was partially dictated by the construction of the room, which included a free-standing structural column. A projection booth in the shape of a peninsula was used to hide the column and divide the room into two zones—one for meetings, and one for walkthrough briefings.

Charts, made of magnetic characters on vinyl-covered metal walls, are updated frequently to compare actual progress with schedules. Maps without backing are posted in order to utilize magnetic characters that designate present and future features

*John E. Stacy, Jr., "From KCS to KCI: Kennedy Space Center-type Control Room Is Focal Point for Development of Kansas City International Airport," *NASA Technology Application Bulletin,* Midwest Research Institute, Kansas City, October 1971.

of the airport construction site. Cork paneled areas are used to display temporary data. A display shelf is also included for models of structures.

Rear projection audiovisual equipment is used to view progress and architectural drawings and renderings. A console-podium has a remote control capability that can be used from a table or standing. A random-access 35-mm slide projector and a 16-mm movie projector can be controlled from the console. In addition, accent spotlights, blackboard lights, and a tape recorder can be controlled from the console, and a portable videotape player and a television monitor are available.

According to the NASA bulletin, the center cost $16,000 to construct. It is, in essence, a programmable conference room with all the data and features necessary to inform visitors, brief officials, and hold required meetings of the KCI management team (see Figure 9-9 for a floor plan of the center).

The NASA Tech Brief cited earlier offers the following guidelines for developing a Management Information Center.

> Centers of this nature can be developed for many purposes: the control of capital improvement projects; management of large city-federal programs such as model cities, alcohol safety action projects, or criminal justice system improvements; or any priority mission of government or industry. The "management of change" is the general goal for use of such a facility.
>
> Regardless of the objective, certain guidelines for development of Management Information Centers should be considered:
>
> 1. Decide on the mission for such a facility. If it is to cover several projects, it should have more convertible display surfaces, such as sliding panels.
> 2. Don't forget the facility is just a focal point for decision makers. Information systems and organizations must often be revised to provide the data essential to support the room. Meetings must be regularly scheduled.
> 3. Conveniently locate it for the busiest users, but slightly off the beaten path for privacy—no telephone to disrupt meetings.
> 4. Size according to average number of meeting participants, but allow enough space for other attendees.
> 5. Furnishings can be plain, but must be functional. If attendees are to view screens and displays on various walls, swivel and tilt chairs are needed.
> 6. Supplementary room lighting, such as accent spotlights for display, is generally needed. Room-light dimming and zone

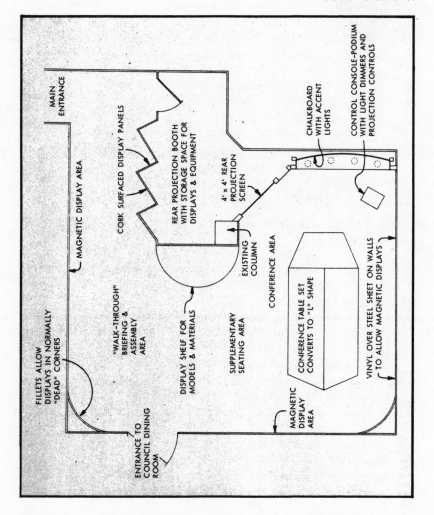

Figure 9-9. Floor plan of Kansas City International Airport Management Information Center. Overall dimensions are 28 × 30 feet.

MAIN ENTRANCE

MAGNETIC DISPLAY AREA

CORK SURFACED DISPLAY PANELS

REAR PROJECTION BOOTH WITH STORAGE SPACE FOR DISPLAYS & EQUIPMENT

4' × 4' REAR PROJECTION SCREEN

CHALKBOARD WITH ACCENT LIGHTS

CONTROL CONSOLE-PODIUM WITH LIGHT DIMMERS AND PROJECTION CONTROLS

EXISTING COLUMN

CONFERENCE AREA

FILLETS ALLOW DISPLAYS IN NORMALLY "DEAD" CORNERS

"WALK-THROUGH" BRIEFING & ASSEMBLY AREA

DISPLAY SHELF FOR MODELS & MATERIALS

SUPPLEMENTARY SEATING AREA

ENTRANCE TO COUNCIL DINING ROOM

CONFERENCE TABLE SET CONVERTS TO "L" SHAPE

MAGNETIC DISPLAY AREA

VINYL OVER STEEL SHEET ON WALLS TO ALLOW MAGNETIC DISPLAYS

control over accent lights are beneficial. Controls should be convenient to the speaker.

7. Contact several local sources for ideas on display surfaces, magnetic materials, and audiovisual equipment. Tailor the design to meet the unique needs of your facility and your mission. Consider the cost and convenience of maintaining any displays or audiovisual methods as part of your selection criteria. Don't overlook the $8\frac{1}{2}$-in. × 11-in. transparency with an overhead projector as a quick means of projEcting normal reports.

8. If slides and films are to be part of the normal communication capability of the room, the rear screen is a real asset, as it keeps noise and heat of equipment out of the room and allows unobstructed view in only slightly diminished room light. Remote-control capability for such equipment by the speaker is generally required. Multiple screens are sometimes used for more complex and dramatic presentations.

9. In addition to classic audiovisual equipment, consider the merit of videotape to bring the latest status or problem back from the field. A computer terminal is also a potential element of such a room if your organization has a computer data bank and telecommunications capability.

10. Consider security control for sensitive information and equipment. A lockable rear projection room is often adequate.

The NASA Tech Brief also listed several benefits of a center such as that developed for KCI:

- It is the catalyst for a total project management approach, which includes organization, management systems, and reporting methods.
- It is a convenient repository for easily referenced data on the project—goals, responsibility for tasks, and progress.
- It stimulates a real team management spirit with free exchange of data about plans, status, and problems.
- It is a "programmed" conference room that makes periodic project review meetings both productive and well attended.
- It allows decisions to be based on consistent and current information.
- It facilitates briefing of VIPs, civic groups, and new team members.
- It offers a convenient source of data and graphics for use by the media to inform the public.

■ It provides visible evidence of good management practices.

The KCI Management Center worked out so effectively that the Midwest Research Institute was contracted to install a similar facility in the Kansas City city hall for management and control of a $2.5 million Alcohol Safety Action program, a federal demonstration project. The results of this center have also been very good.

10

Financing
Capital
Improvements
Through Bonds

IS your local government faced with large, long-term requirements
to finance needed capital improvements? In times when significant
"no" votes on bond issues are the norm nationwide, how does a
local government go about passing a major capital improvements
bond issue? These questions and many others were answered in
Raleigh, North Carolina, as citizens approved a $43.3 million Capital
Improvements Bond Referendum. This bond issue, approved by
three-to-one in a majority of the categories, was both the largest
single municipal bond issue ever approved in Raleigh and the largest
ever approved for a municipality in the State of North Carolina.
In this chapter, we have used a case study to map the systematic
and procedural steps taken by city administrators and elected public
officials to obtain citizen approval of this major bond issue. As

a result of this documentation, it is hoped that other local government officials may learn how to use similar approaches in their jurisdictions.

THE ISSUES

The Raleigh Capital Improvements Bond Issue consisted of four separate issues to be voted on in a special referendum called for early October. A "yes" or "no" vote was possible on any of the four issues. These four issues and a brief description of each were as follows:

Water System Improvement. ($12.4 million)—Raleigh's future water supply will come from the Falls of the Neuse storage reservoir on the Neuse River. This project, however, cannot possibly be completed in time to guarantee that Raleigh will not have a serious water shortage. Therefore, emergency water storage must be available for an interim period. Also, the spreading out and continuing growth of the city requires that large water feeder mains be added to deliver the water with sufficient pressure and volume. Public utility service charges will provide the funds to pay the necessary debt related to this improvement.

Sewer System Improvement. ($23.4 million)—The city of Raleigh believes that no one, including itself, should be allowed to dump waste into creeks and rivers. The city's sewage treatment plant, in operation for over 15 years, can no longer clean up all the waste draining from the city. If the community is to meet its responsibilities, a larger and more modern plant and larger sewage outfalls and collecting lines are urgently needed. Public utility service charges will provide the funds to pay the necessary debt.

Street System Improvements. ($5 million)—Population increases mean more cars, which require new and larger streets on which to travel. Thoroughfare surveys and studies show that Raleigh must provide a new and larger street system. Provided funds are available, many major street projects are ready to commence. These funds will also pay the city's part in a number of planned state and federal highway projects. Furthermore, each year for 20 years, the city has built 3 to 5 miles of streets and still has about 40 miles of unpaved streets to cover. The present debt fund tax levy can absorb this debt without taxes being raised.

Park System Improvements. ($2.5 million)—For a number of years, the city has been buying park lands and building ballfields, tennis courts, and similar projects out of the annual operating budget (recreation tax levy). Some federal funds have been received to assist in this effort. The park system needs a number of community centers to provide more programs for the people. In addition, two of the city's largest parks are in need of major rebuilding. The community centers and major improvements cost more than the annual operating budget can handle, so bond financing is needed. A three-cent tax levy will pay back the required debt for these added capital improvements.

MODUS OPERANDI

Although preliminary and advanced planning had been proceeding on the Capital Improvements Bond Issue for several years, the final detailed planning for the exact items to be included did not culminate until July. At this time, Raleigh's assistant city manager for programming and budgeting made a comprehensive presentation of the capital improvement needs over a five-year period to the city council. This presentation, which was a public meeting with the press encouraged to attend, defined the needs in the four areas previously outlined. In addition, several other needs and additional possible sources of funding were identified. Such items as additional fire stations, improvements and additions to public buildings, and future sanitary landfills were also discussed. Because the city council determined that these latter items could undoubtedly be financed from a recently enacted additional 1¢ sales tax, on a pay-as-you go basis, they were eliminated from the bond issue. At this presentation, a 12-page handout, outlining the needs in the four defined areas, was made available to the council, the press, and other interested persons. Maps of the proposed improvements were also used.

During the week after the presentation, the exact wording of the bond referendum was written by city administrators and the city council. In the first week of August, a special meeting of the city council was called to establish a date for the bond vote. The referendum was set for the second Tuesday in October, and the aggregate amount of the proposed issue was established as $43.3 million.

As soon as the date was established, the planning for the campaign to sell the issue to the voters swung into high gear.

The mayor, city manager, assistant city manager for programming and budgeting, and planning director met to begin forming the strategy for the campaign. At this meeting, it was decided that the assistant city manager for programming and budgeting would manage the efforts, with the mayor spearheading the entire campaign. The city manager was to seek outside assistance from a major local university in developing campaign media material, and the planning director was to begin work on an informational brochure and slide presentation for citizen groups. The assistant city manager for programming and budgeting was to prepare an interim informational pamphlet until a more formal brochure could be developed and printed.

At this meeting, other major items were discussed, including:

1. A central campaign theme or slogan to be used on all informational materials was selected by the mayor: "Vote for Your Future."
2. White and red were to be used as campaign colors wherever possible throughout the campaign.
3. An immediate purchase order was placed for 10,000 white-on-red campaign buttons imprinted with the campaign slogan (see Figure 10–1).

Figure 10-1. Example of City of Raleigh capital improvements bond referendum campaign button and bumper sticker.

4. An immediate purchase order was placed for 5,000 white-on-red bumper stickers imprinted with the campaign slogan. Care was exercised to order the all-plastic sticker that could be easily removed when the campaign had ended (see Figure 10-1).

5. It was decided to contact other cities with recently successful bond issues to determine the methods used in their campaigns.

At several subsequent meetings, held during the next week, the following decisions were also reached:

1. The informational campaign was to be spearheaded by the city council rather than the traditional group of appointed community leaders. It was determined that a Committee for Capital Improvements would be named at a later date. This committee would obtain campaign contributions from citizens and organizations in the community, but it would not carry on the campaign per se. The committee was to consist of several previous mayors, city councilmen, and other business and community leaders.

2. A local volunteer experienced in mass media advertising would be named by the mayor and given responsibility for developing and placing paid media advertising. This was to include the following:

- Developing a paid mass media advertising package and budget to cover the entire campaign.
- Developing radio, television, and newspaper paid advertisements exclusive of the spots being developed by the local university.

3. The design for the multicolor informational brochure developed by the city planning department was approved and an order for 35,000 brochures was placed at a local printer (see Figure 10-2).

4. A monthly mailing machine labeler was to be purchased to imprint the bond issue slogan on all city correspondence.

5. A "shotgun" or areawide approach of conducting the informational campaign in the community was to be used rather than concentrating on selected key groups.

The campaign would have these previously undiscussed attributes:

1. In late August, the city officially requested their bond attorneys in New York and the State of North Carolina Local

Government Commission to approve the city's proposed bond financing program.

2. A special meeting of the city council was called on August 30 to file the necessary debt statement and to adopt the necessary bond ordinances for authorizing a $43.3 million bond issue and for authorizing its announcement in all local newspapers.

3. A meeting of all civic club and community organization presidents and chairmen was called for the evening of September 1. At this meeting, the assistant city manager for programming and budgeting gave the same presentation as he had given to the city council when it was decided to proceed with the campaign. In setting up this meeting, individually typed and signed letters from the mayor invited the representatives. As a matter of interest, original, individually typed letters, rather than form letters, were used for all correspondence throughout the campaign. The advantages of this approach were felt to warrant the extra cost and effort involved. At this meeting, the mayor asked each organization represented to allow someone to make a five- to ten-minute presentation to their entire group in support of the upcoming bond issue. As a follow-up to this meeting, letters were sent to all attendees thanking them for their interest and offering brochures for their members and for speakers at their future meetings. Letters were also sent to those organizations that did not attend the meeting, soliciting their support and requesting permission either to make an informational presentation before their group or to send brochures.

4. The office of the assistant city manager for programming and budgeting was designated as the focal point for all bond issue informational material. Brochures, buttons, bumper strips, and other material were centralized in this office and were mailed or hand-delivered daily to interested organizations throughout the community, including financial institutions and businesses. As presentations were made before civic clubs or community organizations, brochures, buttons, and bumper strips were handed out to the members.

5. "Vote for Your Future" bumper strips were placed on all city vehicles. Although some local citizens protested this method, it was successfully defended by a majority of the city council as "a proper approach."

6. A billboard displaying the bond issue slogan and the referendum date was donated by a local outdoor advertising agency and placed in a strategic, heavily traveled location.

Figure 10-2. Example of City of Raleigh capital improvements bond referendum informational brochure.

SUMMARY OF FACTS

Purpose	Amount
WATER SYSTEM	$ 12,400,000
SEWER SYSTEM	23,400,000
STREET IMPROVEMENTS	5,000,000
PARK IMPROVEMENTS	2,500,000
	$ 43,300,000

Street bonds can be repaid from the present tax debt levy.

Of the remaining, only $2,500,000 will affect the ad valorem tax rate. It will require an estimated 3¢ tax beginning with the 1972 fiscal year. This means that at the home with a market value of $20,000 for real and personal property would be taxed only $3.00 per year (or 25¢ per month).

The $35,800,000 water and sewer bonds will be paid from an estimated 30% increase in utility charges. If your water bill is now $6.00 per month it would increase to $7.80.

★ ★ ★ ★ ★

BOND ELECTION
October 12, 1971

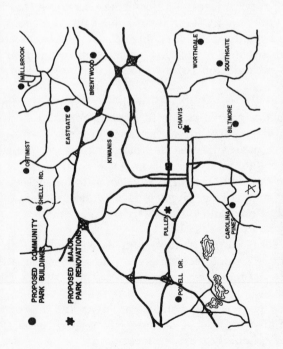

● PROPOSED COMMUNITY PARK BUILDINGS

✹ PROPOSED MAJOR PARK RENOVATION

PARK DEVELOPMENT IS BEING DEMANDED BY CITIZENS OF ALL AGES!

The expansion and development of the City park system is one of the most critical needs facing the City. A major effort is required in addition to the pay as we go annual funding from the present 10¢ tax levy.

These new bonds are needed to construct major improvements, such as community centers, and to rebuild two of the oldest and most used parks, Chavis and Pullen.

THESE $2,500,000 IN BONDS WOULD REQUIRE NO MORE THAN A 3¢ TAX LEVY.

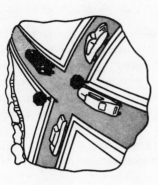

EACH YEAR OVER 5,000 CARS ARE ADDED TO THOSE NOW USING OUR STREETS.

During the next 5 years, the improvements to our streets and Thoroughfare Plan paving program will require $12,000,000 to $13,000,000.

Most of this money will be available through State sources such as the gasoline tax refund.

The $5,000,000 bond funds requested will supplement these funds and enable our street improvement projects to be continued more rapidly.

THESE BONDS CAN BE REPAID FROM THE PRESENT TAX LEVY.

RALEIGH'S PRESENT WATER SUPPLY IS DANGEROUSLY LOW!

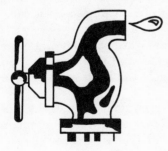

- Raleigh's water supply to the Neuse River Water Plant has reached a critical stage, calling for emergency action to provide carry-over storage until the large lake is built by the U.S. Corps of Engineers.

- The age of the original treatment plant demands repairs and updating of equipment.

- The Neuse River Plant was built for planned expansion and the second stage of its development is now urgently needed.

- A recent engineering study indicated a need for many new lines joining the two water plants and improving the water distribution throughout our area, thus stabilizing pressures and providing adequate fire protection water.

- THESE $12,400,000 IN BONDS WOULD BE REPAID FROM THE INCREASE IN WATER RATES.

RALEIGH'S SEWAGE TREATMENT PLANT IS OPERATING OVER-CAPACITY!

Raleigh's pollution problems must be solved to protect our environment in the city. Our present waste treatment plant is at maximum use and cannot be economically expanded. A new treatment plant must be constructed on the Neuse River to improve and supplement our waste treatment. Large connecting sewer lines must also be constructed.

THESE $23,400,000 IN BONDS WOULD BE PAID FOR FROM THE INCREASE IN WATER AND SEWER SERVICE CHARGES.

7. Subsequent to the September 1 meeting with the civic and community organizations, the assistant city manager for programming and budgeting presented to all city department and division heads approximately the same information given to the city council and civic club presidents. Each attendee was encouraged to explain the need for the bond issue to his employees and to take an active part in disseminating information during the bond campaign.

8. The assistant city manager for programming and budgeting was to schedule all bond issue group presentations and was to keep a calendar of commitments. A city councilman and a city administrator were to make as many presentations together as possible.

9. The assistant city manager for programming and budgeting was to prepare several sets of simplified flip charts or large poster cards to outline briefly the major bond issue elements. These charts or cards were to be used by persons making the bond issue presentations and were to be used temporarily until the slide presentations could be readied. The charts subsequently proved so successful, however, that they were used extensively throughout the campaign, and the slides were used only minimally.

10. A special bond campaign information issue was to be prepared in "At Your Service," the city's monthly water bill stuffer. This stuffer reached over 33,000 people.

11. A special notice was to be prepared in the "Communicator," the biweekly city employee paycheck stuffer, urging all city employees and their families to support the bond campaign.

12. During the latter stages of the campaign, a "Good Morning Flyer" was to be prepared for hand-delivery to each citizen's doorstep on the eve of the referendum (see Figure 10–3). Signs reflecting the same information were placed approximately 50 feet away from each voting precinct. These chores were accomplished by the Raleigh Jaycees and by volunteer groups of interested citizens working at the precinct level. The precinct signs were placed between 4 and 6 A.M. on the morning of the referendum.

13. Various civic and community organizations, such as garden clubs, the Raleigh Chamber of Commerce, and the Raleigh Merchants Bureau, were encouraged to support the bond issue in their organization newsletters.

14. Organizations were encouraged to announce their support of the bond campaign to the news media by issuing a "Statement of Support." This statement usually was printed by the newspapers (morning and evening), and during the latter stage of the campaign,

Today is the day to
vote for all four
issues in the City
Bond Election.
Water. Sewer.
Streets. Parks.
...Have a nice day.

Paid for by the Committee FOR Capital Improvements

Figure 10-3. Capital improvements bond referendum campaign "Good Morning Flyer."

it was used in newspaper advertisements paid for by the Committee for Capital Improvements.

15. The various local news media were encouraged to discuss the bond issue on their programs and in their writings. They complied well, and during the latter stages of the campaign, coverage became quite intensive. A Sunday morning two-page "Bond Issue Question and Answer" article appeared in the Raleigh *News and Observer,* the area's major newspaper. This article had been based on a taped interview of elected and appointed officials conducted in the editor's office. Editorials by both the Raleigh *Times* and *The News and Observer* supported the bond issue, and feature articles fully outlined its attributes.

THE CAMPAIGN

During the weeks that followed the initial presentation to the community leaders on September 1, the bond campaign swung into high gear. Although much of the campaign was of the grass-roots variety, the city council and the city administration bore the bulk of the campaign effort, with the mayor and the assistant city manager for programming and budgeting spearheading these efforts.

During this six-week campaign, approximately 120 informational presentations were given to civic clubs and community organizations, the vast majority of which was given by the mayor and the assistant city manager for programming and budgeting. Sometimes, five or six presentations were given in one day, with the day starting with early morning breakfast meetings and ending well after midnight with neighborhood gatherings. The campaign stressed that sincere and responsive answers be given to questions. In cases where they were not readily available, answers were obtained the next day, and the person raising the question was either written to or called. In addition, a "Hot Line" telephone, set up in the assistant city manager for programming and budgeting's office, was advertised in both local newspapers and on television and radio, and citizens were urged to call to get the facts on the bond issue.

Early in the campaign, a recently elected city councilman opposed the bond issue, primarily because of the sewage treatment and water supply portions of the bond. His public opposition soon dissolved, however, after several face-to-face confrontations with the mayor and other members of the city council.

Two other community organizations started out in opposition, but only one of these carried their opposition all the way through the campaign. This latter group based most of its opposition on alleged inequities in the structure of the water rate.

The city council maintained throughout the campaign that a study of water and sewer services rates and charges would be conducted by independent outsiders before customer charges would be increased to pay off the water and sewer bonded indebtedness. This study was authorized by the city council subsequent to the bond campaign and, as promised, was completed and acted upon.

WHAT CAN SUCCESS BE ATTRIBUTED TO?

The overwhelming success of Raleigh's bond campaign can be attributed to the following:

- Thorough preplanning for the bond issue.
- Thorough planning for the bond campaign.
- Sincerity on the part of all city officials involved to make the needs known to the people.
- The mayor's forthright and untiring personal leadership, assisted by the city's top administration. The mayor's charisma had a tremendous positive effect on the success of the campaign.
- Responsiveness to questions asked by citizens on any city-oriented issue at the grass-roots meetings.
- Effective dissemination of information to all levels in the community.
- Organized support from community leaders and groups.
- Support of the mass media.
- Adequate financial support via the Committee for Capital Improvements.
- Last, but by no means least, HARD WORK.

THE AFTERMATH

After the results of the bond campaign were in, the work was still not completed. Hundreds of "thank you" letters were sent to everyone who participated in the campaign. As before, these were individually typed and signed by the mayor.

In addition, at a subsequent city council meeting, plaques and certificates were presented to those persons who played the most active roles in the success of the campaign.

11

Construction Management and Incentive Contracting

PUBLIC sector organizations are under increasing pressure to save time and money in developing new public facilities. Inflation, the energy crisis, strikes, and generally more complex facility requirements, however, have made these goals more difficult to achieve.

CONSTRUCTION MANAGEMENT

Construction management, an alternative to traditional building processes, seeks to save time and money primarily through better coordination and management. Many private developers and federal agencies, including the General Services Administration (GSA) and the Department of Health, Education and Welfare—along with many state and local governments—have found that construction management saves time, money, and aggravation.

In many instances, construction management has produced impressive savings. GSA reports design and construction time savings of up to two years, and several public sector organizations report time savings of more than six months. These savings have accrued by reducing the impact of inflation, cutting costs for interim construction loans, reducing contingency amounts in contractor bids, and shortening rental periods for temporary quarters prior to occupancy. Certain techniques available through the use of construction management make a major contribution to these savings. For example, value management, discussed later in this chapter, can be used effectively to produce consistent savings of 8 to 1 over the cost of its use.

With the construction management approach, a construction manager coordinates the building process and acts as a fiduciary for the owner, which makes the project a cooperative team effort rather than an adversary proceeding, a situation that is not uncommon in public sector construction. These relationships are backed up by the Critical Path Method, Program Evaluation and Review Technique, detailed cost estimating, and cost accounting. These techniques often require computers, and a competent construction manager will use them with great effectiveness to control his project.

The construction management approach increases usefulness in proportion to the complexity and cost of a project. It can be used on a cost-effective basis for complex projects costing $3 million and more. On the other hand, individual elements of the approach, such as value management, may yield significant cost benefits on projects costing $1 million and less.

Some public developers perform in-house construction management; most, however, contract this service from an outside firm. In cases where construction management was unsuccessful, problems were traceable to an ineffective manager or to unworkable and ambiguous contractual relationships.

This chapter was developed to guide public sector organizations in their evaluation of construction management for their particular needs. It describes the several forms of construction management and provides a process by which public administrators can determine whether or not and how to use construction management. The process will help any interested public development agency to employ a good construction manager under the right contract. In this chapter, administrators will find guidelines for evaluating, selecting, and contracting for construction management services. Jurisdictions without extensive construction experience may need to choose an experienced consultant to assist them with the decisions.

The Need for Construction Management

Disciplined, yet flexible, management of budgets, costs, schedules, and participant involvement in complex public construction projects has become increasingly important for state and local governments and for public agencies. The need for construction programs that are completed on schedule and at reasonable cost has been heightened by demands for additional public facilities and tight construction budgets.

Increasing costs of materials and labor, environmental regulations, high interest rates, materials shortages, supply fluctuations, energy conservation, and regulations for using minority contractors have dramatically increased in importance in recent years.

In traditional public construction, a governmental organization, acting as owner, performs overall project administration, direction, scheduling, monitoring, and management. In this capacity, the agency can be termed "project manager." The owner contracts with design professionals to prepare drawings and other design documents and with general contractors to do the construction work. The general contractor normally subcontracts most of the structural, mechanical, electrical, and interior work to other firms.

Coordinated management of major building projects frequently is a weak aspect of traditional public building projects. Many in the field, for instance, note that under the system the general contractor (seeking to make a profit on a fixed contract amount) is in an adversary position to the owner and to the design professionals. For example, although it could be beneficial, the contractor does not provide cost-saving input to the project's design phase. Others note that when the design and construction phases are totally separate and sequential, the total time for the building process may be unnecessarily long, raising costs and producing a facility that may be partially obsolete even before it is completed. Still others believe that by lengthening development time the sequential nature of design and construction phases reduces the flexibility to adapt to new developments in technology and to forecast construction problems or fluctuations in labor and materials price.

Public sector organizations also lack experienced, in-house personnel to manage major projects. Furthermore, if the public agency does not anticipate a large continuing construction program, it may be unable to justify hiring the necessary staff. Placed in this position, the agency may have no alternative but to turn to outside professionals for project and construction management expertise.

The Construction Management Approach

Construction management, developed as an alternative to the traditional building process, is especially applicable to the organization and management of major and complex construction projects. Because the construction management approach may assume many different forms, public agencies have used it on a variety of construction projects, including buildings, roads, waste water plants, and transit systems.

In each application, the basic thrust is to develop a team approach, which coordinates the working relationships of the public agency developer, project design professionals, and an organization termed the "construction manager." The objectives of these new team relationships are to coordinate the building process, to reduce adversary relationships, and to deal with problems promptly when delay could bring on cost overruns.

Construction management differs in several important ways from traditional public sector construction. First, a construction manager is involved as a multifaceted professional group that provides project management services and administers construction. Second, the construction management augments the capabilities of project design professionals with its own construction expertise. Third, emphasis is placed on integrating design and construction schedules, cost estimating, and cost accounting as management tools, making the construction manager responsible for their use. Fourth, many of the responsibilities traditionally assumed by a project's general contractor are given to the construction manager. Finally, awards are frequently made for multiple prime construction contracts, rather than subcontracting by a single general contractor.

Although these are major changes, existing legal constraints are still met, and several basic project functions remain essentially intact. Public bidding procedures can still be used for all actual construction work. In fact, the construction manager approach generally increases competition by opening up the process to a greater number of qualified bidders. The project design professionals are still responsible for all design decisions, with concurrence from the owner. The owner retains final control of the building process, although he or she is often more involved in project decisions.

Finally, construction management relationships can be developed to provide the owner with a contractually guaranteed limit of construction costs. As mentioned above, individual construction contracts can be publicly bid in a fixed price nature. In addition, the construction manager's contract can include several guarantees for total project cost, although it may be counterproductive to require these guarantees.

How Construction Management Works

Construction management refers to a type of contractual and professional working relationship initiated by a building owner for the project design professionals and the construction manager. The approach can be applied to one particular facility or to several related facilities within an overall construction program. The construction manager may be an individual or a group of individuals on the owner's staff. More frequently, however, the construction manager is an outside firm or firms working as an agent of the jurisdiction under a professional services contract on a specific construction project.

Many variations of the construction management approach have been used by private developers and public construction agencies. Because of the special characteristics of each major building project and the rules and regulations specific to each jurisdiction, no one relationship is best suited to meet the particular needs of all jurisdictions. A broad overview of construction management services through the predesign, design, and construction phases of a project is provided below. The aim here is to indicate the kinds of services a construction manager can provide rather than to specify any hard and fast rules.

Construction management is most effective when employed from a project's predesign stage through construction and to final occupancy. Although construction management services can be employed for only a single phase of a project, the benefits of the approach may not be fully realized.

Predesign Phase

If the public sector organization determines to use an outside group, the construction manager may be placed under contract even before the project design professionals are selected. In fact, one of the first functions of the construction manager may be to assist the organization in contracting for the project architect/engineer. On the other hand, if the design firm is selected first, it may assist the owner in contracting for construction management services. Either way, it is essential that the construction manager and the design professionals work closely together with nonconflicting contractual responsibilities. Some developers avoid this problem by contracting with project design professionals to provide construction management services.

During a project's predesign phase, the construction manager can aid in planning, programming, budgeting, and scheduling and in correlating the input with the public agency's requirements for the project. The construction manager may also assist in preliminary budget analysis and in site selection. Perhaps one of the greatest contributions construction management can make during the predesign phase is to review basic requirements for the facility with the owner and the design professionals, thereby ensuring that the owner's real needs are met effectively within the allowable budget.

During the predesign phase of a project, the owner can use the construction manager's expertise and diversity of possible services to complement the capabilities of the in-house project managers and the project design professionals. Because each public agency has individual needs, each will require different services from its construction manager. Care must be taken before design and construction management agreements are signed so that all necessary predesign functions are completed without conflict or overlap by either the owner, the design professional, or the construction manager.

Design Phase

Many who have used construction management believe that its greatest benefits occurred during the project's design phase, because flexibility still remains for major cost- and time-saving modifications. At this stage in the building process, the construction manager's job is to provide continuing project management, to coordinate the building process, to develop schedules, and to review designs and specifications all aimed at saving the owner construction time and money. Another important job is to develop cost models and component budgets.

During a project's design phase, the construction manager is not responsible for actual design decisions; although the construction manager will review designs, final decisions are made by the design professionals and the owner. The construction manager's prime responsibilities are to keep design activities on schedule, to develop construction schedules, and to provide expertise to reduce and control costs. The cost-control function of the construction manager has two very important elements: cost estimating and value management.

Construction management places greater emphasis on cost estimating as a management tool than does traditional project administration. The construction manager independently reviews estimated and actual construction costs, often using computers extensively. Construction cost control (and budget control) is a primary, not a secondary, function of the construction manager. The construction manager's familiarity with the costs and typical cycle times of labor and materials is usually greater than that of most design firms. Throughout the design phase, the construction manager provides regular cost estimates to the project design professional and to the local administration as a major feedback for evaluating whether or not the design is within desired cost boundaries. On certain projects, the construction manager will have a representative work full time in the design professional's office to expedite the exchange of information on cost estimates.

Although value management, the second design phase approach to cost control, is discussed here as a distinct form of cost control, many construction management organizations integrate it into their overall cost-control services. Value management is an organized and vigorous analysis to find what is needed to achieve essential functions at the lowest total cost, consistent with needed performance, quality, reliability, aesthetics, safety, and operation. Value specialists routinely expect that suggested project savings will exceed the cost of their services by a factor of 8 to 1. The GSA Public Buildings Service reported $10 million in savings for 1974 from value management programs with a return on its investment of nearly 13 to 1.*

Construction management organizations are well suited to provide value management advice, as they use a wealth of construction and design knowledge to independently look at design progress. On the basis of initial cost and projected maintenance costs, typical value management includes advice on the proper size of heating and cooling equipment for life-cycle cost and energy savings, on

*FY 1974 Value Management Annual Report, Public Buildings Service, U.S. General Services Administration.

choosing the most economical structural system, on modifying a design to speed construction sequencing, and on the most economical interior finishes and partitions.

Much of the construction management activity that simultaneously occurs with design is directed toward scheduling and coordinating the construction process. The construction manager prepares overall project schedules, including both design and construction phases. Great emphasis is placed on these schedules as management tools to increase project efficiencies. As design progresses, the construction manager develops a plan for separating construction work into an integrated set of contracts, frequently separated by construction disciplines—heating, electrical work, finishes, and so forth. On the other hand, it may be desirable to separate some work in terms of assemblies within the facility. This would be appropriate if a given assembly (for example, an air diffuser with built-in lighting) could best be installed by a single contractor with multiple capabilities (for example, heating and electrical work).

Other concerns affecting the decision to separate construction contracts include laws or policies on the use of local or small businesses and minority contractors. Overall, the construction manager develops a construction contract plan in order to ensure that all work is contracted in the owner's best interest. As prerequisites, each construction firm must be able to carry out its portion of work efficiently, and problems such as overlapping trade jurisdictions must be avoided.

As the plan for separating construction work is developed and approved by the owner, the construction manager develops bid packages, conducts briefings, and finally assists the owner in selecting competent firms that have submitted reasonably low bids.

Construction Phase

Although the construction phase is discussed as a separate activity, construction management actually integrates both design and construction schedules into one smooth process. In doing so, the construction manager usually reduces the total time between the start of design and the completion of construction, saving the owner considerable cost and time. Technically, this approach is called "phased design and construction," or simply "phasing." ("Fast tracking" is often used in popular jargon; however, it is misused.) Because phased design and construction have been difficult to carry out within the traditional building process, public agencies and private developers often use the construction management approach. Grant constraints and other financial reasons more commonly prevent phasing in traditional project arrangements than do technical constraints.

The procedure for phased design and construction works as follows. Long lead time material (e.g., steel) and equipment often will be procured early in the design phase. Similarly, off-site fabrication of special assemblies and components will be started at an early stage. Then, as design progresses, construction contracts for various portions of the facility, such as excavation, foundations, and steel work, will be competitively bid and let so that each portion of construction can be initiated at the earliest possible time. In this way, procurement and construction actually begin before the design phase is complete.

Some public agencies may have difficulty starting construction under phased design and construction procedures. For example, local, state, or federal rules or regulations may require that all design documentation be complete before construction begins or that nearly all construction work be let as a single lump-sum contract. In several cases, however, public jurisdictions have found that these constraints are subject to interpretation or may be modified for the project at hand.

A similar problem can arise with current building permit and plan review procedures. Several governments have made administrative changes in building code procedures to accommodate phased design and construction. The changes enable partial building permits to be issued ("foundation-only" or "structure-only"). Because the modified procedures, although successful, create more work for the building regulatory agency, permit fees for phased design and construction may be higher than for the traditional building process.

Although phased design and construction is routine under construction management, it is not necessary. Before a decision is made, the jurisdiction should consult with the project design professional, because the designer should have a solid conceptualization of the project at an early stage, and it may increase the firm's workload. Legal counsel also should be contacted.

During construction, the construction manager is responsible for administering progress. In public sector construction, the construction manager frequently does not perform any of the actual construction work in order that all such work will be bid for competitively and that possible conflicts of interest are avoided.

However, the responsibility to administer the construction contracts is usually tied in with a series of related functions, including, but not limited to, cost accounting, overall control of the construction site, site security, maintenance of records, and inspections. It should be noted that the construction manager's inspections are in addition to the periodic inspections made by project design professionals and by regulatory officials and are, in general, more frequent and more detailed.

INCENTIVE CONTRACTING*

Incentive contracting is another systematic method that public sector organizations can use to improve delivery and reduce cost. It can be used with or without construction management.

An incentive is defined as a stimulus to desired action. An incentive contract motivates the contractor to earn more compensation by achieving better performance and by controlling cost. The incentive arrangement also must reduce compensation if desired performance and cost control are not achieved; compensation is therefore more accurately related to value received.

To be meaningful, an incentive must create some specific and favorable effort that would not otherwise have been initiated. It is significant to note, however, that even if incentive contracting is only applied under *appropriate circumstances,* even if it is of the *proper type,* and even if it is *properly structured,* the incentive contract will be ineffective if contract clauses and administrative practices are inappropriate.

The incentive contract should communicate the goals of the public sector organization to the contractor and should motivate the contractor's management to convey the jurisdiction's (customer's) objectives within the contractor's organization. The effectiveness of these communications must be continually examined and assessed. An incentive should always be structured empirically.

By adjusting the contractor's profit to the customer's value of the actual work completed, compared to the contract's target profit and performance goals, incentive contracting motivates the contractor to perform in the best interest of the customer. Two concepts are involved: the motivation of the contractor and the value to the customer.

*"Incentive Contracting Guide," U.S. Department of Defense and National Aeronautics and Space Administration, Washington, D.C., October 1969.

Basic Principles

Profit is the basic motive of business enterprise. However, profit per se is not the only motivation. The typical government contractor has become accustomed to thinking that profit is as necessary an element of price as are material, labor, overhead, and other expenses. Skill at the negotiating table may often determine the profit level in the same way that it determines the amount of dollars assigned to key cost factors. Generally, contractors will optimize—not maximize—profit.

The profit motive is the essence of incentive contracting. In other words, incentive contracts increase the contractor's profit when cost (and sometimes performance and schedule) levels are attained that are more beneficial than expected (target), and they penalize the contractor by reducing profit for less than expected levels. In stressing these profit-making aspects, however, the contractor does not discount the importance of the following extracontractual incentives: (1) future business; (2) profits on other contracts being performed at the same time*; (3) prestige and goodwill; (4) maintenance of engineering and/or production capability; and (5) excellence for its own sake. These factors should be considered prior to making awards and, when possible, while structuring the incentive sharing provisions, because, with any particular contractor, these factors may outweigh the short-term profit incentives.

Without extensively discussing the various theories underlying the incentive concept, it is sufficient to talk about *rewards and penalties* that may be applied to cost, performance, or schedule. In a cost-only incentive contract, the incentive applied to cost is interrelated to performance and schedule (i.e., the sharing ratio applies to a given performance level upon which the estimated, or target, cost is based). It is generally assumed that the relative values of cost, technical performance, and schedule remain constant; however, in incentive structures these values rarely remain balanced, because the sharing ratio is not normally related to a given set of performance conditions as it should in a cost-only incentive contract. Naturally, in a multiple incentive contract, it seldom does apply to a set of performance conditions.

Although penalty incentive is simply the counterpart of reward,

---

*By absorbing a portion of the fixed overhead expense on *this* contract that otherwise would be absorbed by other contracts he has underway, the contractor could increase his profit margin on those other contracts.

in many cases penalty incentives arouse negative emotions or attitudes. For this reason, the contractor may object to a penalty-only incentive, although either the reward-only or the penalty-only approach may be the better motivator. Traditionally reward incentives are applied for cost under target and penalty incentives for cost over target in a cost-incentive-only contract, particularly in the federal government (for example, the Department of Defense and the National Aeronautics and Space Administration). The practical effect is the same, of course, where the ranges of fee and of incentive effectiveness are the same.

The rewards and penalties in a cost incentive contract (or the cost-sharing arrangement) are usually expressed as a percentage ratio. This applies equally to either a cost-plus-incentive-fee (CPIF) or a fixed-price-incentive (FPI) contract. A 60/40 incentive share line in the contract means that of every dollar of cost above the target of the contract the public sector organization pays 60 and the contractor pays 40. Therefore for every dollar of cost under target, the public sector organization saves 60 cents and the contractor earns an additional 40 cents. The precise dollar amounts of the compensation adjustment are determined by this formula after the contract is completed.

State or local laws or regulations may have an impact on the state or local organization's ability to contract with a reward/penalty or incentive approach. However, two examples of incentive contracts that have been successfully used by local governments in two different states are described later in this chapter.

Selection of Contract Types

Recognizing that the federal government needs flexibility, federal regulations provide a wide range of contracts to purchase a large variety and volume of supplies and services. Generally, there are two basic categories of contract: firm-fixed-price and cost-plus-fixed-fee. Firm-fixed-price contracts are characterized by a price that (1) represents full payment for the work; (2) meets minimum standards of performance; and (3) is delivered by a specified time. Cost-plus-fixed-fee contracts, on the other hand, are characterized by an estimate of the contract cost, with the buyer agreeing to reimburse the seller for all allowable costs that are deemed necessary to complete the work. Between the extremes—in terms of the degree of cost responsibility—are variations of the two categories. The firm-fixed-price contract is at one extreme, with the contractor assuming full cost responsibility and therefore having a maximum profit incentive; the cost-plus-fixed-fee is at the other end of the spectrum, with the contractor assuming minimal cost responsibility and having no reason to increase profit or control costs.

Effective pricing and sound procurement practices require discrimination and judgment in selecting and negotiating the *right* type of contract. While federal procurement regulations state that the firm-fixed-price contract is the preferred type for harnessing the profit motive, because the contractor accepts full cost responsibilty, do not assume that it is always the right contract. As stated in the Armed Services Procurement Regulations Manual for Contract Pricing:

> Sound procurement requires use of the right contract type. The best, most realistic and reasonable price in the world (for the particular requirement at hand) may turn sour if the contract type is wrong.

In addition, the best-structured incentive arrangements may become completely ineffectual if the type of contract and the contract price combine in such a way as to eliminate any possibility that the contractor will earn a greater profit by cost savings or performance improvement.

This is especially true in the area of research and development contracting because of the nature of the work, the usual lack of definitive requirements, and the inability to measure technical objectives. The inability to measure risk frequently necessitates the negotiation of a cost-plus-award-fee or a cost-plus-fixed-fee contract. The development effort following the contract definition phase, however, can frequently be accomplished under incentive (fixed-price-incentive or cost-plus-incentive-fee) contracts or firm-fixed-price. Because this area does not usually concern most state and local governments, it may not be a large problem in such organizations.

Some rules of thumb for the selection of contract types are:

- *Cost-Plus-Fixed-Fee* is appropriate where "level of effort" is required or where there are high technical and cost uncertainties.
- *Cost-Plus-Award-Fee* is appropriate where conditions for a cost-plus-fixed-fee are present but where improved performance that cannot be measured objectively is also desired.

- *Cost-Plus-Incentive-Fee* (*Cost Incentive Only*) is appropriate where a given level of performance is desired, where confidence in achieving that performance level is reasonably good, and where technical and cost uncertainty is too excessive to use a fixed-price incentive.
- *Cost-Plus-Incentive-Fee* (*Multiple Incentives*) is appropriate where expectations of achieving an acceptable performance are good but improvements are desired and where technical and cost uncertainties are too excessive to use a fixed-price-incentive.
- *Fixed-Price-Incentive* (*Cost Incentive Only*) is appropriate where confidence in achieving performance is high and where cost and technical uncertainties can be reasonably identified.
- *Fixed-Price-Incentive* (*Multiple Incentives*) is appropriate where improved performance is desired and where technical and cost uncertainties are reasonably identifiable.
- *Firm-Fixed-Price* is appropriate where performance has already been demonstrated and where technical and cost uncertainties are low.
- *Firm-Fixed-Price* (*with Incentives Added*) is appropriate where improved performance or schedule is desired and where technical and cost uncertainties are low.

Elements of Basic Incentive Contract Types

As previously mentioned, two basic contract types are usually available throughout the procurement cycle—fixed-price and cost-plus-fixed-fee—with incentives providing variations. The two most commonly used incentive types are cost-plus-incentive-fee and fixed-price-incentive.

The following elements appear in the basic contracts: *Cost-plus-fixed-fee:* estimated cost and fixed fee; *cost-plus-incentive-fee:* target cost, target fee, maximum fee, minimum fee, and share ratio; *fixed-price-incentive:* target cost, target profit, ceiling price, and share ratio; and *firm-fixed-price:* price (cost and profit).

The sharing line is limited by the "range of incentive effectiveness," or the range of cost sharing from the most pessimistic to the most optimistic cost point and from the amount of profit assigned to the cost incentive (fee pool). There are no hard and fast rules that require a 70/30 or a 75/25 share line. In addition to the mechanical control of the range of incentive effectiveness and the fee pool on the share ratio, the share line should reflect a profit incentive arrangement that will motivate cost control. In cost-only incentive contracts, it may be enough to say that the steepness of the share line is a crucial point for negotiation. The share line should be consistent with the degree of technical and cost uncertainties inherent in the work to be done.

The contract negotiator should be concerned with the contract under consideration, not with overall average profits or with incentive profit ranges on past contracts. Further, the negotiator should not use inappropriately or unreasonably wide ranges of incentive effectiveness or unrealistic minimum/maximum fee positions. A clear and detailed definition of the technical objectives and a method for measuring the achievement of these objectives are almost always more important than the "precise" target cost and target profit.

Relationships of Incentive Contracting and Pricing Policies

Pricing principles are not abandoned when an incentive contract has been selected. Cost uncertainties, whether or not due to technical unknowns, are considered when the type of incentive contract and the variety of pricing arrangements are determined.

There are uncertainties in the pricing of any contract. As these uncertainties increase, contract selection moves farther away from the firm-fixed-price position, because both cost and performance uncertainties are usually eliminated. However, even if the confidence level in cost is not high and the uncertainties are known and recognized, the risk can still be made more acceptable, and a contract can be negotiated that imposes a significant cost responsibility. The probabilities that the uncertainties will occur are not the only concerns: one benefit of incentive contracting for both public sector organizations and contractors is the discipline that requires better contract and program definition. Better definition begets better pricing.

The Armed Services Procurement Manual No. 1 for Contract Pricing points out that one cannot expect the actual cost of performance to be exactly as predicted. The incentive contract deals with the variations from predicted costs, and the infinite variety of available incentive structures may be used to motivate performance to result in what the cost "should be."

The (estimated) cost in an incentive contract is established because of several variable factors, including (1) the public sector organization's price objective; (2) the contractor's price objective;

and (3) the negotiation as a tool of contract pricing. Bargaining between the buyer and seller involves many factors other than cost and profit, and it should also involve certain extracontractual factors, although target cost should represent that point in the range of possible costs that the parties to the contract agree is the "most probable."

The target cost objective includes the same mutually determined estimate of costs for a level of effort that would have been determined for any type of contract. However, in an incentive contract, the target cost is only a point in a range of possible costs, which, from the most optimistic to the most pessimistic, is determined before the target cost objective is established. During contract negotiations, the target point may change as facts are revealed, and the variation between the target and the projected cost points may change during the life of the contract. Variances in final realized cost are included in the very concept of incentive contracts. Moreover, the negotiated target cost and the actual cost are not directly comparable between individual contracts, although the validity of the target cost may be assessed by examining the causes of deviation.

Any attempt to correlate target cost and actual cost must be done in light of what the realized prices might have been.

The confidence in the target cost position (variation from target cost) is not the sole or even the primary criterion for determining the selection of either a cost-plus-incentive-fee or a fixed-price-incentive contract. Many more important factors, such as technical uncertainty, come into play. Obviously, when there is great technical uncertainty, cost uncertainty will result, which combines to dictate the selection of a cost-reimbursement type of contract.

Confidence in predicted cost is evaluated in terms of the risk of various situations within the range of incentive effectiveness or the range of probable cost and performance outcomes. For example, situations may arise where there is a high probability of a minor cost underrun, a low probability of an extensive cost overrun, or a high probability of a large overrun. These differences should be reflected in the range of incentive effectiveness and in the sharing ratio.

As stated previously, the mutually determined point that represents target cost presents an equal probability of cost over or under target; however, this did not refer to equal magnitude of the variance from target. It would be wrong to assume that there would be equal probabilities of variance from target and of various cost positions between minimum and maximum costs. This is demonstrated by the fact that too often every factor is equal or balanced (for example, cost range ±25 percent; cost fee ±4 percent; performance fee ±2 percent; schedule fee ±1 percent.) This equal balancing normally reflects a failure to evaluate the probable outcomes.

The incentive-sharing arrangement, which is the slope of the share line, should be negotiated on the basis of the target cost and the probability of various cost outcomes. When the probability for technical achievement is high, the fact that there is a high probability for a large cost variance does not dictate the use of a cost-plus-incentive-fee contract. The probability of a large variance only affects the range of cost incentive effectiveness. Thus, there may be a possibility of a +25 to +30 percent or a −10 to −15 percent variance from target cost in either a cost-plus-incentive-fee or a fixed-price-incentive contract; at the other extreme, there may be a high probability of only a +15 percent or a −10 percent variance from target cost in either type of incentive contract.

In selecting contract type, technical uncertainties are far more significant than cost uncertainties. Where there is a high probability of technical failure (and therefore cost uncertainty), any fixed-price type contract, other than a level-of-effort type, should be avoided. However, this is an infrequent occurrence in most nonfederal public sector organizations that let contracts.

While it is true that the confidence in both technical and cost outcomes should be very high in firm-fixed-price contracts, generally, technical uncertainties should influence the choice between fixed-price-incentive and cost-plus-incentive-fee contracts. A fixed-price-incentive contract should be used only when there is a reasonably high expectation of technical success.

Because probability is not constant during the life of a project, it is very important in pricing to consider the probability of the occurrence of a technical change within the cost range. The identification of cost-based probability distributions can be a very complex process involving technical capabilities that are not generally found in contracting offices and project organizations.

The pricing arrangement should never have an adverse impact on technical performance under any type of contract. When pricing and negotiating are based on accepted procedures for estimating and pricing, a realistic target cost results, which supports technical performance. In a very practical sense, the incentive contract bridges the gap in appropriate contractual structure after research through systems development. The negotiation and establishment of pricing ranges and equitable sharing rates should not have a negative impact on technical performance. Inappropriate narrative "restraints," such as technical contractual language instead of clearly defined technical objectives, change the pricing structure and can adversely affect performance in unforeseen situations. The possibilities for this undesirable overemphasis will generally increase where there has not been a free and open exchange between the technical and procurement personnel—either in the public sector organization or by the contractor.

The preceding discussion on incentive contracting has presented the basic methods that are employed by the Department of Defense and by the National Aeronautics and Space Administration. Sophisticated incentive contracting is not widely used in nonfederal public sector organizations. However, two rather elementary types of incentive contracts have been successfully utilized by the cities of Philadelphia, Pennsylvania, and Raleigh, North Carolina. The remainder of this chapter will be devoted to a discussion of the practices that they developed.

Philadelphia, Pennsylvania*

The city of Philadelphia wanted new vandal-resistant parking meters, which were very important to the city's revenue base, to be delivered quickly. The city incorporated both reward/penalty incentives into the city's experimental contract, which required the city to pay the contractor a set or fixed premium for early completion of work.

Following a city council decision to raise parking rates from five to ten cents per hour, the city elected to replace 13,000 existing parking meters with new vandal-resistant units. Because it was obvious that the earlier the new meters could be installed the more revenue the city would receive, the city's managing director appointed a top-level committee to control and expedite the project. This committee was composed of representatives from the managing director's office and from the purchasing, collections, streets, and police departments. The coordinating committee was chaired by the deputy procurement commissioner of the city.

The committee had three major parking meter manufacturers present their products and preliminary proposals, each of which

*This section was developed from "Using Incentives in Purchasing," by Thomas A. Miller and Edward P. Flood, originally printed in *Nations Cities,* June 1971.

left two of his company's meters for the city to examine and test.

In accordance with normal purchasing procedures, the committee developed preliminary specifications to meet its needs. These specifications incorporated the most desirable features of each manufacturer's sample meter.

At the earlier committee presentations, only one manufacturer had stated that he could deliver and install the required 13,000 meters within approximately five months from the awarding of the contract. The others had estimated that it would take nine and twelve months, respectively.

The committee decided that a six-month period would optimize competition among suppliers, installation of the meters, and financial benefits to the city.

In order to avoid financial loss from uneven or delayed installation, the committee decided to put a reward/penalty incentive clause in the contract. A premium payment was to be made for early completion, and a penalty of $1/meter/day was to be assessed for each meter installed six months after the day the contract was executed. The premium was based on the city's calculations of the probable premium paid for early completion and the increased revenue derived from these new meters.

On the basis of the data collected and analyzed, bids were solicited, with the following premium clause written into the solicitation.*

In order that the benefit of the new parking rates be promptly realized, it is the intent of the city that the new meters be installed and operating at the earliest possible date. To that end, the contractor may earn a premium for expeditious delivery and installation. The basis for the premium shall be as follows:

a. The contractor will be required to begin installing the new meters purchased under this contract within 75 days of the date of the purchase order.

b. The contractor will be expected to maintain a reasonably uniform rate of meter installation.

c. Upon completion of the installation, and provided the balance of the meters not requiring installation are delivered before the end of the six months, the contractor shall be paid a premium of 5¢ per meter for each operating day (excludes Sundays) on which the entire meter installation is in service and operating

*Most municipal attorneys believe that a reward/penalty clause for an incentive-type contract must be written into the bid solicitations so that all prospective bidders are aware of its existence. In the opinion of the authors, it is illegal to put an incentive into the contract without it having first been in the bid solicitation.

prior to the contract completion date. This premium shall be paid upon the total number of meters installed and shall be computed as follows:

Contract completion date − actual completion date = total days.
Total days − Sundays = net premium days.
Net premium days × number installed (approx. 13,000) × 5¢ = premium.

   d. No allowance will be given for delays due to strikes, weather, or other causes referred to as "Acts of God" with reference to application of the premium clause.

The three meter manufacturers who had appeared before the committee submitted similar bids, price-wise, in response to the solicitation.

The contract was let to the low bidder at a contract price of approximately $650,000. The contract was to be completed within six months from date of letting, although installation work began in about 30 days and was completed eight weeks before the end of the contract period. Because the contractor "beat" the completion date, he earned a premium of about $25,000.

However, additional revenue of approximately $250,000 was produced for the city.

In many ways, the incentive clause in Philadelphia's parking meter contract was unique. Frequently, purchases or construction contracts cannot be directly related to additional revenue produced through early completion of a project. However, if money can be saved, costs avoided, or productivity increases quantified, a reward/penalty incentive contract can offer real benefits to a public organization.

However, if no clear financial savings are discernible, there could be disadvantages. Placing unnecessary emphasis on delivery or early completion might so restrict competition in bidding that the public sector organization might actually suffer, according to the Miller–Flood report.

Raleigh, North Carolina

The City of Raleigh, N.C., developed a fixed-fee-plus-incentive contract* for some of its urgent capital improvements projects.

*James L. Mercer, "Try Incentive Contracting," *American City* [*and County*], November 1972, p. 83.

This type of contract draws on contracting criteria established by the National Aeronautics and Space Administration and by the Department of Defense.

The city first used the incentive clause in a street improvement contract. A school needed the street on a specific date. By working day and night, the street contractor "beat" the city's estimated tight completion schedule by three days and won a $300 incentive award. A maximum award of $1,000 would have been possible had the project been completed ten days ahead of schedule.

Penalty vs. Reward

As with most government contracts, the city had used penalty clauses for *not* meeting completion dates. In the special provisions section of a typical capital improvements contract, the city historically included the following two penalty paragraphs:

> *Completion date:* That portion of the work included in this contract involving the construction of (project) between (location a) and (location b) is to be completed by (date), ready for use.

> *Liquidated damages:* Liquidated damages for failure to complete that portion of (project) as specified in paragraph 1 above will be ($ penalty) per calendar day after (project completion date).

However, the city now frequently includes a reward clause for completion ahead of schedule. The following paragraph appears in some of its more critical capital improvements contracts:

> *Early completion incentive:* For each calendar day that the above specified project is completed prior to (project completion date), the contractor will be paid $100 as an incentive to complete (project). This incentive payment will be limited, however, to ten calendar days.

In some instances, the paragraph also lists the reason for providing the incentive. For example, "This is a street project needed to serve a school prior to school opening on (date)."

Incentive contracting on selected projects has proved both beneficial and cost-effective. Basically, the city uses the early-completion incentive clause only on critical capital projects, but the practice has yielded excellent results.

Problems of Penalty-Only

The Department of Defense and the National Aeronautics and Space Administration's Incentive Contracting Guide* describes the penalty incentive as simply the opposite of the reward incentive. The guide warns, however, that there are numerous instances where penalties arouse emotions or attitudes that make a contractor reluctant to accept the agreement. The most widely applied incentive contract has the traditional method of utilizing reward incentives for cost results under target and penalty incentives for cost results over target in a cost-incentive-only contract.

Incentive contracting, even on a limited and simplified scale, can also benefit local governments. The City of Raleigh has proved to itself that this is an acceptable and viable tool for municipal contracting, one that is readily accepted by the city council, the citizens, and the contractors.

Among the important advantages that incentive contracts provide are:

> Incentives provide a planning discipline for the buyer's employees. When an incentive contract is to be negotiated, the analysis of requirements is more thorough and the work statement is more precise. Thus, incentive contracts provide the buyer with better program cost information than do cost reimburseable contracts. Because target costs are more realistic, they permit better financial planning and budgetary control, and reduce the likelihood of large cost overruns.

> Incentive contracts tend to make both the buyer and the contractor more cost-conscious, which probably results in indirect cost savings.

> Incentive contracts clearly communicate the buyer's objective to the contractor. They attract special management attention to the objectives (of the contract) and explicitly show their relative importance. . . .

> When it is possible to associate activities of individuals with specific contracts, incentives (regardless of their amount) provide a useful tool for motivating contractor employees†

---

*"Incentive Contracting Guide," DOD/NASA, 1969.

†Gordon Milliken and Edward J. Morrison, "Aerospace Management Techniques: Commercial and Governmental Applications," A Report prepared for the National Aeronautics and Space Administration by Denver Research Institute, November 1971.

Selected Sources of Further Information on Construction Management*

American Consulting Engineers Council. "Something Better than Turnkey," Seminar Proceedings, March 7, 1974. 1165 15th Street, N.W., Washington, D.C. 20005.

American Institute of Architects. *Construction Management* (8213) (Tape Cassette). Publication Sales Department, 1735 New York Avenue, N.W., Washington, D.C. 20006. $12.50.

Associated General Contractors of America. "Owners Guide: Building Construction Contracting Methods" (11 pages). 1957 E Street, N.W., Washington, D.C. 20005. 25¢.

Associated General Contractors of America. *CM for the General Contractor: A Guide Manual for Construction Management.* 1957 E Street, N.W., Washington, D.C. 20006. $19.95.

Associated General Contractors of America. "Construction Management Guidelines" (10 pages). 1957 E Street, N.W., Washington, D.C. 20006.   25¢.

Atkinson, Ian Edward. *Construction Management* (New York: American Elsevier, 1971).

Begley, Francis D. *Project Management for Construction Superintendents* (Toronto: Saunders of Toronto, Ltd., 1970).

Bonny, John Bruce, and Frein, Joseph. *Handbook of Construction Management and Organization* (New York: Van Nostrand–Reinhold, 1973).

Clough, Richard Hudson. *Construction Contracting,* 3rd ed. (New York: John Wiley and Sons, 1975).

Cleland, D. L., and King, W. R. *Systems Analysis and Project Management* (New York: McGraw-Hill Book Co., 1968).

Deatherage, George E. *Construction Scheduling and Control* (New York: McGraw-Hill Book Co., 1965).

Douglas, Clarence J., and Elmer, J. Munger. *Construction Management* (Englewood Cliffs, N.J.: Prentice-Hall, Inc., 1970).

Foxhall, William B. *Professional Construction Management and Project Administration* (New York: Architectural Record and the American Institute of Architects, 1972). $12.50.

The GSA System for Construction Management. U.S. General Services Administration, Public Buildings Service.

Guide for Project Applicants: Construction Management Services, Technical Handbook for Facilities Engineering and Construction Manual—2.4. June 1975. Available without charge from HEW regional offices or: Director, Office of Federally Assisted Construction, OFEPM, Department of Health, Education and Welfare, 330 Independence Avenue, S.W., Washington, D.C. 20201.

Hackney, John W. *Control and Management of Capital Projects* (New York: John Wiley and Sons, 1965).

Heery, George T. *Time, Cost and Architecure* (New York: McGraw-Hill Book Co., 1975).

O'Brien, J. J. *CPM in Construction Management* (New York: McGraw-Hill Book Co., 1971).

Pilcher, Roy. *Principles of Construction Management for Engineers and Managers* (New York: McGraw-Hill Book Co., 1966).

Royer, Kine. *The Construction Manager* (Englewood Cliffs, N.J.: Prentice-Hall, Inc., 1974).

Volpe, Sonnino Peter. *Construction Management Practice* (New York: Wiley–Interscience, 1972).

*Suggested readings from "Using Construction Management for Public and Institutional Facilities, Public Technology, Inc., Washington, D.C., 1976.

12

Word Processing Systems

AS governments provide services that have increased in volume and complexity over the years, paperwork has expanded concomitantly. In order to handle this paperwork efficiently, many governments have conducted studies on how to improve the productivity of secretarial staffs. And a technique known as "word processing" has evolved.

"Word processing" designates a sophisticated, automated typing and stenographic center. Basically, most word processing systems work like this:

In order to dictate a letter, an administrator picks up his regular telephone, dials a predesignated number, and dictates his letter. The letter is recorded on a magnetic belt on a PBX Recorder located in the word processing center, which is special room. A word processing secretary removes the magnetic belt from the PBX Recorder, places it on a transcriber, and types the letter in draft form. As the letter is being typed, it is recorded on a magnetic tape or card.

After a draft of the letter is typed and the corrections are made, the proper stationery is entered to produce the required number of copies of the final letter. The paper is properly positioned by the secretary, and the letter is "played out" on the automatic typewriter at a rate of more than 150 words per minute.

The letter is then hand-delivered to the administrator, who either signs it or makes changes. If changes are made, only the changes are retyped, because the original letter is still recorded on the magnetic tape or card.

A word processing system improves quality, centralizes typing, increases the speed and the quality in producing bulk mailing, and improves overall organizational efficiency. Typewritten documents are produced three to five times faster than by conventional methods.

The secretaries who remain are able to devote more time to administrative support, because their typing workload has been significantly diminished, if not completly removed. These administrative support secretaries can also dictate into the center, thereby relieving their supervisors of much routine work.

The objective of word processing is to place the pressure of processing administrative paperwork on the system, not on the secretarial personnel.

Word processing systems necessitate major changes in personnel assignments and office procedures. Although such systems are not without start-up and morale problems, the benefits that have accrued to the seven cities and two counties described in this chapter suggest that government officials would do well to consider such a system.

As citizens demand more services and as revenues become more scarce, governments must find more efficient and effective delivery systems. This chapter describes an innovative approach to handling one facet of government: administrative paperwork.

A new approach to processing the vast amounts of administrative paperwork has been developed in recent years. This new innovation, called a "word processing system" has revolutionized the standard method of having a secretary in each office. This system has been extensively implemented in the private sector and is becoming increasingly popular in various governmental organizations.*

This chapter surveys the word processing systems and their

---

* J. L. Mercer, "Word Processing in Local Government," Management Information Service Report, Vol. 5, No. 3 (Washington, D.C.: International City Management Association, March 1973).

results in seven cities and two counties geographically dispersed throughout the country: Fort Lauderdale, FL; Sioux City, IA: Omaha, NB; Raleigh, NC; Middletown, OH; Waco, TX*; Everett, WA†; Maricopa County, AZ‡; and Wake County, NC. In addition, several private sector installations also are reviewed.

NEED for a SYSTEMATIC APPROACH to PAPERWORK PROCESSING

In recent years, the United States, with all its technological advances, has experienced a veritable explosion of paperwork. At the present time, it is estimated that originators create over 1 million pieces of paper every minute—each of which also must be filed.

As governmental units have grown, secretaries and other clerical and administrative personnel have been added as needed. Although only one-third or one-half of a secretary was required, a full secretary had to be hired. In many instances, existing secretaries could have done the extra work, but because of logistics or built-in resistance by supervisors, it was impractical or impossible. These secretaries were not only assigned typing but also were expected to serve as receptionists, answer telephones, set up meetings, and perform other routine "Gal Friday" tasks.

In the average office, distribution of work was unequal, clerical staffing was uncontrolled, and much professional time was lost because of insufficient clerical support and reliance on costly and inefficient methods of input preparation. In addition, the working environment was usually uncontrolled, which led to underspecialization of clerical staff. This latter fact frequently contributed to work that was of poor quality. However, because of the status attached to having a personal secretary, attempts to change the system have met with strong resistance.

With revenue sources shrinking and demands for services increasing, many governments are faced with a very real challenge: "Find more efficient methods of handling office paperwork!" In

*M. M. Calvert, "Word Processing Frees Officers from Clerical Work, *Law and Order*, July 1971.

†Jack V. McKenzie, "Everett's Automated Typing Center Puts 25% More Police in the Field," *Western City*, July 1971, pp. 26–27.

‡"More Words and Less Girls for the County Attorney's Office," *The American County*, October 1971.

two of the cities surveyed here, Sioux City and Raleigh, city administrators were under edicts from their city councils to develop more efficient systems vis-à-vis the continual hiring of more clerical staff. In Raleigh, the city council froze the hiring of secretaries until a study of a more efficient system could be conducted. In several of the cities and counties surveyed, increased clerical personnel costs provided considerable impetus for changing to a more efficient processing system.

THE FEASIBILITY STUDY

If a government is interested in surveying its paperwork processing system in order to improve efficiency, how does it proceed? Who conducts feasibility studies? What do they cost? Questions such as these automatically occur to government officials as they examine their administrative paperwork operations.

Most of the cities and counties surveyed for this chapter considered several possible avenues for conducting their feasibility studies, including using internal staff, hiring independent outside consulting firms, or relying on various systems and equipment manufacturers.

In a majority of the local governments surveyed, equipment suppliers were selected to make the feasibility studies because they offered certain advantages. They would, for example, conduct the studies at no cost to the cities or counties; recommend systems that were more efficient and effective than existing ones; supply and install the systems; assist in the training of the supervisors, secretaries, and organizational principals; assist in writing operating procedures; and maintain and repair the systems after they were installed.

The major disadvantages concerned total objectivity and the amount of equipment *actually* required.

Before agreeing to conduct a study of an organization's administrative paperwork processes, most suppliers usually ask the organization to write a letter stating the objectives of the study and requesting that it be conducted at no cost to the organization. As an example, Raleigh's objective was to

> Provide improved economy or improved efficiency and effectiveness
> to the communication processes of the City of Raleigh Government
> at the earliest possible opportunity.

In addition to the above, a supplier usually makes some requests of the organization to be studied. Raleigh, for example, was asked that (1) top management be involved in the study and implementation phases of the possible center, and (2) the organization demonstrate a willingness to implement new systems and procedures, realizing that this might mean some significant changes in people, systems, and procedures.

Prior to conducting the study, the organization should inform its employees about the study, telling them why it is being conducted, that their jobs are not threatened (if, in fact, this is true), and that their full and complete cooperation should be provided.

In the mechanics of the study, several techniques are normally used, which include:

- Task lists prepared and written by the clerical personnel being surveyed.
- Interviews with department heads, supervisors, and clerical personnel.
- Observations by surveyors.
- Review of typing and paperwork applications.
- Review of organization and floor charts.
- Use of "action paper" (precarbonized paper used behind every item typed for a specified period of time, such as one week).
- Review of projected new employees.

Using the above techniques, the surveyors usually prepare a work distribution chart, which is effective for preparing a task summary of the amount of typing, shorthand, filing, copying, posting, telephone answering, and other secretarial tasks being performed by the clerical staff.

In Raleigh, for instance, the overall task summary showed that 37 percent of the average secretary's day was spent typing, 14 percent answering the telephone, 7 percent filing, 7 percent in research and analysis, 5 percent on shorthand, and so forth.

A work distribution chart can usually identify the limitations and weaknesses in the existing system. Such items as unequal work distribution, uncontrolled clerical staffing and working environments, and loss of professional time can be readily identified and often quantified. The amount of time spent on input, which consists of longhand, shorthand, or machine dictation, can also be determined. Table 12-1 shows the average time devoted to dictation and transcription.

In organizations that use a great deal of longhand, the input

Table 12-1. Average dictation and transcription time for various input methods.

Medium	Dictation (wpm)	Transcription (wpm)
Longhand	10	20
Shorthand	18	14
Machine dictation	22	18

SOURCE: Adapted from "Cost of a Business Letter at $4.47 for 1977." Copyright © 1977, the Dartnell Institute of Business Research, Chicago, Illinois.

preparation time consumes a large portion of any job. This is referred to as "make ready" time (see Figure 12-1, top). The objective is to reduce this "make ready" time by using more efficient input devices, such as dictating machines.

Figure 12-1 (bottom) depicts a situation in which the "make ready" and "put away" portions of a task have been reduced, and the "do" portion has been increased by using more efficient input and output devices. Too many different tasks for one person lead to increased "make ready" and "put away" times. A more controlled working environment with fewer tasks leads to greater "do" time.

After the results of the study have been categorized and analyzed, the surveyors try to answer several important questions:

Can we as the supplier meet the organization's stated objective?
What will be a feasible plan of action for the organization to follow?
Can the typing functions be affected?
Will word processing fit in the organization?
Are the anticipated results worth the expended efforts?

Figure 12-1. Two ways of performing tasks.

Too many different tasks:

Make ready	Do	Put away

A better controlled working environment:

Make ready	Do	Put away

If in fact the study provides affirmative answers to these questions, the supplier then makes a series of recommendations to the organization.

In a majority of organizations, and in the seven cities and two counties surveyed for this report, equipment suppliers recommended the installation of word processing systems to improve efficiency. The configuration of the recommended systems varied, of course, depending on the needs of the particular governmental unit. (See Figure 12-2 for a complete breakdown of the system configurations of the cities/counties surveyed here.)

RESULTS OBTAINED with WORD PROCESSING

What has been the result of implementing word processing systems in these seven cities and two counties? Although some start-up problems occurred, a certain amount of which are to be expected, the overall results have been favorable.

Here are brief comments relative to the actual (A) or expected (E) results in each of the nine cities/counties surveyed.

Fort Lauderdale, Florida (Responsible Officials: City Manager and Central Services Supervisor)

- Increased productivity of secretarial personnel (A).
- Will forestall hiring of additional clerical personnel (E).
- Future savings will accrue from lessened departmental typewriter and dictation equipment requirements (E).
- Every document free of typewriter errors (E).
- Typewritten documents produced three to five times faster than by conventional methods (E).
- Documents stored on magnetic tape for reference, revision, or later use (A).
- Improved quality through automation of present composer equipment, plus savings of 25 to 30 percent in paper and offset press time (E).

Sioux City, Iowa (Responsible Official: City Manager)

- Discontinuation of three secretarial positions through attrition (A).
- City manager's staff of scretaries reduced from three to one (A).
- Turnaround time for a normal letter is 60 to 90 minutes (A).

Figure 12-2. A survey of local government word processing installa-tions.

City/County Governmental Unit	1972 Population (Estimated)	Form of Government	WORD PROCESSING SYSTEM EQUIPMENT CONFIGURATION					Length of Time Center Operating as of 9/1/72	Center Serves Citywide	Center Serves One Department Only
			MTST*	MCST†	Leased or Purchased	Number of Operating Shifts	Number of Personnel in Center			
Fort Lauderdale, Fla.	139,590	C/M[a]	3		L	1	3	3 months		X[c]
Sioux City, Ia.	85,925	C/M[a]	3		L	1	3	21 months	X	
Omaha, Neb.	347,000	S/M[b]	11		L	1	12	8 months	X	
Raleigh, N.C.	130,000	C/M[a]		8	L	1	10	1 month	X	
Middletown, O.	48,767	C/M[a]		5	L	1	5	7 months	X	
Waco, Tex.	95,326	C/M[a]	3	3	L	3	9	25 months		X[d]
Everett, Wash.	53,622	S/M[b]	3		L	3	5	Prior to 7/1/71	X	
Maricopa County, Ariz.	967,522	County Manager	7		L	1	7	Prior to 10/1/71		X[e]
Wake County, N.C.	229,006	County Manager		7	L	1	8	12/1/72		X[f]

[a]C/M — council/manager form of government.
[b]S/M — strong mayor/council form of government.
[c]Serves six departments, excluding police. Other departments are being phased in.
[d]Serves police department only.
[e]Serves county attorney's office only.
[f]Serves department of social services only.
*Magnetic tape selectric typewriter.
†Magnetic card selectric typewriter.

- Generally, department heads have accepted system but would prefer own individual secretaries (A).
- City did not accept full recommendations of equipment supplier initially but plans to add extra equipment (A).
- Took nine months to one year to get center into operation from date of original commitment (A).
- City manager highly recommends system and is very satisfied with it (A).

Omaha, Nebraska (Responsible Official: City Clerk)

- Took about one year to get center into operation from date of original commitment (A).
- Reduced secretarial staff in middle management ranks by ten employees, who were put on availability list to be transferred to other departments as needed (A).
- Of eleven typists originally placed in center, three had to be changed due to lack of mechanical ability (A).
- Had greater success by converting one department at a time to new system rather than by doing it all at once (A).

Raleigh, North Carolina (Responsible Officials: Assistant City Manager for Programming and Budgeting and Word Processing Supervisor)

- Took about ten months to get into operation from date of original commitment (A).
- Nine secretaries were promoted into the center from existing staff (given 5 percent pay increases after a three-month training period). Supervisory position was newly created and filled from within (A).
- Three department heads vigorously resisted giving up secretaries to the center but finally agreed reluctantly (A).
- Net estimated deferred savings over old system will be $52,241 per year (E).
- Supervisor attended one-week word processing manager training session prior to center start-up (A).
- Considerable supervisory time is needed (four to six months) prior to center opening for training of personnel, writing of procedures, schooling of dictators, and so forth (A).
- Telephone company was not able to provide all requested telephone linkages when needed (A).
- Center serves 18 departments and does most of the typing formerly assigned to 61 clerical people (A).

- Monthly rental cost of system is about $2,000 (A).
- Prior to word processing, 50 percent of input preparation had been in longhand, 30 percent in shorthand, and only 20 percent via machine dictation (A).

Middletown, Ohio (Responsible Official: Administrative Assistant)

- Took more than five months to get center into operation from date of commitment (A).
- City is extremely pleased with results and plans to expand center's coverage (A).
- All personnel were assigned from existing city staff (A).
- Word processing supervisor doubled as payroll clerk in the beginning stages but became full-time supervisor when this was found inefficient (A).
- Word processing supervisor had to spend 40 hours per week for five months before the center opened to interview dictators and to prepare procedure manuals (A).
- Close coordination with the telephone company was required to get necessary linkage equipment installed. This equipment required considerable lead time (A).
- PBX system required testing for at least one week before actual start of dictation to get bugs out of telephone company equipment (A).
- About 100 dictators were trained and it was then found that they did not know how to use the system even with detailed instruction and procedure manuals. For example, some dictated report columns vertically rather than horizontally (A).
- Some people would not use the system, preferring the old way. City manager's office informed the employees that the office would no longer accept reports, letters, or requests not typed by the word processing center (A).
- Typewriters will be removed from various departments shortly after center becomes operational (E).
- Attrition is to take care of excess secretarial staff (E).
- Each department had to adopt a standard format for all correspondence (A).
- Center strives for 100 percent accuracy, a three-hour turnaround time, zero complaints, and conformance with established procedures (E).
- Center supervisor attended one-week word processing manager training session (A).

- Supervisor will be tactful with dictators but must make them conform with the procedures (E).
- Start-up costs totaled $9,468, of which $5,191 was direct cash outlay (A).
- Monthly cost of operation is about $5,000 to $6,000 (A).
- Savings during first year were the result of attrition rather than layoff (E).
- Intangible savings in dictator's time and increased secretarial time to perform administrative functions has resulted (A).
- Original letters that get reader's attention can now be sent (A).

Waco, Texas (Responsible Official: Chief of Police)

- Police reports can be filed via public telephone without the patrolman leaving his beat. If necessary, the report can be ready in just minutes after dictation (A).
- Employees can work without interruptions (A).
- Police department is turning out 1,200 to 1,500 reports each week without accumulating any backlogs (A).
- Documents are flawless, and uniform formatting and quality have been achieved (A).
- Every report generated by the police department, except motor vehicle accidents, is dictated for processing through the center (A).
- Priorities can now be assigned to any report, and the finished document can be available within minutes after dictation (A).
- Turnaround time for routine reports has been substantially reduced from two or three days to a few hours (A).
- Juvenile officers' and other detectives' man-hours spent on paperwork have been reduced by 20 percent (A).
- Through report automation, up to 20 percent more time in the field is being realized (A).
- Word processing has contributed to an overall increase in the efficiency of the police department (A).

Everett, Washington (Responsible Official: Finance and Budget Director)

- Patrolmen now dictate via the nearest pay telephone reports that they once had to write in longhand at the station (A).
- Detectives and watch sergeants dictate into portable units, often at the scene of an investigation, the reports they formerly returned to the police department to type (A).

- Police "office time" has been cut, and availability of police manpower on the street has been increased more than 25 percent (A).
- With its staff of five, the word processing center meets the city's overall typing needs, for which twelve typists had originally been requested on a decentralized basis (A).
- Before word processing, department heads had been handwriting memos or doing their own typing. Also, policemen were spending up to 50 percent of their time producing reports, and a backlog of typing existed in other departments (A).
- A conservative first-year savings of $5,500 was realized through the implementation of word processing (A).
- The center operates from six A.M. until midnight using three staggered shifts seven days a week (A).
- Early implementation problems included changeover, redirecting workflows, and form revision. Closer monitoring of incoming work and the processes through which it passed was required to correct these. In addition, it was discovered that the center required its people to plan ahead more regarding deadlines and work schedules (A).
- Work currently being processed in the center includes police reports, letters, memos, tabular reports, council minutes, annual reports and budgets, street construction specifications, purchase orders, inventories, and correspondence with citizens (A).

Maricopa County, Arizona (Responsible Officials: Administrative Assistant to County Attorney and Communications Center Supervisor)

- County attorney's office had formerly used 32 secretaries to produce typed work for 42 attorneys (A).
- With word processing, over 80 percent of all typing is now accomplished in the communications center, with seven typists and seven magnetic tape typewriters. The remaining 25 secretaries do nominal amounts of typing as well as all the administrative tasks for the attorneys (A).
- The county attorney's office is handling a greater load of civil and criminal cases and is saving money at the same time (A).
- With the installation of a new communications center, it is now possible to stay ahead of the paperwork generated by increased county case loads (A).

- With the previous system in effect for 50 years, there existed a high imbalance of work between secretaries, duplication of typing documents, excessive proofreading by both attorneys and secretaries, excessive clerical interruptions, and an office space problem (A).

Wake County, North Carolina (Responsible Officials: County Manager and Word Processing Supervisor)

- Center went into operation on December 1, 1972 (A).
- Center serves county social services department only. Eighty case workers and ten administrative personnel dictate into the center (A).
- Center supervisor attended one-week word processing manager training session (A).
- No results available (A).

WORD PROCESSING OFFICE LAYOUTS

Because of the heat and noise factors associated with having a number of pieces of automatic equipment in one room and because of the potential psychological effects of doing repetitive typing day after day, as well as other human and physical considerations, the office layout for word processing is very important.

One equipment supplier believes that the physical layout of the word processing center is so important to the overall success of the system that a customer packet entitled *Planning the Office for Word Processing** has recently been prepared. This packet includes a magnetic board and characters for planning an office layout, a flow charting and a layout template, a tape to be used for defining the work flow, graph paper, and a booklet giving suggestions on physical layouts that reflect the experience that the company has gained from installing numerous word processing centers.

The office-planning manual discusses several areas that need attention and specifies minimum requirements for properly implementing a word processing center. These areas and requirements are:

---

* "Planning the Office for Word Processing," IBM Corp., Office Products Division, Franklin Lakes, N.J., 1972.

1. *Minimum Space Requirements*
   Magnetic tape, card, or composer typewriters require 64 sq ft per unit, including operator and aisle.
2. *Office Layout*
   Office plan selected should:
   a. Provide smooth flow of paperwork.
   b. Minimize operator distractions.
   c. Ensure that center personnel can see other employees to avoid a sense of isolation.
   d. Provide adequate electrical outlets to allow flexibility in arranging equipment and furnishings.
3. *Center Electrical and Safety Requirements*
4. *Temperature, Humidity, and Ventilation Requirements*
5. *Center Lighting and Acoustical Requirements*

Nonstatic carpet is almost always recommended for a word processing center, as is some type of accoustical wall treatment to absorb some of the sound being generated by the equipment. Some centers in the private sector have even used carpet effectively on wall surfaces.

If many windows are present in the center, brapes are usually recommended to absorb sound and reduce glare.

In some of the local governmental units surveyed, centers have been placed in existing facilities with few renovations. In others, an office has been specifically designed.

Fort Lauderdale started out on one floor and then moved to another to obtain additional work space. Middletown's processing operation is decentralized, with two small centers in two separate buildings. Middletown is considering a third decentralized center in the near future to serve the police department exclusively.

In Raleigh, a room 32 ft by 52 ft has been renovated specifically for word processing. A carpet and drapes have been installed, and bright contemporary office furniture and equipment have been placed in an "open landscape" type of environment. One wall is decorated with a modern mural, and a large supply cabinet that blends with the decor has been specially constructed.

Local budgetary considerations, office space availability, time, and needs have usually had a great bearing on center layout. Some centers, particularly in the private sector, have placed modular units around each secretary. Others have stayed with an "open landscape" layout.

PERSONNEL CONSIDERATIONS

Proper selection and placement of personnel in the center are probably the most important considerations in implementing a word processing system. This fact was confirmed by virtually every local goverment surveyed.

When the City of Raleigh was considering a decision regarding the implementation of word processing, the personnel office surveyed several organizations to determine the relationship of the positions assigned to the word processing center to other clerical positions within city government.

Raleigh contacted the following organizations to determine the prevailing practice:

> Sioux City, Iowa (municipal government)
> Omaha, Nebraska (municipal government)
> State of North Carolina
>> State Personnel Office
>> Attorney General's Office
>> Memorial Hospital
>> Department of Motor Vehicles
> Cameron-Brown Company, Raleigh, North Carolina

From this survey, the following conclusions were reached:

1. Employees working in word processing must be highly trained and should have experience with transcribing equipment.

2. Salaries of equipment operators in the word processing centers were the same as or many times higher than clerk-stenographer salaries. For instance, the State of North Carolina places the Clerk-Typist III at one 5 percent increment higher than the Clerk-Stenographer II level.

3. The supervisor of the center must be unusually competent. In all the centers contacted, the supervisor is the key to the system's success.

4. Persons going into the program are usually promoted into the word processing center; in nearly all the organizations contacted, experienced transcribers or stenographers moved into higher classifications. In the state offices, inexperienced operators started at a trainee level and after training and a short adaptation period moved to the higher classification. Not only is this a morale booster and an incentive to become a part of the word processing center,

but the end result places the highly trained operators into this very important job.

5. The supervisory position is usually higher than the highest-level secretary, because the position is a management-type position and requires supervisory and technical skills.

On the basis of this survey, the following recommendations were approved and adopted by the Raleigh city council:

1. The word processing center secretaries should be classified as Clerk-Typist III, provided that inexperienced clerk-stenographers and clerk-typists are placed in a trainee step for a period of time to become more experienced with the equipment. Clerk-Typist IIIs would be allocated to Paygrade 22, with an annual starting salary of $5,160 per year (1972 rate).

2. The supervisor should be placed in Paygrade 27, which has a starting salary of $6,600 per year (1972 rate).

3. First and serious consideration should be given to present city employees for positions in the word processing center. However, it is recommended that all positions be advertised in local newspapers to ensure that the best-qualified persons are selected for the positions.

In Middletown, Ohio, salaries of center personnel were as follows:

Center Supervisor $6,798–$8,554 (1972 rate)
Center Secretary II   6,493– 8,170 (1972 rate)
Center Secretary I   5,924– 7,452 (1972 rate)

By comparison, a patrolman in Middletown earns between $8,968 and $10,655 a year (1972 rate).

The consensus seems to be that the secretaries in the center should be given the feeling that they are being treated in a "special" way. Such things as attractive work surroundings, extra pay incentives, and so forth, help to overcome the monotony of a routine typing job and the stigma attached by some secretaries to a "steno pool."

IMPLEMENTATION HINTS

What suggestions can be offered to public or private sector organizations considering word processing centers.

Richard A. Clark, administrative assistant, Middletown, Ohio, offers a very succinct and thought-provoking comment:

To any city which is planning on implementing Word Processing, we would give the following two pieces of advice: First, do not try to do it yourself. Some equipment manufacturers supply good equipment, but they do not set up the system for you. We found that Word Processing is not just typewriters and dictating machines, but is a concept which changes established ways of doing things, and requires procedures, training, controls, reporting, and evaluation.

. . . Second, we would not recommend that a city try to implement the concept, without the total commitment of the top management. Word Processing will destroy the social office concept. Department heads will be told they will no longer have private secretaries, and they will be forced to become members of a team with efficiency as a goal, and they will resist it.*

Jack V. McKenzie, finance and budget director, Everett, Washington, writes:

Essentially, we have adopted the 'gradualist' approach, permitting all who are interested to see the efficiency and convenience of the new system, but forcing no one to adopt it. We recognize that a transition of this type is traumatic because we are asking users to go from the auto age to the jet age in one leap. As a result, we still haven't gotten all the typewriters off the desks to the degree we should. But the city's total secretarial staff has stabilized and the Word Processing Center is one of the major factors.†

Some organizations, primarily in the private sector, have found that word processing has caused some problems of new-task orientation for the secretaries left behind in the offices.

In its corporate headquarters in Franklin Lakes, New Jersey, the IBM Corporation has established an organizational concept whereby word processing secretaries report to word processing supervisors and administrative secretaries are grouped in unenclosed centers next to the departments to which they report. This gives the administrative and word processing secretaries new career paths in that they can advance to jobs in both first- and second-line management. In addition, the administrative secretaries are avail-

*Richard A. Clark, letter to author, 1972. Cited in "Word Processing in Local Government," op. cit.
†Jack V. McKenzie, "Everett's Automated Typing Center Puts 25% More Police in the Field," *Western City,* July 1971, op. cit.

able to handle work for other departments when they are needed. IBM now has 140 secretaries doing the work of 172 secretaries.*

The City of Raleigh has found that taking the time and effort to plan and prepare both the employees and the center has increased the morale of the employees and the effectiveness of the center. In fact, the center has been so successful that additional personnel and equipment have been added, and a second shift is currently being planned to add new police applications.

Several local user organizations have been formed around the country to disseminate information on word processing. One such organization, the International Word Processing Association, with headquarters in Willow Grove, Pennsylvania, serves the needs of word processing users and potential users through seminars and literature distributed to its members.

Below is a checklist of items to be considered when implementing a word processing system:

1. Survey the present paperwork processing system, paying particular attention to its efficiency. All employees involved in the survey should be informed in advance of the purpose of the study.

2. Examine whether word processing can increase paperwork efficiency. An equipment supplier will probably be required to make this evaluation and to recommend the required equipment configuration.

3. If, from an equipment standpoint, a word processing system seems appropriate, carefully consider the personnel changes and start-up dimensions. Present secretarial personnel will need training, and managers will have to adapt to new ways of working.

4. Give attention to the office layout for word processing. With several pieces of automatic equipment in one room and the psychological effects of several secretaries grouped together, office layout is very important.

5. Select and place the required personnel for the word processing center. Attention must be given to the relationship of the positions assigned to the center and other clerical positions.

6. Implementation may well occur gradually, permitting top management to see the benefits of the system within a department or two before establishing it organizationwide.

7. Don't forget to go back and address the reorganization of

* John J. McGlynn, "IBM's Conversion to Word Processing," *Professional Management Bulletin*, October 1971.

the administrative secretaries that have been left behind. They still have very key functions to perform and must also have career paths to follow.

QUESTIONS and ANSWERS about WORD PROCESSING

Below are several questions that have been raised by potential users of word processing systems. Every attempt has been made to answer each question as objectively and straightforwardly as possible:

Q: What are the psychological effects of the new system?

A: As we mentioned earlier, many department heads and administrative personnel will resist the system. Many of them seem to feel that they are being personally affronted, because they may be losing a secretary. Also, many feel that they are being forced to use a new system that they do not want. Some fight this system as much as they do any progress toward more control or efficiency. They rationalize this by saying, "The system will never work!" or "I'll sabotage the new system by deluging it with busywork!" Many never do this consciously, but the resistance is still there. To combat this, the groundwork for the system must be carefully laid, and management must support the system from the outset. The reason for improving the decor and working environment in the center itself is to help overcome the psychological effects on the center secretaries.

Because secretaries are doing repetitive typing day after day, boredom could result. Attractive layouts using carpets, modern furniture, and so forth, can help alleviate or forestall this problem. Also, allowing secretaries to deliver finished work to originators gives them a break from the center routine and allows them to talk with other people.

Q: Do the word processing secretaries have enough work to do?

A: In almost every organization surveyed, they had more than enough work. There was usually some backlog for each worker. One of the ways to ensure that there is enough work is to remove existing typewriters from the offices. This forces all typing into the center. However, this must be done gradually, so as not to swamp the center. In many of the organizations surveyed, the demand for the center's services was more than it could handle except by a gradual phase-in of work. Dictators frequently find that it is easier and more convenient to pick up the telephone and dictate a memo or letter than to wait for a secretary. This increases utilization of the center.

Q: How do word processing secretaries get along with the supervisor of the center?

A: Basically, a supervisor–subordinate relationship exists in the center. Some supervisors have personnel problems, other do not. If good management practices are utilized, all should go rather smoothly. Some adjustment problems occur when a secretary is forced to transfer from an individual office to the center. She may have been the only secretary in her previous position. Now she is merely one of many, which can cause problems and must be handled carefully. Also, if the center supervisor is a woman and the secretary formerly worked for a man, this could be a potential problem.

Q: Are employees actually laid off by the word processing center, or do they move into new careers? If so, what are these careers?

A: Personnel cutbacks are usually handled through attrition, the method used in the vast majority of organizations surveyed for this chapter. The secretaries that are left behind typically have assumed new roles as administrative assistants to their supervisors. Instead of spending the bulk of their time typing, these secretaries now gather statistics, prepare budgets, dictate letters into the word processing center to answer routine correspondence, and so forth. The major problem is to ensure that these secretaries' contributions to the organization are meaningful. In some instances, the administrative secretaries have been organized much like the word processing secretaries, with one common supervisor. In this way, they serve the needs of the entire organization better, and they are in line for a supervisory position, as are the word processing secretaries. Many pitfalls can occur in this area, however, and much work must be done to ensure that these administrative secretaries have meaningful duties. Most of the current literature admits that this is a difficult problem to handle, because the needs of each organization, as well as its logistics and physical constraints, have a great bearing on how effectively these administrative secretaries can be handled.

Q: If employees are not laid off, how are financial savings achieved?

A: Herein lies one of the biggest pitfalls that must be avoided when dealing with equipment suppliers and salesmen. In most of the organizations surveyed, deferred or intangible savings had accrued; few savings were immediate. Because attrition takes care of excess employment, personnel savings are seen only over several years. Because of word processing, most organizations do not hire additional secretaries nor are existing secretaries replaced when they leave. Also, key personnel gain, because they now have more administrative support time than ever before and because their typing is handled in a more efficient manner. These savings must be balanced against the lease or the purchase cost of equipment. Although savings result from implementing word processing systems, they usually are not visible until after the first year.

Q: What percentage of all government typing is done by word processing centers? Does the top executive participate in the system, or does he retain his own private secretary?

A: In a majority of the organizations surveyed that have citywide word processing operations, about 60 to 80 percent of the typing is being done in the center. Because word processing has only recently been implemented in most of these organizations, this percentage will probably increase.

In most instances, the city manager participates in the system. It was noted earlier that the city manager's secretarial staff in Sioux City, Iowa, was reduced from three to one as a result of word processing. In Raleigh, N.C., the city manager uses the system extensively but has also retained his own private secretary. Because most city managers' secretaries are often administrative assistants, it is doubtful that all secretaries will be removed from the chief executive's office as a result of word processing.

Q: Have any government organizations studied the system and then decided not to adopt it, or adopted the system and then abandoned it? If so, why?

A: On the basis of this brief survey, no organizations, public or private, considered adopting the system but did not do so. If the feasibility study is truly objective, though, this must occasionally occur. Organizations and situations must certainly exist where word processing will only add to the cost and difficulty of processing paperwork. Potential users are again cautioned to be wary of overeager salesmen. Likewise, no organization could be found that adopted a system and then subsequently dropped it, although it is certainly possible that this has occurred. Several organizations, primarily in the private sector, have experienced such morale and personnel problems because of word processing that they have considered dropping it. A closer analysis in these cases has found that center personnel had not been properly classified, resulting in unusually high turnover, which led to overly high backlogs of work. By restudying and reclassifying these jobs, however, the centers have achieved success.

13

Systems in
Day-to-Day Operations

THIS chapter presents the basic concepts of several management systems approaches that can be valuable to public sector organizations, because they offer greater efficiency and effectiveness. Various systems approaches in the hardware and software areas also are discussed as well as a potpourri of relatively simple and unsophisticated systems approaches.

Day-to-day public management is one area where systems approaches have been slow to develop and to be implemented. However, it is an area where significant economic gains can accrue through proper applications of the management systems approach.

HARDWARE SYSTEMS

Several public management systems have been developed in the hardware area to meet expressed needs of public sector managers, particularly those in the local government fire service field. The fire service field has been slow to innovate and utilize the

210

management systems approach in their operations. The three hardware systems described in this section are recent efforts that are just now being accepted. All three systems were developed by manufacturers with the assistance of Public Technology, Inc., the Washington-based research and development arm of state and local governments.*

NPO Automated Flow Control System†

The automated flow control system for the standard pumper apparatus enables the fire service to control the flow of water at the nozzle rather than at the engine, thereby increasing the safety and effectiveness of firefighting operations.

When the firefighter nozzleman determines his desired flow rate, a transmitter located between the hose and the nozzle is activated and sends a coded radio signal to a receiver on the pumper. The radio signal activates the system, which automatically adjusts the variable flow valves and engine speed, thereby rapidly and accurately providing the selected flow rates. The nozzleman is able to call for more water instantly or to shut off the flow to his line without affecting other lines.

If the fire pumper malfunctions because of excessive temperature, low battery voltage, low oil pressure, or pump cavitation, the automated system warns the firefighters by sounding an alarm and pulsing the water, thereby allowing enough time to correct the problem. Finally, if the automated system itself malfunctions, the engineer can immediately revert to manual operation.

Firefighters currently regulate water flow by signaling the engineer stationed at the pumper by hand or by radio. However, this method is slow or inaccurate during rapidly changing conditions, ties the engineer to the pumper, and creates hazardous conditions for personnel.

Grumman Aerospace Corporation of Bethpage, N.Y., in conjunc-

---

*Public Technology, Inc., was chartered in 1971 by the International City Management Association, National League of Cities, U.S. Conference of Mayors, National Association of Counties, National Governor's Conference, and National Association of State Governments. The executive directors of these six organizations serve on Public Technology's board of directors. Public Technology's mission is to bring better technology to bear on the high-priority technical needs of state and local governments.

†"NPO Automated Flow Control System," Product Awareness Brochure, Public Technology, Inc., Washington, D.C., 1974. The material discussed in this section is based on the information in this brochure.

tion with Public Technology and a user requirements committee,* has designed and developed a system, to the requirements specified by the committee, for automating the water flow control function of the pumper apparatus. Grumman Allied Industries, Inc., is producing the system for local governments.

The system has undergone an extensive series of tests by Grumman to ensure its safeness, strength, and reliability under severe handling and environmental conditions. Moreover, it has been field-tested by the New York City and Long Beach, California, fire departments.

Giving control of the water flow to the nozzleman was one of the top priority problems defined by 80 local governments in 1970. Grumman Aerospace Corporation approached Public Technology and convinced them that they possessed the management and technical resources to successfully design and develop an automated flow control system. Grumman has a strong record of performance for designing and building highly reliable systems in which men's lives are at stake, such as high-performance aircraft and the lunar module used on the Apollo space program. Some of the command and control principles and techniques developed for the lunar module were incorporated into the automated flow control system.

Public Technology organized a User Requirements Committee to advise and guide the system's development. The system, which costs about $12,000–$13,000, automates two outlets on a pumper. The cost-effectiveness of the units are realized through:

Better utilization of personnel.
Increased equipment and personnel safety.
Property saved by faster initial response.
Reduced operations and maintenance costs.

This system represents a significant breakthrough in increasing efficiency of firefighting methods.

Applications of the Automated Flow Control System

As mentioned earlier, firefighters currently regulate water flow by signaling the engineer, who is stationed on the pumper, by voice, hand, or radio. The engineer must receive and understand

---

*A user requirements committee is usually made up of local government representatives, including general and functional management, budget, finance, operating, and union personnel.

the signal and then manually adjust the pumper. This system relies on open communications between the nozzleman and the engineer, which is often difficult to maintain at the fireground because of high background noise, distance, voice traffic, and darkness. The current method gives slow response to rapidly changing fire conditions, ties the engineer to the apparatus, and creates conditions that are hazardous to personnel.

The automated flow control system was designed to answer the need of the fire service to put positive, direct control of the water flow in the hands of the nozzleman. This allows for smoother, more efficient operation, which ultimately increases safety and effectiveness.

The nozzleman, communicating directly with the pumper, calls for water and has it flowing through his hose in seconds, thus allowing him to put water on the fire once he is in position. He also is able to maneuver inside structures before the line is fully charged, thus enabling him to get to the face of the fire much more quickly and efficiently. Time, especially during the initial phase of fire attack, is of the utmost importance.

During fireground operations, the firefighter often has to advance or withdraw lines quickly in response to rapidly changing conditions. Under the conventional system, this presented a serious problem. If the nozzleman shuts off his hose at the nozzle, he is left with a stiff, unwieldy hose to maneuver around walls or obstructions. If he has the engineer shut off flow to his line at the truck, he must rely on the engineer, remote from his location, to restore flow at the proper time and at the proper level. Both alternatives are inefficient and dangerous. The automated flow control system allows the nozzleman to shut off his flow at the pumper, then reestablish it at the desired rate when he has taken up his new position.

Under current methods, when multiple hoses are in operation from one pumper truck, the lines are not independent of one another. A change in flow in one line affects the flow in others. One important and time-consuming task for the engineer is to balance the flow among the lines. This is difficult because calculations are required for such factors as nozzle elevation and length of hose. When sudden changes in flow occur on one line (such as a bail being closed) pressure surges affect the flow to other lines. The automated flow control system maintains the flow in each automated line separately. Shutting down or changing flow in one line does not affect the flow in the others.

During the initial stage of fire attack, the engineer must rapidly perform several tasks to start water flowing to the fire. He must locate a source of water and connect it to the pumper. He then starts, balances, and maintains flows to the various lines at the direction of the nozzleman and the officer. The automated flow control system frees the engineer to perform other vital firefighting tasks during the critical initial phase. Once the pumper is connected to a water supply and the system is activated, the engineer is, for example, free to man a second attack line, monitor more than one pumper, assist in raising ladders, or provide first aid.

Cost Justification Criteria

In actual use, the automated flow control system has proved cost-effective for the following reasons:

1. Fire service productivity has been increased by enabling the engineer to perform additional tasks.
2. Personnel and equipment are safer, because the nozzleman can rapidly and accurately control water flows, and he knows about impending malfunctions of the pumper.
3. Total property loss has been reduced by getting water on the fire more quickly, thereby keeping small fires small.
4. Property damage from water has been reduced as a result of more accurate control of water flow.
5. Operating and maintenance costs have been reduced. The highly reliable air-activated governor significantly reduces maintenance. The quick-responding engine governor system reduces fuel consumption and engine and pump maintenance.

Probeye® Infrared Viewer*

At a meeting at the Kennedy Space Center in 1970 to discuss technology applications in the public sector, a number of local governments defined a common need for a fire service operations tool with the following capabilities:

1. Detect first-order fires through the heat radiated or conducted through walls, floors.

*"Probeye Infrared Viewer," Product Awareness Brochure, Public Technology, Inc., Washington, D.C., 1974. Probeye® is a registered trademark of the Hughes Aircraft Company.

2. Detect and locate fire or smoke victims in dark or smoke-filled environments.
3. Provide orientation to firefighters in identifying the physical characteristics of dark or smoke-filled rooms (doors, windows, furniture, and other obstacles).
4. Identify residual hidden "hot spots" during overhaul operations.

Probeye®, developed by the Hughes Aircraft Company in conjunction with Public Technology, is the earliest commercially available device that has all these operating capabilities. Basically, it uses thermal radiation to give a clear view of objects, even when there is no light, by projecting images onto a built-in screen. The unit is a product of infrared technology used by the Department of Defense in weapons systems.

As mentioned above, the need for such a device was first articulated by local officials. The city of Anaheim, California, led the search for this device. The development of the equipment was monitored by a user requirements committee comprised of local fire officials to ensure its conformity to actual operating conditions.

Some of the more important performance specifications of Probeye® are:

Portable and lightweight (just over seven pounds).
Water and shock resistant.
Compatible with firefighters' existing protective breathing equipment.
Requires minimal training for use.
Easily operable by one person.
Usable for four hours before recharging.

In addition to its fire service applications, Probeye® has other uses for local government operations.

1. Building and electrical inspections (Probeye® locates potential trouble spots such as overloaded wires or switches).
2. Electric utility plant maintenance (Probeye® detects high-voltage heat buildup that can interrupt service).
3. Police operations (Probeye® is useful as a vision enhancement device for night surveillance).

Probeye® costs about $3,575, but its cost-effectiveness is

realized through the following benefits of time, manpower, and safety:

1. Cuts property damage by allowing firefighters to more rapidly locate an interior structural fire.
2. Increases the speed and accuracy of the search for victims.
3. Decreases the risk of injury to personnel by enabling firefighters to identify obstacles in total darkness or in heavy smoke.
4. Because Probeye® can detect heat behind and within walls and floors, it eliminates property damage and operating costs caused by rekindles.
5. Permits the officer in charge to direct and complete overhaul operations more quickly and efficiently.
6. The public image of the fire department is improved because of the other benefits.

Scott Air-Pak 4.5 Firefighters' Breathing System *

The National Aeronautics and Space Administration, Technology Utilization Office, sponsored the development of a much needed improved firefighters' breathing system. The Lyndon B. Johnson Space Center, Crew Systems Division, with its expertise in life-support equipment for astronauts, conducted the development and testing program, supported by Scott Aviation Company and others. Public Technology, under contract to the Technology Utilization Office, provided local government inputs through a user requirements committee.

Scott Aviation Company has introduced the first commercially available breathing apparatus primarily based on this development and testing program. However, other manufacturers have expressed an interest in incorporating the design innovations into their products.

The need for improving the firefighters' breathing system is related to the following problems:

1. Department of Labor figures show that firefighting is one of the most hazardous occupations in the United States.

---

*"Scott Air-Pak 4.5 Firefighters' Breathing System," Product Awareness Brochure, Public Technology, Inc., Washington, D.C., 1975.

2. Every year 50 percent of the nation's paid firefighters sustain some injury. *

3. Respiratory injuries, such as smoke inhalation, toxic atmospheres, and oxygen deficiency, account for 10 percent of these injuries. *

4. Although fire departments have been equipped with self-contained breathing apparatus for several years, the trend of respiratory injury is rising.

5. Firefighters do not fully utilize their breathing apparatus because it is heavy and bulky and it restricts maneuverability.

Improving firefighters' breathing apparatus was given the highest priority by municipal officials at the National Aeronautics and Space Administration-sponsored meeting organized and conducted by Public Technology in 1970. The purpose of that meeting was to identify local government problems that might be solved by applying advanced technology. The city of Boston had previously identified firefighters' breathing equipment as an area needing significant improvement, and one in which technologies generated by the space program might be readily applied.

Public Technology assembled a user requirements committee made up of fire service professionals and city administrators to define the user needs and to provide assistance to the National Aeronautics and Space Administration and its subcontractors during the development of the system. The user requirements committee established the requirements for an improved breathing system, and their inputs ensured that the design would be acceptable to the fire service and to the cities from both an operational and an economic perspective.

The Johnson Space Center explored several alternative design concepts with the user requirements committee before selecting the system that best met the user's needs. An open-loop system was chosen because significant improvements in weight, bulk, and duration could be achieved with high reliability, ease of maintenance and operation, and relatively low intial and recharging costs.

The prototype has been extensively tested to determine if it meets qualification demands and various regulatory agency requirements. This system has been subjected to a six-month field

*1973 Annual Death and Injury Survey, International Association of Fire Fighters, Washington, D.C., cited in "Scott Air-Pak 4.5 Firefighters' Breathing System."

test in which the prototype was used as first-line suppression equipment in some of the world's busiest and most diversified engine and ladder companies in Houston, Los Angeles, and New York. This allowed the system to be proved in actual firefighting conditions. Comments from personnel who have used the system have been overwhelmingly positive. Firefighters have been most pleased about improved maneuverability and reduced fatigue.

The Scott Air-Pak 4.5 is based primarily on the prototype design, but it was further refined to take advantage of the experience gained in the field testing. Changes also have been made to accommodate higher production volumes. The units cost about $550 to $700 apiece (about 10 percent higher than conventional units).

In order to utilize the new system, the pressure vessels must be refilled to 4,500 pounds per square inch (psi) with high-quality breathing air. In some areas, it may be possible to have bottles filled to the correct pressure and purity by local air supply sources. If the public sector organization wants to charge its own bottles, this may be accomplished by: (1) a cascade system from commercially available high-pressure air vessels; (2) a booster station added to the current air compressor station; or (3) a high-pressure (5,000 psi) air compressor station with an air purification system. Jurisdiction size, air use rates, location, and several other factors determine the best method.

Most fire professionals who have viewed the prototype units agree that it represents a significant advance in firefighters' safety equipment. They believe that these units would reduce the cost of fire protection by reducing the firefighters' injury and lost time rates. The firefighter will suffer less discomfort and fatigue by using this unit and will thus be able to be more effective in firefighting situations. The Scott Air-Pak 4.5 Firefighters' Breathing System improves firefighters' performance by:

- Reducing fatigue and stress under emergency conditions through reduced weight, profile, and breathing resistance and better weight distribution.
- Improving mobility and maneuverability in performing fire suppression, forcible entry, and overhaul operations.
- Increasing visibility and communication through improved faceplate.

In addition, firefighters are safer as proved by:

- Reduced number of respiratory injuries.
- Reduced number and duration of sick leaves.
- Reduced number of disabilities in addition to increased service longevity.

This section has briefly presented several hardware systems that can increase the efficiency and effectiveness of day-to-day public sector operations. Although the three examples have been developed primarily for the fire service, new and improved hardware systems undoubtedly occupy a valuable place in an operating manager's systems approach. Other hardware systems currently being developed include the following.*

Short-Range Communications System for Fire Services

Objective: To develop a short-range, portable radio for command and control during firefighting. Major features will include lower cost and reduced size and compatibility with protective clothing and apparatus.

Improved Pavement (or Pothole) Patching Material

Objective: To develop an all-weather permanent street-patching material for potholes, cracks, and surface patches. An improved cold-patching material called Sylvax U.P.M.† is currently being tested and evaluated in several jurisdictions throughout the United States. Early results obtained through full freeze and thaw conditions indicate that this material is about twice as cost-effective as standard cold-mix materials. Although not a system per se, this material applied in a systematic way with a new approach to street maintenance operations (to be described in the next section) produces significant cost-effective benefits.

Underground Pipe and Conduit Locator System

Objective: To develop an instrument for locating underground utility lines, both metallic and nonmetallic, to greater depth and accuracy than is possible with existing equipment. A device, based on the concept of downward looking radar, is currently being developed and will be tested and evaluated by a user requirements committee.

---

*Current projects of Public Technology, Inc.
†Sylvax U.P.M. is distributed by Sylvax Chemical Corporation, Great Neck, New York.

Improved System for Rapid Detection of Enteric Bacteria

Objective: To develop a device for rapidly and accurately detecting the presence of enteric bacteria in water samples. Current methods require 24 to 48 hours. This device would obtain a more accurate analysis in less than four hours. In addition, this approach would be less labor-intensive than present methods, would be portable, and would detect bacteria in any aqueous solution.

Improved Street-Striping System and Materials

Objective: To develop a more easily applied and removed, cost-effective street-striping material that has improved durability and wet-night reflectivity. The material and systematic process being considered are proprietary to the manufacturer, but the process involves the molecular grafting of materials to the surface and an improved systematic approach to application and removal.

This section has described some hardware systems that are currently available or under development; there are, of course, many others. All these systems, if properly applied, can help public sector managers conduct their day-to-day operations in a more cost-effective and less labor-intensive manner.

SOFTWARE SYSTEMS

In addition to these hardware systems, numerous software systems exist that can be of significant value to public sector managers. Frequently, hardware systems require some software for proper implementation. However, for our purposes, this section will only consider software systems. Several of the following systems were developed to meet expressed public sector needs. Although federal grants and contract funding were involved, most of the development efforts were managed by Public Technology.

Fire Station Location System *

The fire station location system, developed by Public Technology, was designed to evaluate and form public policies and to make

---

*"Fire Station Location Package," Chief Executive's Report, Public Technology, Inc., Washington, D.C., 1974. This package and the reports associated with it were developed by Public Technology as a community management option in fire service management under sponsorship of the Department of Housing and Urban Development, Office of Policy Development and Research. The material discussed in this section is based on these reports.

strategic management decisions about the adequacy of fire station locations. The system is applicable to both present and planned station locations. Its basic premise is that station locations should be determined by the time it takes a fire engine to respond to a fire (response time) rather than on arbitrary distance requirements. In this way, jurisdictions have the most fire protection for the least investment. As structured, the system relies on a jurisdiction's strong interest and on top management's commitment to the evaluative effort. The system uses a project team composed of fire officials, support staff, and representatives of top management. The project gives a focal point for fire officials and public sector administrators to agree on the level of service that is to be provided to a particular jurisdiction.

The fire station location system determines the least expensive alignment of fire stations necessary to meet local fire protection requirements. It allows a municipality to meet local administrators' and fire officials' long-expressed need for a fire suppression approach that recognizes and responds to response time as the single most important ingredient in saving lives and property. Depending on local conditions, the number and alignment of fire stations may be less, more, or the same as a jurisdiction has.

The fire station location system was developed and tested by nationwide local administrators and fire officials. This system has provided most of these communities with substantial savings, ranging from $150,000 to $600,000 in annual operating costs when measured against outmoded, arbitrary distance requirements.

System Operation

The package is structured around a computer program that locates fire stations on the basis of response time, which is defined apart from any specific location proposal or national standard.

Local government personnel survey their community to collect data on hazards to life and property. Requirements for a quick response may be determined by the type and the age of each structure, frequency of use, and other factors. Additional data are collected on possible fire stations and characteristics of the local street system.

On the basis of this analysis, local administrators and fire officials specify how fast fire apparatus must respond to a fire alarm or other service call. This constraint is termed the "response-time requirement." Computer-generated data summaries, are then used to measure the consequences of alternative proposals:

- A detailed description of the streets and highways that are used by fire equipment.
- A list of the fastest route from each potential station site to each point where a fire could occur.
- An analysis of the capability of each existing or potential station site to meet response-time requirements.
- A list of station site assignments by first, second, and third responding locations that are available to protect different areas.

It is important to note that the precise values change as the response-time requirement is varied across a broad range. Local administrators and fire officials can then use the information base to compare alternative proposals.

Careful interpretation yields a clear understanding of the available options. Decisions are made by interpreting the imbalances between the "supply" of station sites and the "demand" for fire protection. Decision makers select the proposal that best meets local objectives for fire protection.

System Implementation

A local project team that is responsive to community priorities is set up to implement the various system components which include orientation and training sessions, documents, forms, worksheets, computer programs, and, if necessary, technical assistance from Public Technology.

First, the project team develops a searching attitude toward the fire station location proposals. Because of the magnitude of the costs involved, it is clearly in a local government's interest to question any new proposal. The following questions are based on the need for objectivity in fire station location.

- Do the existing stations provide adequate coverage?
- Do we have enough fire stations? Too many? Too few?
- Are the mutual-aid agreements up to date?
- Is consolidation feasible?
- Should stations be relocated to account for shifting patterns of growth and deterioration?
- When a station responds to a fire, are other stations available for backup within a reasonable time?
- How can we ensure that any plan developed now won't be obsolete in a matter of months or years?

- How receptive will other municipal departments, such as planning and finance, be to this plan?
- What are the comparative costs? Are any savings indicated?

Second, the project team defines local needs for fire protection, thereby obtaining a baseline for the effectiveness of current stations. Various proposals for station consolidation, relocation, new construction, or planning alternatives can then be assessed. The project team determines which of the following applications best fits their community needs.

To Measure the Effectiveness of Current Deployment

The first use of the system is to describe the status of current fire protection arrangements.

The baseline information is used to decide whether current protection provides the desired results or whether other alternatives must be studied.

To Compare Alternative Site Options

It is essential that the options available to a community be identified and organized in an understandable manner. There are four broad possibilities: (1) consolidation or reduction of the total number of stations; (2) replacement on the same site; (3) relocation to a new site; and (4) new construction.

The first and third options assume that one or more stations must be closed, but in replacement and relocation decisions, the total number of sites is held constant.

To Determine Effects of Annexation or Development

Either action usually involves new station construction. However, this could be offset by relocating existing stations.

To Plan for the Future

In general, the system can be used to gauge the impact of decisions that could affect existing coverage.

This can include public works projects, zoning changes that affect land costs, and so forth.

Third, the project team determines whether or not a proposal satisfies the response-time requirement. Under some plans, the actual travel time to a particular hazard may be longer than the response-time requirement. This situation is displayed prominently in the computer-generated data summaries. However, there may be an acceptable backup available from second and third responding locations. Thus, the administrator has a trade-off that balances the interests of a specific neighborhood with the interests of the total community.

Measuring and attaining the response-time requirement are the objectives of system implementation, the results of which will differ with various alternative station site configurations. However, any proposal that affects one or more stations can have an impact on an entire community.

The system provides an overview of all stations simultaneously (and gauges the effects of specific decisions on the entire community). The proposal that comes closest to meeting the response-time requirement and the other applicable constraints is usually the one to implement.

Finally, the project team calculates the benefits of system implementation. An illustration of benefits identified from previous applications by Public Technology is as follows:

Objectivity
- An objective analytical tool that utilizes up-to-date approaches to fire suppression.
- Geared to flexibility and an orientation to performance.
- Avoids arbitrary distance requirements derived from custom. Substitutes response time as the key criterion.

Fire hazard analysis
- Incorporates both life saving and property protection as important objectives.
- The beginning of a systematic approach to assessing community needs for fire protection.
- An understanding of basic fire protection needs that is based on fact and careful analysis.

Full fire protection
- Whenever feasible, emphasizes using existing facilities.
- New facilities located on need rather than on traditional formulas.
- Maintenance or improvement of fire protection coverage.

Improved equipment routing
- Up-to-date analysis of the street transportation network.
- Stresses accessibility to potential hazards.
- Provides a basis for assigning second and third responding locations to particular hazards.

Flexible station location

- Provides for detailed examination of specific fire station location options.
- Requires systematic approaches to interdepartmental cooperation and public facility planning.
- Improves placement of capital facilities, with a positive impact on the utilization of equipment and personnel.

Documented cost advantages

- Some savings from $150,000 based on the anticipated savings in annual operating costs.
- Provides a basis for relating costs to fire incident records and response-time requirements.
- Builds a strong information base on which parallel studies can be effected more quickly and at less cost.
- Staff acquires a strong background in analytical approaches to public facility problems.

This system has now been implemented in several local governments throughout the country, and significant cost-benefits have been reported.

Equipment Management System*

The equipment management system allows public administrators and equipment managers to decrease the operating and maintenance costs of motorized equipment, to improve efficiency, and to maximize availability through decreased downtime.

This system is founded on computer-based information and aids in the development and the management of public policies. Effective monitoring and evaluation of motorized equipment management are the ultimate objectives of system implementation. The effectiveness of the system depends on top management's use of the reports that are generated.

The system is usually implemented by a start-up project team composed of top management representatives, equipment fleet

*"PTI/APWA Equipment Management Package," Chief Executive's Report, Public Technology, Inc., Washington, D.C., 1976. Financial support to develop and test this package was shared by Public Technology; the Department of Housing and Urban Development, Office of Policy Development and Research; and the American Public Works Association. The material in this section is based on information in this package.

officials, and support staff. The system output allows administrators and equipment managers to reach an objective understanding of inventories, staff levels, and replacement policies that are appropriate to their public sector organizations.

This system provides detailed information on equipment operating and maintenance characteristics, which enables officials to keep the minimum number of vehicles in service for the maximum amount of time at minimal cost. Depending on local conditions, the system determines if the equipment fleet size, staff levels, or replacement rates should be less, more, or the same as an organization has.

Maintaining detailed records of vehicle utilization by various organizational units within a jurisdiction is a complex task. Effective management analysis of the present and historical costs of fuel, parts, labor, and commercial expenditures usually requires a computerized information system.

The equipment management system was developed and tested by local public officials and equipment managers across the country. The computer programming was performed by local government staff, with Public Technology coordination. Most communities involved thus far indicate that the system helps them hold the line on equipment management costs by improving their statistical and cost-accounting procedures.

System Operation

The equipment management system is composed of a set of computer programs, worksheets, and forms, which provide complete documentation to support the project team. Government personnel collect data, which are then prepared for the system. Forms are generated by the users and transmitted to the jurisdiction's own data-processing facility. The forms include repair orders, fuel usage, and other data necessary for computer operation.

Following the data-collection phase, the system modules are used to generate a series of reports in the following seven categories:

Equipment inventory
Fuel
Repairs
Preventive maintenance
Billing
Vehicle replacement analysis
Parts inventory control

Although the basic or prime modules of the system are for equipment inventory, fuel, and repairs, these are used the least if the system is to be effective. The system's greatest value is in the sharing of data by each of the modules, resulting in comprehensive reports that strengthen management analysis.

Most module reports are produced monthly and transmitted to system users. Some reports are generated only when requested. The system also retains information that can be useful for special reports.

The equipment management system produces reports that pool information from the complete set of modules. These comprehensive reports present a picture of the operating and maintenance costs and of the characteristics for individual pieces and classes of equipment. This output is used in support of cost-accounting and performance evaluations.

The equipment management system does not make decisions. Careful interpretation of the computer-generated data summaries provides a better understanding of the status of motorized equipment. Decision makers develop the management guidance that meets local objectives for service delivery.

System Implementation

The system is implemented by a local project team, which is responsive to community priorities. The system components include: training and orientation sessions, documents, forms, worksheets, computer programs, and technical assistance if necessary.

A project leader, appointed by the jurisdiction, pulls a team together to implement the system. Because of the coordination involved, the project leader should be appointed from the executive staff level. In some jurisdictions, the chief executive, department head, or fleet manager may fill this role. Additional members of the project team are drawn from data-processing and other relevant departments and disciplines.

First, the project team develops a searching attitude toward equipment management. Because of the magnitude of the costs involved, it is clearly in a public sector organization's interest to question the status of current operations. The following questions help top management determine the adequacy of its existing system:

1. Is there an excessive amount of equipment out of service?
2. What controls and audit information exists on fuel disbursements?

3. What types of repairs are causing the highest outlays for labor and parts?
4. Is there an adequate periodic program for maintaining optimal equipment performance and decreasing equipment downtime?
5. Do equipment billing rates recover maintenance and operating expenses?
6. Are certain pieces of equipment being used for purposes that increase maintenance costs and downtime?

Second, the project team accurately defines local needs for an equipment management system. The answers to the above questions will establish a baseline for management decision requirements. Various proposals for system modification, department reorganization, inventory control, fleet expansion, equipment replacement, and staffing can then be assessed. The project team is guided by the applications listed below:

To minimize equipment downtime
 Preventive maintenance schedules.
To minimize equipment operating and maintenance costs
 Detailed fuel mileage and operating costs.
 Detailed repair characteristics and maintenance costs.
To decrease the high costs of parts inventories
 Identification of obsolete parts.
 Identification of frequently disbursed items.
To compare equipment performance
 Detailed operating and maintenance characteristics for classes of equipment and using agencies.
 Detailed equipment usage characteristics.
To determine optimum replacement cycles
 The effect of mileage on operating and maintenance characteristics.
 The depreciated value of equipment.
 Maintenance cost characteristics for each class of equipment.
To decrease clerical duties
 System preparation of interdepartmental billings.
 System scheduling of periodic maintenance.
 Production of cost-accounting records.
To perform historical analysis
 Trends in individual equipment operating characteristics and costs.

Trends in organizational equipment operating and maintenance characteristics and costs.

Trends in equipment class operating and maintenance characteristics and costs.

Third, make whatever changes are implied for implementing the new system. The programs and procedures are flexible and can be modified as necessary. On the other hand, modification of operating procedures may be needed to utilize the full potential of the system. A mix of system modifications and procedural changes is the most common method. As a result of this systematic approach, the administrator has a trade-off available that balances different kinds of benefits, technological and organizational, depending on local needs.

Finally, the project team calculates the benefits of package implementation. The following benefits can be expected from current applications:

Objectivity

An objective tool using up-to-date approaches to equipment management.

Builds a strong information base on which to rest top management decisions.

Geared to flexibility and an orientation to performance.

Describes garage operations for top management evaluation.

Improved equipment management

Increased data utilization.

Increased control of operations.

Centralized fleet information.

Analytically oriented reports.

Accuracy and timeliness

Increased accuracy of input/output data.

Improved reporting elements.

Increased flexibility of report generation and distribution.

Provides machine-readable data for other data-processing applications.

Documented cost advantages

Improved budgeting decisions, with positive impacts on equipment and personnel.

Provides a basis for comparing costs with the experience of other jurisdictions.

Provides staff with a strong background in systematic approaches to equipment management problems.

Increases equipment availability at decreased costs.

System flexibility for organizational flexibility.

This system has undergone extensive real-life testing by PTI and is now ready for wide dissemination and implementation.

Street-Patching Operations Decision System*

The problem of maintaining streets is highly visible and often becomes a political issue for local elected officials. Yet little attention has been devoted to evaluating current street maintenance operations and considering new ways of providing the service.

Management must be provided with methods for assessing street maintenance operations and for evaluating the impact of alternative modes of operation, new materials, or new equipment. These new methods will help management determine where improvements can be made and which alternatives will be most cost-effective.

This systematic approach provides such a method for street-patching operations. It does not include street construction or reconstruction, curb repair, and snow and ice removal, all of which are part of overall street maintenance operations. The process itself is not complex, and the required data are obtainable from available street department records. This process has been tested by street departments in a number of local governments, with surprisingly successful results. When used with an improved pavement-patching material (see the discussion of Sylvax U.P.M earlier in this chapter), this system can typically produce significant cost-benefits.

The cost of street maintenance in local governments is increasing rapidly. In 1976, it was estimated that local governments spent in excess of $2.5–$3 billion for maintaining municipal and county roads. Labor rates are increasing considerably, and the price of asphalt is also going up. As a result, in order to maintain current budget levels, street departments have cut back on major repair and reconstruction projects and on resurfacing with asphalt overlays in favor of patching individual potholes, which is less expensive.

*"Street Patching Operations Decision Process," A report prepared by Public Technology, Inc., Washington, D.C., under the auspices of the Urban Technology System, was sponsored by the National Science Foundation. The material in this section is based on this report.

Moreover, the level of pothole patching has increased, because inadequate patching materials and techniques require considerable repatching. Northern cities estimate that one pothole may be repatched as many as fifteen times during the winter season before a permanent patch can be installed in the spring.

The methods, materials, and equipment generally used for street patching have not changed significantly for many decades. Standard hot-mix, if applied properly under the right conditions, provides a permanent patch; however, installed under cold or wet weather conditions, hot-mix provides only a temporary patch that has to be replaced. In addition, because hot-mix manufacturers generally close down during rainy or cold days or seasons, when large highway construction projects, their primary business, shut down, local governments are then forced to use temporary cold-mix for patching operations.

Public Technology has spent considerable effort and resources to develop improved materials for street patching, and has just completed field-testing a commercially available material called Sylvax U.P.M. in 27 jurisdictions across the country. Public Technology wants to find a material that can be installed easily under all weather conditions and will yield a permanent or at least more durable patch than the standard cold-mix patch currently being used. The results of the field-test program are currently being assessed and will be available shortly.

To improve patching materials, chemicals are blended with asphalt to increase the adhesion and flexibility of the patching material. This process increases materials costs. In order to properly evaluate the cost-effectiveness of using improved but more expensive patching materials, Public Technology has developed a systematic method for calculating the total cost and performance impacts of using these new materials: the street-patching operations decision system.

Objectives of the System

The street-patching operations decision system breaks down street-patching operations into three basic components: labor, materials, and equipment. The system allows a jurisdiction to determine and to analyze its current street-patching costs and to evaluate the impact of proposed changes. The analysis of current costs and performance suggests ways in which costs can be reduced or performance can be improved.

Typical questions that are answered by evaluating total cost for each alternative and by comparing the results of each possibility against current cost might include: Should we use Material A or Material B for winter patching? Should we deploy our six people as two three-person crews or as three two-person crews? How does an extra truck on Crew C affect overall cost?

The system also serves as a useful management control tool. In developing the system, it was found that certain costs could be conveniently written in terms of "output factors," which are measures of installed tons of material per labor hours or equipment hours using commonly available street department data. These factors do not reflect absolute standards of performance (although data indicate that average output factors are remarkably similar for various jurisdictions) but provide the manager with a local relative standard against which he may evaluate improvement or degradation within his own operation. To use the system as a management control tool simply requires weekly, monthly, or even quarterly street-patching cost evaluations of the existing operation, critically looking for significant changes.

While the system does evaluate alternative operations, it does not specifically address the conversion costs of changing street-patching operations, such as selling old and buying new equipment or redistributing or reducing labor because of increased productivity. It is designed to determine the total costs in terms of labor, materials, and equipment of current operations and to evaluate the estimated operation costs of proposed changes. In order to determine the costs of phasing out current operations and phasing in new methods, additional calculations are required.

Improved Emergency Communications and Dispatching System Handbook

Because of the efforts of 27 technology agents participating in the National Science Foundation-sponsored Urban Technology System (see Chapter 16), many local governments realized that they had to improve the communications and dispatch functions of their emergency services.

Such a computer-assisted joint-dispatching system should be capable of comparing incoming calls with available units; selecting the most logical units to respond to any given address; selecting the most logical units to respond to second, third, and fourth assignments; and relocating idle units.

Such a system should have the following attributes:

An integrated communications center.

Alternatives to land lines.

Vehicle-to-vehicle communications.

Hard copies of communications—in vehicles and at stations.

An interface with other communications media for high-rise evacuation.

Enroute transmission of fire suppression data, including:
Building plans.
Hazardous materials.
History of previous calls.
Information about other responding units.

An interface with the 911 emergency telephone service, if appropriate.

A recording system for dispatch communications.

Simplified dispatch systems, including:
Efficient, spectrum management.
Predispatch diagnostics.

Information-retrieval capability in mobile units.

An interface with vehicle location monitoring.

Digital communications.

A tie-in with emergency pull boxes and roadside call boxes.

The Urban Technology System program, under the management of Public Technology, is developing a handbook for public sector managers that is to include: (1) system requirements; (2) assistance in selecting the preferred system concept; (3) a program plan; and (4) information for preparing the request for proposal and the proposal review process. Tucson, Arizona, has agreed to lead the development of the handbook, with most of the effort being provided by the Aerospace Corporation and Texas A&M University.

Although this systematic approach to emergency communications and dispatch is only in its early stages, it promises to assist public sector managers to evaluate and to reach decisions about their efforts.

Parks Resource Allocation System*

The parks resource allocation system was developed by a technologist in Akron, Ohio, and by a professor at Kent State University.

*E. L. Herman, "Parks Management System / Resource Allocation System," Brief No. 5, Urban Technology System, Public Technology, Inc., Washington, D.C., August 1975. Mr. Herman is the technology agent in Akron, Ohio.

The basic elements of the problem, the approach taken, and the early results are described in this section.

Problem. The Parks and Recreation Bureau of Akron, Ohio, is responsible for maintaining about 70 parks that are two acres or larger plus a number of smaller facilities. Determining the optimum mix and the allocation of maintenance resources (mowers, trucks, tractors, equipment operations, laborers) has been a continual problem for management. In addition, determining the impact of a proposed new park or a change in the level of resources, or even justifying more resources, is extremely difficult.

Solution. The problem surfaced after the initial Urban Technology System problem-identification process. A project team was formed under the leadership of the technology agent to consider alternative solutions. It was decided to take a management science approach, which mathematically models the parks maintenance function and then employs the model to allocate resources optimally and to project the impact of changes in the number of parks, equipment, manpower, and so forth. A consultant from Kent State University was employed, and assisted in developing the model and the solution. The system was applied to the Southwest District of Akron, and operational reports were immediately produced. After experience with the procedure, some refinements were made, and it was learned that adding cost data made the system much more valuable. The program is being extended to all park districts in the city.

Impact. The system has been valuable to the management of the Parks and Recreation Bureau. The initial runs identified bottlenecks and equipment constraints that had in some cases been suspected and that can now be quantified in the budget. In addition, the process of developing the model was educational, because management gained the ability to scrutinize its operations in a structured and rigorous manner.

Savings. The system will provide significant savings, because the parks maintenance function can be managed more efficiently and the situations where excess resources are employed can be eliminated. Estimates of savings will be made after experience has been gained during citywide implementation.

Transferability. The modeling technique, the solution procedure, and perhaps the computer program could be transferred essentially intact, although model parameters would be unique for each location. In addition, the system potentially can be generalized to apply to any operation that uses a large variety of resources for a complex set of tasks. If this generalization is accomplished, the system will have a wide application and a high degree of transferability.

Public Technology, under the auspices of the Urban Technology System program, has received a major HUD grant to develop the Akron model into a transferable package.

MANAGEMENT SYSTEMS for DAY-to-DAY OPERATIONS

This section presents brief discussions and descriptions of several rather simple but effective management systems.

Energy Conservation Systems and Approaches

Several energy conservation efforts currently underway or being planned by jurisdictions participating in the Urban Technology System (see Chapter 16) are listed in Table 13-1. Responding to high-priority local needs, these efforts are being conducted by on-site scientists and engineers participating in the program as technology agents. Not all of the approaches are management systems per se, but all are attempts to reduce energy consumption and thereby reduce costs.

A public building energy conservation program in the Town of West Hartford, Connecticut, focused on reducing energy usage in the heating, ventilating, air-conditioning, and electrical systems of public buildings. The final report, to be published shortly by Public Technology, will include a case history of the West Hartford experience and guidelines on how other local governments can conduct similar energy conservation programs.

Under the sponsorship of the Research Applied to National Needs Program of the National Science Foundation, Public Technology has recently developed a comprehensive Energy Conservation Guideline and Management Report for state and local governments. The reports discuss the need for energy conservation, describe how to plan conservation programs, discuss the organization of local resources, provide suggestions for implementing conservation measures, and describe approaches to assessing energy program results.* The reports have been widely disseminated and utilized by state and local governments throughout the country.

*"Energy Conservation: A Management Report for State and Local Governments," Public Technology, Inc., Washington, D.C., March 1975. Supported by Research Applied to National Needs Program, National Science Foundation.

Table 13-1. Urban Technology System energy projects.

Jurisdiction	Type of Project	Project Description	Project Status (Early 1976)
Jersey City, N.J. (See fuller discussion in Chapter 16.)	Energy conservation in public buildings	Demonstration and evaluation of cost-effective devices, such as time and zone controls for heating and lighting.	Contract with ERDA* and team of Jersey City and the Aerospace Corporation. Contract value approximately $250,000. Two-year work effort currently underway.
	Energy conservation-boiler modification	Modification to housing project boilers to increase efficiency. Changes include automated breaching dampers, tubulator installation, air dampers, and operating procedures. The Dwyer kit will be used to test and evaluate efficiency periodically.	Hardware procurement of $3,000 has been made. Exxon Corporation supported this effort and has written a report. It has an interest in developing an awareness package for other jurisdictions.
	Total energy system	Replace existing boilers in a hospital with a new total energy system—gas turbine generator and waste heat usage.	Proposals for this activity are being considered. $600,000 cost.

Sioux City, Iowa	Energy conservation in municipal buildings	City-sponsored activity to study and make recommendations for improvement to the central steam system. Modifications will be made to pumps, radiator values, and thermostats.	Study is complete. Budget allows for implementation.
West Hartford, Conn.	Energy conservation in public buildings	City-sponsored program to conserve energy in public buildings.	Implementation phase to reduce energy cost in public buildings has started. This effort was preceded by the study and analysis of 11 buildings. Total program costs are 225,000.
St. Petersburg, Fla.	Solar energy in public housing	Solar energy grant application to Dept. of Housing and Urban Development to heat water for a public housing project.	Project funded for $9,000.
Nashville, Tenn. (Metro)	Energy conservation in municipal buildings, street lights, and water and sewage pumping stations	Metro government-sponsored effort to reduce energy use by providing a public awareness program, light reduction program, revised electrical system network, analysis of water and sewage pumping operations, and emergency equipment.	Reduced electrical consumption by 20 percent. Ongoing program (see Chapter 16 for fuller description of this program).

Table 13-1. *Continued.*

Jurisdiction	Type of Project	Project Description	Project Status (Early 1976)
Pueblo, Colo.	Energy conservation in public housing and public buildings	City-sponsored program of de-lamping and public awareness information.	Program is complete.
	Solar energy in residential buildings	Grant application to Department of Housing and Urban Development to install and evaluate solar energy systems for residential heating and hot water heating.	Project is funded for $16,000.
Akron, Ohio	Energy Conservation public buildings	City-sponsored program using the TRACE system. (TRACE is a computerized approach to determining energy loss. It was developed by the TRACE Corporation.)	· Used TRACE on one building and verified effectiveness. Plan to apply to other new buildings.
Tucson, Ariz.	Solar-heated fire station	Design and build with city funds a solar-heated fire station.	This project is currently waiting for commitment of city funds.

Kettering, Ohio	General energy conservation and solar energy program	Citywide programs that include conversion of air-conditioning units to heat pumps, increased insulation, thermostat controls, motor vehicle modifications. Investigations into solar energy.	Programs currently underway. Council approved $83,000 for activities. Solar program discontinued because of lack of available funds.
Henrico County, Va.	Energy conservation in new office buildings	Work involved requesting from the architect/engineer maximum energy conservation measures during construction, such as variable value air system and heat transfer equipment. Also, automation system to monitor HVAC systems, light control, and electrical load shedding.	Work is complete.
Pasadena, Calif.	Energy conservation in public buildings	Broad program of energy-conserving measures for public buildings and city vehicles. Public awareness and review of city building codes.	Proposal to ERDA has been prepared by the city and the Aerospace Corporation. $250,000 effort.

*Energy Research and Development Administration. Developed from the Urban Technology System program.

Fire-Training Simulation System*

The fire-training simulation system provides realistic and cost-effective training for fire service personnel. The simulator is a visual system that uses a specially constructed two-stage overhead projector in combination with a standard 35-mm slide projector. The system simulates certain fire situations in a classroom, thereby eliminating the need to be at the scene of an actual fire.

One stage or platform of the overhead projector is used to project a reddish-orange flickering light that produces the illusion of fire. The other stage or platform projects a gray light that gives the illusion of smoke.

The projection of a 35-mm slide of a residence, commercial building, automobile, and so forth, provides the basis for the simulation exercise. The overhead projector images are superimposed on the 35-mm transparency images.

At the start of training, the 35-mm transparency is projected first. The fire and smoke lights are restrained by a carbon film light trap on the overhead projector. The operator of the simulator can project fire or smoke onto selected areas of the 35-mm situation slide (roof, windows, doorways). This is accomplished by removing small areas of the carbon from the film on the overhead projector. The simulator operator can also extend the fire horizontally or vertically, expose different areas of the 35-mm situation slide, create explosions, and so forth.

As a fire company responds and fights the fire properly, the fire and smoke lights can be restricted, giving the appearance that the fire is being extinguished and that the proper ventilation is taking place. Communications systems are also provided for simulation of fireground communications by trainees and for coordinating the simulation between the simulator operator and the training officer. Sound also is fed into the communications system to simulate sirens, background sounds, and so forth.

Although only recently developed and not widely applied, this simple system promises to improve firefighters' training. Compared

*Edward E. Wright, in collaboration with Richard C. Dietz and Gerald E. Miller, San Diego Technology Action Center, "A Fire Training Simulator," A Report, Urban Observatory Press, San Diego, California, February 1976. In cooperation with the California Innovation Group and the Research Applied to National Needs Program of the National Science Foundation.

with alternative fire-training simulators, this device is tremendously cost-effective.

"Flying Squad" Firefighting System*

Problem. Many local governments have recently been confronted with new federal regulations that reduce work weeks for firefighters. The alternatives include paying overtime for long work weeks, hiring more personnel under existing criteria to avoid paying overtime, or revising manpower utilization practices to achieve shorter work weeks without reducing fire suppression effectiveness.

Solution. The City of St. Petersburg, Florida, with the assistance of its technology agent, undertook an in-depth review of its fire services, including facility location, utilization of equipment, and manpower allocation criteria. One major result of the review has been the implementation of "flying squads" of manpower that are available to supplement regular fire companies. The flying squads have been created by borrowing manpower from existing companies. At any given time, three flying squads of six men each are available for assignment. At least one of these squads is assigned wherever a structural fire occurs within the city.

Impact. The flying squads were implemented in late July 1975. Proven results are: Increased manpower at fire scenes; in one case, the flying squad arrived on the scene first. The rapid assembly of manpower is providing for faster control of fires, and has allowed the department to release equipment that is enroute to the fire scene more quickly. The flying squads have also been equipped with and trained in the use of Probeye® infrared hot-spot locators, thereby enhancing their ability to identify the central areas of fires.

Savings. The flying squads provide a service level that would have required approximately 44 additional men under previous assignment practices. St. Petersburg estimates that the additional manpower would have cost $500,000 per year.

Transferability. The flying squad concept is broadly transferable and provides major benefits in terms of assembling manpower, handling special fire suppression equipment, and so forth. The

*Edmund J. Boyle, "Fire Service Innovation," Brief No. 25, Urban Technology System, Public Technology, Inc., Washington, D.C., August 1975. Mr. Boyle is the technology agent in St. Petersburg, Florida.

potential impact must be estimated in relation to current practices at each specific jurisdiction.

Systematic Approach to Police Manpower Scheduling*

Problem. The police department of Arlington, Texas, typically scheduled police personnel manually. Under these circumstances, lengthy rescheduling was necessary whenever special assignments or illness disrupted the original schedule. The police department wanted to automate the scheduling to reduce the time that it took and to provide better insight into the impact of schedule changes.

Solution. The technology agent, working with a representative from Texas A&M University, initiated action to organize the scheduling process. As the scheduling process was analyzed, it became clear that the number of alternative schedules was reasonably small and that they could be readily catalogued in handbook form. The handbook contains ready-made schedule patterns for various numbers of available personnel. The supervisor selects the schedule pattern that matches the number of personnel available and assigns individuals accordingly.

Impact. The manual is expected to facilitate scheduling and rescheduling significantly.

Savings. Cost savings have not been assessed, because the emphasis is establishing meaningful control of the scheduling process. However, it is expected that cost savings will accrue, because the time expended in making and revising schedules will be reduced.

Transferability. The potential exists for transfering this approach. Although the handbook can be understood in approximately one half hour, it was tailored to local requirements in Arlington. Other public sector organizations might modify the handbook to include additional or different schedule patterns.

Card Parking System†

Problem. Three major problems are associated with urban parking-meter systems: collection, maintenance, and vandalism. Because

*John Bayles, "Police Manpower Scheduling," Brief No. 7, Urban Technology System, Public Technology, Inc., Washington, D.C., August 1975. Mr. Bayles is the technology agent in Arlington, Texas.

†John Ewen, "Card Parking System," Brief No. 40, Urban Technology System, Public Technology, Inc., Washington, D.C., February 1976. Mr. Ewen is the technology agent in Jersey City, New Jersey.

the related costs for these operations are rapidly increasing, net revenues are reduced. In Jersey City, New Jersey, equipment damage alone in 1974 was $14,000, without considering the loss of revenue and repair costs.

Solution. The technology agent researched various parking systems in the United States and abroad to find one that would address these problem areas and reduce operating cost, increase net revenue, and be accepted by businessmen and citizens. A card system was found in Tel Aviv, Israel, that appeared to meet these requirements. A cost comparison of this system with the city's existing metered system revealed that net revenue could be increased by 15 to 20 percent.

Impact. The Jersey City Parking Authority conducted a test implementation. A decision is being considered whether or not to implement the system on a full-scale basis.

Savings. Based on the technology agent's analysis, an $82,000 increase in annual net revenue can be expected for Jersey City's 2,200-parking-meter system.

Transferability. The system is well documented and can be implemented easily; however; the cost-savings trends may differ from site to site because of the degrees of vandalism and parking-meter usage.

Fuel-Monitoring System*

Problem. Oklahoma City became aware that 200,000 gallons of gasoline per year were not being accounted for, a situation that was aggravated by a doubling in the price of gasoline. Looking forward to ever-increasing costs, it was decided to place the dispensing of fuel under tighter control.

Solution. The technology agent investigated a computerized gasoline-dispensing system. The system was justified, the alternatives evaluated, and a request for proposal was submitted. The computerized system could also maintain vehicle mileage records when fuel was dispensed, thus providing an improved records system for equipment maintenance. The computerized system could be designed to interface directly with the city's main computer.

Impact. The total system cost $136,000 and will be amortized

* James R. Carter, "Fuel System Monitor," Brief No. 42, Urban Technology System, Public Technology, Inc., Washington, D.C., February 1976. Mr. Carter is the technology agent in Oklahoma City, Oklahoma.

in three years through personnel and fuel savings. The 15 dispensing locations will be available 24 hours per day with no attendants. At the same time, losses of fuel to unauthorized vehicles will be stopped, and the interdepartmental accounting for fuel use will be improved.

Savings. Estimated savings of $50,000 per year will pay for the $136,000 system. After three years, the $50,000 per year can be regarded as true savings. Data-processing savings from the automatic transmission of information to the main computer are expected to be $3,000 per month.

Intangible benefits include improved control of fuel and reduced energy expenditures by the city.

Transferability. The request for proposal and subsequent evaluation used by Oklahoma City are applicable to other governments. Several commercial firms offer such a system, although design and installation will be unique to each jurisdiction. Standard procurement practices are adequate to obtain this system.

Refuse Collection System Revision*

Problem. The Refuse Section of Evanston, Illinois, Street and Refuse Department had been operating with the same routing structure for over 15 years. During that time, a transition was made from open-back trucks to 16-yard rear loaders, and a conversion to 25-yard rear loaders is currently underway.

Initially, refuse disposal was handled by a city incinerator and a landfill inside the city limits. In the last two years, the incinerator and the landfill have been closed. All refuse is now taken to a landfill some 13 miles away.

In spite of these drastic changes in collection, equipment, and disposal techniques, no corresponding changes in procedures or route loading had been instituted.

Solution. The technology agent made a thorough study of the existing system. He determined the levels of service, the inefficiencies in the system, the labor and management constraints and problems, an agreed-upon definition of a "fair-day's work," and the city's street and alley layout and the limitations it imposed on routing. Based on this information, he developed a report for the city manager and the city council. In it, he outlined his findings

*Richard Nordquist, "Refuse Collection System Revision," Brief No. 3, Urban Technology System, Public Technology, Inc., Washington, D.C., August 1975. Mr. Nordquist is the technology agent in Evanston, Illinois.

and several alternative designs for the collection system, with cost analyses of each. The alternatives included different levels of service, new route structures, and different types of equipment.

The city council adopted the alternative that maintained the same level of service (twice a week) but restructured the routes and used larger trucks where the routes would allow. The routing used in part the Environmental Protection Agency's heuristic routing model.* Most significantly, the plan reduced the number of vehicles, and it reduced personnel from 57 to 36.

The requirements of other city departments for equivalent personnel were also studied, establishing that other departments could absorb the excess refuse personnel. Foremen and supervisors were used early in the study to help define the parameters used in the restructuring. Initially, a problem existed, because equivalent jobs in the street section were considered more desirable, but pay scales were the same. In order to make the two equally attractive, refuse collection jobs were given an extra step increase on the pay scale. Such approaches as these gained the support and cooperation of the foremen, supervisors, and union, allowing the change to take place with a minimum of opposition and few morale problems.

Impact. The new collection system was implemented in May 1975, with remarkably few problems considering the extensive changes. The city now has a much more efficient system without reducing services. The new system also allows better record keeping and reporting for management information, and will eventually adapt the Environmental Protection Agency's Collection Management Information System for continual assessment of operation efficiency and timely correction.

Savings. Savings in the first partial year were approximately $200,000 and in the first full year of operation will be $315,000.

Transferability. The exact solution is of course site specific and not transferable. However, the study and resulting report can serve as models for other jurisdictions.

Underground Leak Detection System†

Problem. Underground leaks in pressurized fluid systems are most commonly detected either by allowing the leak to surface

---

*This model, Collection Management Information System (COLMIS), is available at no cost from the Office of Solid Waste Management Programs, Environmental Protection Agency, Washington, D.C. 20460.

†John Ewen, "Underground Leak Detection," Brief No. 47, Urban Technology System, Public Technology, Inc., Washington, D.C., February 1976. As mentioned earlier, Mr. Ewen is the technology agent in Jersey City, New Jersey.

or by using such acoustical devices as geophones or hydrophones. Both methods are extremely limited in accurately pinpointing the source of the leak, resulting in wasted excavation hours.

Leak surfacing is acceptable if the cover soil is very permeable, thereby allowing detection to occur before damage. The hydrophone and geophone are also effective if the leak is large enough to be heard, if there is no background noise, and if the cover soil is not too deep. These conditions do not usually exist in city areas.

Solution. The technology agent in Jersey City, New Jersey, researched the available equipment and techniques used in other cities and by utility companies. With the help of science advisors from the California Innovation Group, a National Science Foundation-sponsored technology transfer group, an acoustical device was found being used by a western utility company that was superior to the existing equipment. The main difference between this device and the standard equipment is that the acoustical hardware is integrated with an electronic filter bank. The filter bank isolates frequencies associated with high-pressure leaks and drowns out some background interference. In addition to the sound transmitted to the device's headset, a visual display is also read on a sound meter.

Impact. The system was demonstrated in Jersey City to the Water Division personnel. Because ths equipment offered superior advantages over the present methods, the division initiated the necessary procedures to purchase it.

Savings. Considerable savings have resulted from accurate leak location and reduced excavation time, but they have not been documented.

Transferability. Information on this system is available from Jersey City. Also, information on other leak detection techniques, such as the nitrous oxide method, are also available.

Disaster Warning System*

Problem. Following a nearby tornado disaster, the City of Kettering, Ohio, tested its disaster warning system. Because it alerted less than half the citizens, it became obvious that the system needed to be upgraded.

---

*Daniel C. King, "Disaster Warning System," Brief No. 9, Urban Technology System, Public Technology, Inc., Washington, D.C., August 1975. Mr. King is the technology agent in Kettering, Ohio.

Solution. Although a proposal had been received from a signal equipment vendor for installing new sirens, the technology agent in Kettering contacted his counterpart in Topeka, Kansas, which had an effective warning system. Through him, the Topeka Civil Defense director advised Kettering about types of sirens and provided specifications for procurement. In addition, the Kettering technology agent sought assistance from Bolt Beranek & Newman (BB&N), one of the Urban Technology System's backup sites. BB&N considered the terrain, ambient noise levels, and possible wind dispersion in its analysis and recommended some changes in the proposed plan to assure full coverage. Recommendations were made to the city council along with a summary of the data collection.

Impact. The thoroughness of the data and the recommendations convinced the city council to approve both the plan and the necessary funds for implementation and the application for a Civil Defense grant to assist with implementation. Replaced sirens were given to local schools, which further augments the warning system. The city council and the citizens feel much more secure, because they have an adequate warning system.

Savings. No tangible cost savings can be quoted. Savings will depend on loss of life, injury, and property damage in the event of a future emergency.

Transferability. The actual design of the system is site specific. However, the data about the characteristics and the specifications for sirens and the methodology applied by BB&N are transferable. The information has been supplied to other Urban Technology System jurisdictions.

Street-Sweeping System Improvement*

Problem. The overall costs of street sweeping in the Township of Lower Merion, Pennsylvania, had been excessive. Maintenance costs per unit were well above average because of excessive equipment damage and failure. The tons of debris swept per curb mile had been very low. Township officials were interested in purchasing vacuum-type sweepers to improve performance and reduce costs.

Solution. The technology agent arranged for township officials to have several demonstrations and inspections of street sweepers,

*James Reynolds, "Street Sweeping Efficiency Improvement," Brief No. 53, Urban Technology System, Public Technology, Inc., Washington, D.C., February 1976. Mr. Reynolds is the technology agent in Lower Merion Township, Pennsylvania.

including both mechanical and vacuum type. The township street sweeper operators were provided with additional training in operating and maintaining the currently used mechanical sweepers. The technology agent conducted a cost-effectiveness analysis of current township street sweeping procedures. The analysis developed data that indicated that curbed streets could be swept about every eight working days with only two mechanical sweepers instead of the three being used. This conclusion was based on an actual sweeper availability of four hours per day per sweeper, thereby allowing for adequate maintenance time. The training of the equipment drivers in maintenance and operations would provide at least four hours of actual sweeper availability per working day.

Impact. Reducing the sweeper force to two machines manned by trained operators permitted frequent downtown sweeping and sufficient residential sweeping to maintain a high level of street cleanliness. The reduction of "oversweeping" in various parts of the township also increased the tons per curb ratio.

Savings. The elimination of one sweeper and one operator from the street sweeping crew did not alter its effectiveness and reduced operating costs by over $29,000 annually.

Transferability. The data-collection procedures and the cost-effectiveness methodology employed by the technology agent can be used by any public sector organization.

Geographically Based Information System*

Problem. Many records maintained by Independence, Missouri, contained information that would be more useful for planning and decision making if it were aggregated by location. This fact, plus the untapped capabilities of the city's computer, fostered an interest in an information system that could relate various events or information to geographical areas of the city.

Solution. The technology agent recommended that Independence use the Geographic Base File, Dual Independent Map Encoding (GBF/DIME) System. Developed by the U.S. Census Bureau, the system provides an excellent framework upon which to build a city information system. GBF/DIME is one of a wide variety of computer programs, data files, and technical reports that are

---

*Robert Svehla, "Development of Geographically Based Information System," Brief No. 16, Urban Technology System, Public Technology, Inc., Washington, D.C., August 1975. Mr. Svehla is the technology agent in Independence, Missouri.

available to local governments from the Census Bureau at little or no cost. Basically, GBF/DIME encodes on magnetic tape all the streets and city blocks that existed in 1970. Thus, the city can utilize this system, instead of starting its own, thereby saving many man-months of effort. In addition, the city also is using a system upon which the 1980 census will be based. However, the GBF/DIME file has to be updated, as it is based on the 1970 census.

Impact. When the system is fully operational, it helps the city, for example, to identify:

Where the elderly, poor, handicapped, or school-age residents live.
High fire and crime areas.
Dangerous street intersections.
Land use and zoning patterns.
Location of various types of industries.
Areas with high electrical power usage.

Savings. Although indirect cost savings have accrued, it should be viewed as an improvement in the provision of city services.

Transferability. The process used by the technology agent in updating the GBF/DIME files can be utilized by other jurisdictions.

Telephone System Cost Analysis*

Problem. The City of Tucson, Arizona, spent approximately $500,000 a year for telephone service. Of this amount, 71 percent represented charges for the basic telephone service, 13 percent was for long-distance service, 13 percent was for leased-line service, and 3 percent was for installations. The telephone company billed various addresses, refused to show any city account numbers, and provided the billing in an inconvenient form. The city used one person half-time just to organize the telephone bills into a convenient form.

Solution. The technology agent was asked to analyze the telephone system to determine if cost savings were possible. The basic telephone service was analyzed in detail, because it represented

*Robert E. Stutz, "Telephone System Cost Analysis," Brief No. 24, Urban Technology System, Public Technology, Inc., Washington, D.C., August 1975. Mr. Stutz is the technology agent in Tucson, Arizona.

the largest dollar amount and because each of the other cost items required approval before any changes could be made. Comparisons were made between existing rates and increases that the telephone company had requested of the Arizona State Corporation Commission. The technology agent also assisted the city attorney's office to prepare and present the city's objections to the proposed rate increases. His third task was to establish contact with suppliers of alternative services to determine if cost savings were possible and in what areas.

Impact. One immediate result was that the telephone company furnished the billing data in punched card form, which greatly reduced the time required by the accounting department to review the bills. This study also provided information on alternative communication systems and an in-house cost analysis of telephone usage.

Savings. Substantial cost savings were made through this approach.

Transferability. The technology agent documented the activities, and other cities in the Urban Technology System network used similar approaches to reduce their telephone costs.

Records Management System*

Problem. The Finance Department of Metropolitan Nashville/Davidson County, Tennessee, needed a new records management system. For years, almost no records had been thrown away, and records storage was becoming a problem. A system of records management techniques was needed for screening financial data and records, destroying duplicates, and updating retention schedules. A microfilm capability also was required.

Solution. The technology agent began by examining the records in storage. He found that there were many duplicates and that numerous documents were no longer needed and could be destroyed. The metro treasurer, who has overall responsibility for retaining records, and the technology agent met with each division manager and reviewed all forms and documents being used and sent to storage. Preliminary decisions were reached about how long each document should be retained, which ones should be microfilmed, and who should submit the copy for retention.

*Elmer Young, "Records Management System," Brief No. 11, Urban Technology System, Public Technology, Inc., Washington, D.C., August 1975. Mr. Young is the technology agent in Metropolitan Nashville, Tennessee.

After determining what material should be microfilmed, the technology agent investigated microfilm and reader/printer equipment. He and other officials visited several facilities with records management systems, including the Tennessee State Archives, called in equipment manufacturers, and developed a set of specifications that were sent out with a request for proposals. The equipment was subsequently purchased and installed. A Records Management System Manual was developed, including operating procedures and requirements, plus the retention schedules legally required by federal, state, and local governments.

Impact. The new system better serves the needs of the Finance Department. Records can now be retrieved much more quickly, because a lot of material has been removed from storage. This also means better service for those requesting documents.

Savings. The time saved in retrieving documents accrues to the Finance Department; however, new space is now available for other departments.

Transferability. The methods used to evaluate the records management system and the specifications can be transferred to any local government. Local governments can revise the information in the manual to meet their needs and legal requirements.

Library Cataloging System*

Problem. The Library Department of the city of San Jose has a traditional card catalog. The professional cataloging effort plus the clerical support required to produce the cards has been rather extensive. Although support systems such as Card Set had been used, many typists and an offset press operator were needed to do the job.

Solution. The Library Technical Services staff, assisted by the technology agent, reviewed a number of cataloging and card production services. The system offered by the Ohio College Library Center (OCLC) was selected and installed. OCLC has a data base of about 2 million titles, which provides immediate data on more than 90 percent of the titles. When the library is required to do original cataloging, the system assists with pre-edited forms.

Impact. The system has been installed and is operational. The

---

*Monroe H. Postman, "Library Cataloging System," Brief Number 114, Urban Technology System, Public Technology, Inc., Washington, D.C., October 1976. Mr. Postman is the technology agent in San Jose, California.

Figure 13-1. Urban Technology System energy report.

1.0   Purpose:

To establish the policy, system, and procedure for expediting special documents through the required review and approval cycles.

2.0   Organizations Affected:

All departments/divisions

3.0   Policy:

3.1   A special red interoffice mailing envelope called REDEYE has been developed to be used in order to expedite special documents through the review and approval cycles.

3.2   It shall be the policy of the city to review and approve such documents in an expeditious manner.

4.0   Definitions:

4.1   Special Document—A contract, municipal agreement, other forms of agreement, or other types of correspondence or report requiring that the necessary review and approval cycles be completed in an expeditious manner.

4.2   REDEYE—The name given to a system of expediting special documents through the necessary review and approval cycles.

5.0   Responsibility:

5.1   All city department heads; administrative staff; division heads; and other management, supervisory, and professional personnel are responsible for expediting special documents received in the REDEYE red envelopes on a "first thing" basis.

5.2   It shall be the responsibility of the assistant city manager for programming and budgeting to initiate the REDEYE system when needs dictate on all projects dealing with capital improvements, budgeting systems, or citywide systems and procedures.

5.3   It shall be the responsibility of any cognizant management, supervisory, or professional personnel to initiate the REDEYE system in areas other than those outlined in 5.2 only when needs dictate.

6.0   Procedure:

6.1   When it has been determined by any of the responsible persons outlined in 5.2 or 5.3 that a document requires expediting, the document will be run through the normal stamping process and will be placed in a REDEYE red interoffice mailer.

6.2   The name of the next recipient will be written on the outside of the REDEYE red mailer, and it will be hand-carried to the next person in line.

6.3   When a REDEYE red envelope is received, it should be processed immediately, the next name written on the envelope, and the envelope hand-carried to the next recipient.

response time to search requests has been almost instantaneous with a cathode-ray-tube terminal on a leased line. The system produces high-quality catalog cards, which are mailed to the city within a week from systems access. The cards are sorted by outlet (branch) and by category, where required (subject, author, title). The system is also a valuable research tool, and it provides holding data for all member libraries. A magnetic tape is generated at intervals and sent to the city, which indicates all the city's holdings. This tape is used as input to the circulation automation system.

Savings. Three typists and two aides have been reassigned to other duties. The response time of the cataloging process has shown marked improvement over the previous system, and the quality of the product, both in print quality and accuracy, has also been improved. The library staff has estimated the annual savings at approximately $25,000. On the basis of recent billings from OCLC, this is probably a conservative estimate. Furthermore, the transition has been very smooth.

Transferability. The Ohio College Library Center service is available throughout the United States. OCLC is a nonprofit organization. They will assist libraries in adopting their system and, in turn, can supply a variety of output products to meet individual requirements.

REDEYE System for Expediting Special Documents

REDEYE is a system for expediting contracts, agreements, and memoranda through necessary review and approval cycles. This simple system was developed by one of the authors when he was assistant city manager of Raleigh, North Carolina.

REDEYE has as its major attribute a bright red interoffice envelope with an accompanying routing slip. Instructions direct that the red envelope be hand-carried from one person to the next throughout the review and approval cycles. The standard procedure reproduced in Figure 13-1 outlines the major elements of the REDEYE system:

The REDEYE system was implemented in Raleigh and worked rather effectively in improving the time required to review and approve various documents. The system is quite simple and can be used by most jurisdictions that have similar needs.

14

Local Government
Orientation for Citizens—
A Systematic Approach

LOCAL governments are faced with the problem of informing
business and civic leaders and citizens about their various programs,
methods of operations, and financial and other constraints to
delivering services. This is particularly true now, because citizens
want both a greater voice in local decision making and improved
and increased services. Because most local governments are caught
in the cost-revenue squeeze, it is even more important for them
to "get the word out" about how things really are. In this chapter,
we use a course outline to describe a systematic procedure of one
medium-size local government—Raleigh, North Carolina—to educate business, civic, and citizen groups about how their local
government works.

Raleigh officials undertook a unique program, Local Government
Institutes,* to educate the citizens on how and why city government
works.

---

*James L. Mercer, "'Local Government Institute': Raleigh Citizens Learn How
Their Government Works," *Southern City*, December 1971.

The idea for the institutes was originally conceived by the Raleigh city manager and by the community services division of the Raleigh Chamber of Commerce. The Chamber of Commerce committee selected the participants for the first course; the assistant city manager for programming and budgeting prepared the course outline and did the scheduling; and various city administrators made the actual presentations.

In the first institute, 55 participants were selected by the chamber from a cross section of young community leaders. Included in the group were representatives from the Raleigh public schools; Shaw University; St. Augustine's College; North Carolina State University; banking institutions; and other business, industrial, and professional groups.

The course was divided into three phases. The first phase, a basic course on the total city operation, consisted of four two-hour sessions spread over a period of four weeks. The second phase consisted of seven two-hour sessions spread over a period of seven weeks. During this second phase, the 55 participants were divided into five groups and given in-depth training in five areas of municipal government: administration and finance; planning, engineering, and traffic; parks and recreation; public utilities and public works; and police and fire.

Phase three, consisting of one two-hour session, was devoted to techniques of public speaking and preparing presentations. The object of this phase was to prepare the participants to be speakers at various civic organizations and clubs throughout the community. The mayor then sent personal letters to each of the 250 or so organizations in the Raleigh area, informing them that guest speakers were available in five subject areas.

Several months after the first course, the second institute was conducted for about 50 participants who were selected by the Raleigh/Wake County League of Women Voters and by city staff members from a list of citizens who had expressed an interest in attending. In both courses, several new city staff members attended in order to learn about city operations. The second institute was changed in format because of what had been learned at the first course and also because the second group had expressed interests in different areas.

Additional institutes were tailored for special groups, such as the group of 50 Raleigh/Wake County School District Social Studies Teachers. The mayor presented certificates of completion to all participants who attended a majority of the sessions.

The institutes accomplished several objectives. First and foremost, they gave community leaders and citizens a much better understanding of the workings of their municipal government. After completing the institutes, citizens had a better appreciation of the problems, legal limitations, and financial constraints that Raleigh city officials face.

Second, the institutes enabled the city to tell its story in simple terms to interested civic clubs and organizations. City officials assisted the course participants to ensure that their talks were well prepared and that their presentations were factual.

Third, the course of instruction provided city administrators with an opportunity to do some of their own training and public speaking. In addition, city administrators had to review their organizations and operational functions and probably made them look at their operations with an eye toward improvement. The institutes also gave excellent training material to the city for its own personnel and for future institutes.

During the first institute, about 90 percent of the sessions were taped. These tapes were transcribed, and this manuscript was given to course participants at the beginning of later institutes. What follows is the course outline and instructor's guide for the first local government institute on basic municipal government in Raleigh. The foreword read as follows:

The purpose of the Local Government Institute and of this course in Basic Municipal Government is to help Raleigh citizens learn more about their City Government.

The objective of the institute is to provide local community leaders with sufficient informational data relative to local municipal government so that they, in turn, can make factual presentations on the subject to local civic clubs, business groups, professional organizations, etc.

The institute will be presented in three phases over a 12-week period (24 hours maximum of subject study) as follows:

Phase 1. Four 2-hour sessions—general basic municipal government— A familiarization course with the overall City Government operation.
Phase 2. Seven 2-hour sessions in study groups—in-depth municipal government in Raleigh (may be less than seven, but not more).
Phase 3. One 2-hour session—techniques of presentation preparation.

City officials will prepare and make the presentations in the first two phases. The Raleigh Chamber of Commerce will arrange for the presentations in the third phase. Selection of participants will be made by a Chamber of Commerce committee. Use of outside resources such as personnel and materials will be coordinated by the responsible city official making each presentation. A 10-minute break will generally be provided half-way through each session. Because of time constraints, it will be difficult to schedule question and answer sessions during the first phase. Therefore, participants will be asked to write down questions for discussion during the in-depth second phase. Each class session in the second phase will consist of approximately 1 hour and 40 minutes of lecture or discussion around the specified topic for the session. The remaining 10 minutes in the second phase will generally be spent in a question-and-answer period. Field trips may be used to acquaint participants with physical facilities of the City. This outline is to be used as a guide in the preparation and presentation of the course material for all three phases. All of the class sessions will be held in the City Council Chambers, Room 311, Raleigh Municipal Building, corner of Hargett and McDowell Streets, Raleigh. If it becomes necessary to change the meeting place, or time, the attendees will be notified by the instructor assigned for that particular session or by the Chamber of Commerce.

PHASE 1: Basic Municipal Government in Raleigh

General Basic Course
(Approximately 8 hours)

To the Instructor

The broad general Basic Municipal Government Course has been programmed to cover approximately 8 hours of instruction in four (4) two-hour sessions to be spread over a period of one month. While teaching this course, the instructors should follow the lesson plan outlined below:

Schedule—First Session—ADMINISTRATION AND PLANNING

Wednesday, September 22

3:00 PM to 3:10 PM—Introduction to the Course—Course Coordinator, Chamber of Commerce; President, Chamber of Commerce; and Mayor of the City of Raleigh

3:10 PM to 3:35 PM—Introduction to the Course; Council-Manager Plan and Relations; Management Team, Research and Information, Personnel, City Attorney and City Clerk and Treasurer Functions—City Manager

3:35 PM to 4:00 PM—Council Committees, Boards and Commissions and General Municipal Government in Raleigh—Assistant City Manager for Operations

4:00 PM to 4:10 PM—Break

4:10 PM to 5:00 PM—City Planning, Zoning, Subdivision Control and Annexation—Planning Director

Schedule—Second Session—Finance, Engineering, Traffic Engineering, Parks and Recreation

Wednesday, September 29

3:00 PM to 3:25 PM—Municipal Finance—Finance Director

3:25 PM to 3:40 PM—Municipal Engineering Functions—Chief Engineer

3:40 PM to 3:50 PM—Break

3:50 PM to 4:15 PM—Traffic Engineering Functions—City Traffic Engineer

4:15 PM to 4:40 PM—Park Planning, Acquisition, Development, Maintenance and Management—Director of Parks and Recreation

4:40 PM to 5:00 PM—Recreation Programs—Director of Parks and Recreation

Schedule—Third Session—PUBLIC WORKS AND PUBLIC UTILITIES

Wednesday, October 6

3:00 PM to 3:55 PM—Water and Sewer Plants and Systems—Director of Public Utilities

3:55 PM to 4:05 PM—Break

4:05 PM to 5:00 PM—Streets, Sanitation, Garage, Inspections, and Equipment Maintenance Depot—Director of Public Works

Schedule—Fourth Session—Police, Fire and Programming and Budgeting

Thursday, October 14

3:00 PM to 3:40 PM—Police Department Functions—Chief of Police

3:40 PM to 3:50 PM—Break

3:50 PM to 4:25 PM—Fire Department Functions—Fire Chief

4:25 PM to 4:45 PM—Budgeting Systems, Capital Improvements Program and Systems and Procedures—Assistant City Manager for Programming and Budgeting

4:45 PM to 4:55 PM—Review Session—Assistant City Manager for Programming and Budgeting

4:55 PM to 5:00 PM—Where do we go from here?—Coordinator, Chamber of Commerce

PHASE 2: Basic Municipal Government in Raleigh

In-Depth Course
(Approximately 14 hours)

To the Instructor

The In-Depth Municipal Government Course has been programmed to cover approximately 14 hours of instruction in no more than seven (7) two-hour sessions to be spread over a period of about two months. These sessions will be taught to small groups of about ten (10) persons each and are for the purpose of training the student in-depth about specific functional areas of City Government. Each group will have its own topic. Five different topics have been programmed necessitating five separate course formats. Whenever possible, the topic areas have been planned so as not to be presented at conflicting times and so that involvement in more than one topic is possible.

Group 1—Administration and Finance

Schedule—First Session

Friday, October 15—Council Chambers

10:00 AM to 10:15 AM—Introduction—City Manager

10:15 AM to 11:00 AM—Council-Manager Plan, History and Configuration in Raleigh and the Raleigh City Charter—City Manager

11:00 AM to 11:10 AM—Break

11:10 AM to 11:50 AM—Council-Manager Relations and the Role of the City Manager and the City Council—City Manager

11:50 AM to 12 noon—Question and Answer Session

Schedule—Second Session

Monday, October 18—Council Chambers

7:00 PM to 7:20 PM—Functions of the City Council Public Works Committee—Assistant City Manager—Operations

7:20 PM to 7:40 PM—Functions of the City Council Law and Finance Committee—Assistant City Manager for Programming and Budgeting

7:40 PM to 7:50 PM—Break

7:50 PM to 8:30 PM—Description and Functions of the Various City Council Boards, Committees and Commissions—City Manager

8:30 PM to 8:50 PM—Functions of the Raleigh Community Relations Committee—Executive Secretary RCRC

8:50 PM to 9:00 PM—Question and Answer Session

Schedule—Third Session

Monday, October 25—Council Chambers
    7:00 PM to 7:15 PM—City Clerk and Treasurer's Function—City Clerk and Treasurer
    7:15 PM to 8:00 PM—City Attorney's Office and Basic Municipal Law—City Attorney
    8:00 PM to 8:10 PM—Break
    8:10 PM to 8:35 PM—The Research and Public Information Office—Research and Public Information Officer
    8:35 PM to 8:50 PM—The Management Team Concept—Its Origin, Composition and Functions—City Manager
    8:50 PM to 9:00 PM—Question and Answer Session

Schedule—Fourth Session

Monday, November 1—Council Chambers
    7:00 PM to 7:20 PM—Intergovernmental Relations—Intergovernmental Relations Coordinator
    7:20 PM to 8:00 PM—General Municipal Government in Raleigh—The Operating Functions—Assistant City Manager—Operations
    8:00 PM to 8:10 PM—Break
    8:10 PM to 8:35 PM—The Personnel Office—Personnel Director
    8:35 PM to 8:50 PM—The Safety Program—Safety Coordinator
    8:50 PM to 9:00 PM—Question and Answer Session

Schedule—Fifth Session

Monday, November 8—Council Chambers
    7:00 PM to 7:40 PM—Municipal Finance—Finance Director
    7:40 PM to 8:00 PM—Accounting and Internal Auditing—Assistant Finance Director
    8:00 PM to 8:10 PM—Break
    8:10 PM to 8:30 PM—Municipal Purchasing—Purchasing Agent
    8:30 PM to 8:50 PM—Water Billing, Traffic Violations and Data Processing—Finance Director
    8:50 PM to 9:00 PM—Question and Answer Session

Schedule—Sixth Session

Monday, November 15—Room 424, Municipal Building
    7:00 PM to 7:20 PM—Annual and Five Year Operating Budgeting Systems—Assistant City Manager for Programming and Budgeting
    7:20 PM to 7:45 PM—Capital Improvements Program—Management, Budgeting, Program Planning and Control System—Assistant City Manager for Programming and Budgeting

7:45 PM to 8:00 PM—Citywide Systems and Procedures—Assistant City Manager for Programming and Budgeting

8:00 PM to 8:10 PM—Break

8:10 PM to 9:00 PM—General Review Session—City Manager, Assistant City Manager—Operations, Assistant City Manager for Programming and Budgeting

Schedule—Seventh Session

Monday, November 22—Council Chambers

7:00 PM to 9:00 PM—City/County Consolidation—Assistant Director, Institute of Government, University of North Carolina, Chapel Hill

Group 2—Planning, Engineering and Traffic

Schedule—First Session

Tuesday, October 19—Council Chambers

3:00 PM to 3:50 PM—City Central Engineering Functions—Chief Engineer

3:50 PM to 4:00 PM—Break

4:00 PM to 4:50 PM—City Central Engineering Functions—Chief Engineer

4:50 PM to 5:00 PM—Question and Answer Session

Schedule—Second Session

Wednesday, October 20—Council Chambers

3:00 PM to 3:15 PM—Introduction—City Manager

3:15 PM to 4:00 PM—City Planning—Planning Director

4:00 PM to 4:10 PM—Break

4:10 PM to 4:50 PM—City Planning—Planning Director

4:50 PM to 5:00 PM—Question and Answer Session

Schedule—Third Session

Wednesday, October 27—Council Chambers

3:00 PM to 3:50 PM—Subcontracting, Sidewalk Inspection, Coordination with N.C. State Highway Commission and Federal Highway Administration and other Engineering Functions—Chief Engineer

3:50 PM to 4:00 PM—Break

4:00 PM to 4:50 PM—Right of Way Functions—Right of Way Agent

4:50 PM to 5:00 PM—Question and Answer Session

Schedule—Fourth Session

Wednesday, November 3—Council Chambers

3:00 PM to 3:50 PM—Zoning—Planning Director

3:50 PM to 4:00 PM—Break

4:00 PM to 4:25 PM—Subdivision Control—Planning Director
4:25 PM to 4:50 PM—Annexation and Other Planning Department Functions—Planning Director
4:50 PM to 5:00 PM—Question and Answer Session

Schedule—Fifth Session

Thursday, November 11—Council Chambers
3:00 PM to 3:50 PM—Traffic Engineering Functions—City Traffic Engineer
3:50 PM to 4:00 PM—Break
4:00 PM to 4:50 PM—Traffic Engineering Functions—City Traffic Engineer
4:50 PM to 5:00 PM—Question and Answer Session

Schedule—Sixth Session

Wednesday, November 17—Council Chambers
3:00 PM to 5:00 PM—Tour and Explanation of Traffic Engineering Functions—City Traffic Engineer (Bus may need to be arranged for)

Schedule—Seventh Session

Wednesday, November 24—Council Chambers
3:00 PM to 4:00 PM—General Review Session—Planning Director, Chief Engineer and City Traffic Engineer

Group 3—Parks and Recreation
Schedule—First Session

Friday, October 15—Council Chambers
3:00 PM to 3:15 PM—Introduction—City Manager
3:15 PM to 3:50 PM—General Parks and Recreation Functions—Parks and Recreation Director
3:50 PM to 4:00 PM—Break
4:00 PM to 4:50 PM—General Parks and Recreation Functions and Relationship with Park and Recreation Advisory Commission—Parks and Recreation Director
4:50 PM to 5:00 PM—Question and Answer Session

Schedule—Second Session

Friday, October 22—Council Chambers
3:00 PM to 5:00 PM—General Parks Tour—Parks Superintendent (Bus will need to be arranged for)

Schedule—Third Session

Friday, October 29—Council Chambers
    3:00 PM to 3:50 PM—Recreation Programs—Recreation Superintendent
    3:50 PM to 4:00 PM—Break
    4:00 PM to 4:50 PM—Recreation Program—Recreation Superintendent
    4:50 PM to 5:00 PM—Question and Answer Session

Schedule—Fourth Session

Friday, November 5—Council Chambers
    3:00 PM to 3:50 PM—Parks Planning, Acquisition and Development—Parks and Recreation Director
    3:50 PM to 4:00 PM—Break
    4:00 PM to 4:50 PM—Park Planning, Acquisition and Development—Parks and Recreation Director
    4:50 PM to 5:00 PM—Question and Answer Session

Schedule—Fifth Session

Friday, November 12—Council Chambers
    3:00 PM to 5:00 PM—General Tour of Recreational Program—Recreation Superintendent (Bus will need to be arranged for)

Schedule—Sixth Session

Friday, November 19—Council Chambers
    3:00 PM to 4:00 PM—General Review Session *—Parks and Recreation Director, Park Superintendent, Recreation Superintendent
  * The possibility exists of adding a seventh session if the need arises.

Group 4—Public Utilities and Public Works

Schedule—First Session

Friday, October 15—Council Chambers
    1:00 PM to 1:15 PM—Introduction—City Manager
    1:15 PM to 2:00 PM—Water Supply, Treatment, Storage and Distribution Systems—Director of Public Utilities
    2:00 PM to 2:10 PM—Break
    2:10 PM to 2:50 PM—Continuation of Water Systems Discussion—Director of Public Utilities
    2:50 PM to 3:00 PM—Question and Answer Session

Schedule—Second Session

Friday, October 22—Council Chambers
>   1:00 PM to 2:00 PM—Waste Treatment Plant and Systems—Director
>   of Public Utilities
>   2:00 PM to 2:10 PM—Break
>   2:10 PM to 2:50 PM—Continuation of Waste Treatment System Dis-
>   cussion—Director of Public Utilities
>   2:50 PM to 3:00 PM—Question and Answer Session

Schedule—Third Session

Friday, October 29—Council Chambers
>   1:00 PM to 3:00 PM—Tour of Water and Waste Treatment Facilities—
>   Director of Public Utilities (Bus will need to be
>   arranged for)

Schedule—Fourth Session

Tuesday, November 9—Council Chambers
>   10:00 AM to 11:00 AM—Public Works Functions—Director of Public
>   Works
>   11:00 AM to 11:10 AM—Break
>   11:10 AM to 11:50 AM—Public Works Functions—Director of Public
>   Works
>   11:50 AM to 12:00 noon—Question and Answer Session

Schedule—Fifth Session

Friday, November 12
>   1:00 PM to 2:00 PM—Public Works Functions—Director of Public
>   Works
>   2:00 PM to 2:10 PM—Break
>   2:10 PM to 2:50 PM—Public Works Functions—Director of Public
>   Works
>   2:50 PM to 3:00 PM—Question and Answer Session

Schedule—Sixth Session

Friday, November 19
>   1:00 PM to 3:00 PM—Tour of Public Works Facilities (Sanitary Land-
>   fill, Shops, etc.)—Director of Public Works (Bus
>   will need to be arranged for)

Schedule—Seventh Session

Friday, November 26
>   1:00 PM to 2:00 PM—General Review Session—Director of Public
>   Utilities and Public Works

Group 5—Police and Fire

Schedule—First Session

Tuesday, October 19

    7:00 PM to 7:15 PM—Introduction—City Manager

    7:15 PM to 8:00 PM—Police Department—Uniform Division Functions—Major in Charge

    8:00 PM to 8:10 PM—Break

    8:10 PM to 8:50 PM—Continuation of Police Department—Uniform Division Functions—Major in Charge

    8:50 PM to 9:00 PM—Question and Answer Session

Schedule—Second Session

Tuesday, October 26

    3:00 PM to 4:00 PM—Police Department—Investigative Division Functions—Captain in Charge

    4:00 PM to 4:10 PM—Break

    4:10 PM to 4:50 PM—Continuation of Police Department Investigative Division Functions—Captain in Charge

    4:50 PM to 5:00 PM—Question and Answer Session

Schedule—Third Session

Tuesday, November 2

    3:00 PM to 4:00 PM—Police Department—Service Division Functions—Major in Charge

    4:00 PM to 4:10 PM—Break

    4:10 PM to 4:50 PM—Continuation of Police Department Service Division Functions—Major in Charge and Discussion of Other Police Department Functions—Lt. in Charge and Chief of Police

    4:50 PM to 5:00 PM—Question and Answer Session

Schedule—Fourth Session

Tuesday, November 9

    3:00 PM to 4:00 PM—Fire Department Functions—Fire Chief

    4:00 PM to 4:10 PM—Break

    4:10 PM to 4:50 PM—Continuation of Fire Department Functions—Fire Chief

    4:50 PM to 5:00 PM—Question and Answer Session

Schedule—Fifth Session

Tuesday, November 16

    3:00 PM to 4:00 PM—Fire Department Functions—Fire Chief

    4:00 PM to 4:10 PM—Break

    4:10 PM to 4:50 PM—Continuation of Fire Department Functions—Fire Chief

    4:50 PM to 5:00 PM—Question and Answer Session

Schedule—Sixth Session

Tuesday, November 23
>   3:00 PM to 5:00 PM—General Tour of Fire Department Facilities—Fire
>   Chief (Bus will need to be arranged for)

Schedule—Seventh Session

Friday, November 26
>   2:00 PM to 3:00 PM—General Review Session—Chief of Police, Police
>   Majors, Captains and Lt. and Fire Chief

PHASE 3: Techniques of Presentation Preparation

(Approximately 2 hours)

To the Instructor

The Techniques of Presentation Preparation Course has been programmed
to cover approximately 2 hours of instruction in one (1) two-hour session.
This session will be taught to the combined group of about fifty-five (55)
participants. The purpose of this session is to train the participants in
various techniques of presentation and delivery. When the participant
makes a presentation to a civic club or other group, he will have been
schooled in suggested techniques to assist in more effectively getting the
message across.

All Groups—Techniques of Presentation Preparation

Session Schedule

Tuesday, November 30—Council Chambers
>   3:00 PM to 4:00 PM—Techniques of Presentation Preparation—Direc-
>   tor of Information, Carolina Power and Light
>   Company—Film: "Unaccustomed As They Are"
>   4:00 PM to 4:10 PM—Break
>   4:10 PM to 4:40 PM—Discussion of Presentation Preparation Assis-
>   tance Available from City Departments—Plan-
>   ning Director and Research and Information
>   Officer
>   4:40 PM to 5:00 PM—Course Wrap-Up—City and Chamber Officials—
>   Included in this session will be completion of
>   a course critique sheet.

15

Gaining Systems Acceptance Internally

IF a management system is to be effective and if it is to be successful, employees must willingly accept it, support it, and use it. But in many organizations, some employees merely go along with the system because of top or middle management's commitment to it and because they do not wish to lose favor with "the boss." Others continue to fight the new system long after it has been implemented.

Resistance to a new management system, be it hardware, software, or both, may manifest itself in the following ways:

- Outright refusal to use the system—this is particularly true of data processing, word processing, and so forth.
- Conscious or unconscious avoidance of the system—assuming other methods continue to be available.
- Use of the system only when absolutely necessary or when forced to do so by management.
- Dumping the more difficult work onto the new system while assigning the easy work to the older method (assuming this type of activity relates to the particular system and that this option is still available).

Even more damaging to the system is the negativism that is often circulated via the informal organization or the grapevine. Employee car pools, coffee breaks, and office gossip often provide excellent opportunities to "bad mouth" the new approach.

Any new hardware, software, or mixed system, no matter how strong its foundation, must be nurtured in its early stages. Employee negativism in the early stages can leave long-term scars and in some cases can completely abort a new system. Moreover, negative attitudes can be so subtle that they are unnoticed until they have become dangerously powerful and disruptive. If resistance to a new management system is known or suspected, how can management overcome it?

Sheer force is one of the most ineffective techniques. Sometimes top and even middle management issues an edict that "the new system is here to stay, and all employees will use it and will give it their full support." In today's world of participative management, such an approach could do considerable harm.

If directives won't ensure acceptance of the new system, what will? Here are ten successful techniques that have proved particularly effective*:

1. *Assure top and middle management support.* Not only must top and middle management be behind the new system, they must be committed to its workability in the organization. Management support must make itself felt all the way up and down the line, in good periods as well as bad. Problems will occur during the implementation of a new management system, no matter how well the system is planned. Top and middle management must make a strong enough commitment to see it through the rough spots and onto firmer ground.

2. *Keep potential dissenters involved.* One of the best ways to overcome dissent and negativism is to involve the hostile camp in the activity being planned and implemented whenever possible. Request opinions and comments from nonsupporters with regard to possible improvements. People like to believe they are a part of the action and are contributing to the attainment of organizational objectives. If their advice is sought, outright or potential dissenters may feel obligated to adopt a wait-and-see attitude, if not one of wholehearted support. This technique must be applied early in

---

*This list is derived from J. L. Mercer, "The Second Sell," *Word Processing,* April 1973.

to be effective, must be followed throughout the implementation stages.

3. *Thoroughly explain the new system to dispel misconceptions.* People in organizations implementing new management systems approaches to operations or administration often fear they will lose their jobs or be unable to perform effectively under the new system. They frequently believe that they could work better in a "laissez-faire" or "country club" atmosphere but, in fact, they are usually much happier when they can see that they have done a full day's work for a full day's pay. Ensuring that all myths about the new system are dispelled quickly can be accomplished through frequent and widely disseminated status reports, as well as through orientations and question-and-answer sessions. When people fully understand a new system and its concepts and know that they will not lose their jobs—in fact, their jobs can be made easier as a result of the new system—hostility may be transformed into support.

4. *Build mutual trust.* The best way to accomplish this most difficult task is for system supporters to become *you*-oriented. Here are several approaches:

- Meeting with dissenters in their offices—on their home grounds, so to speak—to discuss various aspects of the system.
- Discussing *their* problems and requirements.
- Allaying *their* fears about the new system.
- Discussing *their* reasons for not using, or not planning to use, the new system.
- Doing a lot of *listening.*

5. *Make the system responsive.* This can be accomplished through:

- Quick turnaround—if this is an aspect of the system.
- Top-quality output—if this is an aspect of the system.
- Making the system easy to use.
- Making the system flexible enough to handle unusual requirements (peaks and valleys, rush work).

6. *Organize extra-system support activities to meet other needs more effectively than ever before.* This is one of the biggest bonus techniques of all. If the potential system users can be provided with excellent support from extra-system activities (activities outside those affected by the system itself), the new management

system will undoubtedly be hailed as a tremendous success by potential dissenters. This area deserves a lot of attention in the overall design and implementation phases of a new management system. Extra effort at the right time can result in a tremendous harvest of support when the going gets rough.

7. *Provide incentives to system users.* An awards program, such as a "user of the month" award (if appropriate to a given hardware or software system), may be very effective in building support for the system. If it becomes a status symbol to receive such an award, your goal has been accomplished. Even tongue-in-cheek awards can be helpful in developing competitive channels that will promote a new system.

8. *Build esprit de corps.* Team spirit should be built both inside and outside the arena of the new system, but probably what goes on inside is a prerequisite to outside activity. The main objective is to build an attitude of teamwork. A common goal is usually desirable, such as being the first in an organization to have or make the most or best use of a new management system, the best geographically, or part of a particular bureau or department. It helps if the new system manager is a master psychologist; such activity is akin to coaching an athletic team. Building team spirit is difficult, but look what it has done through the years for the Notre Dame football team and for the U.S. Marine Corps.

9. *Become truly service-motivated.* If the new system can do this effectively, it will have a long leg up on the ladder to success. In the case of an EDP or word processing system, the system supervisor and staff must develop a pleasant attitude of service to the total organization. It is difficult to argue with a friendly smile and willingness to go that extra mile. It is hard to keep this up during times of stress, but a positive attitude can eventually subdue the most hardened critics. This point is less applicable to software systems, such as budgeting and standard procedures.

10. *Never criticize the system yourself.* Even in jest or among your closest colleagues, don't be guilty of criticizing the system yourself. Privately or openly, there will be enough of this without the supporters of the system contributing to it. Be dedicated to the new system even though you may recognize that it has a few shortcomings. A positive attitude can be contagious.

Here are 17 strategies that can be valuable to those who are responsible for management systems development and implementation. This list was developed in a general discussion among the 27 scientists, engineers, Urban Technology System program staff, and consultants from Rensis Likert Associates, who are participating in the National Science Foundation-sponsored Urban Technology System program.*

1. *Listening.* Being an active listener (using such listening responses as I see; I understand) allows the other person to know you are focused on his or her problems. Limiting your own talking, asking questions, not offering solutions until you know the full extent of the problem, buys you more extensive information than a too-hasty response. Interrupting or arguing is distracting to you and the other party and tends to alter your tone of voice in a negative way. The problems may be old hat to you but are often unique and perplexing to the party seeking help. (NOTE: The tone of the conversation will be remembered long after the content is forgotten.)

2. *Doing seedwork for future projects.* Even if no specific project relationship is established now, you may wish to keep the door open for future involvement. By relating possible areas of mutual interest and gaining an awareness of department needs, you provide a channel of communication that can be used effectively at a later date.

3. *Visibility.* You won't be used if the group doesn't know you're around! Get the word out about what you're doing whenever possible. It keeps you in mind as a resource when problem solving must be done. As a person who has had the confidence of other departments and has been effective in resolving problems, you acquire credibility—it's called the "halo effect."

4. *Openness, honesty, trust building.* If you don't know the answer, say so. There is nothing more intimidating than working with someone who can "walk on water." Also, do your best to help find the answer. Keep your commitments. If you can't, share the reasons for not doing so. If you're approached in confidence, respect the person's judgment—he may know better than you that his job depends on your keeping quiet. If the information must be shared, get permission to do so first, or you'll soon enjoy the reputation of being a spy (or worse).

5. *Giving credit to others even if it's your own idea—especially in the media.* Except in rare instances, public sector personnel can use good coverage by the media more than you can. If the

*This material is based on "Notes from PTI Conference—Fort Worth, Texas, March 26, 1975," Summarized by Sandra S. Bauer, Rensis Likert Associates, Ann Arbor, Michigan, unpublished report.

voters feel "their man" is doing an effective job, he's more likely
to remain in office. By helping him, you make him your supporter.
When things get rough, it's nice to have someone in your corner
who has some clout. Get your sense of accomplishment through
implementation of projects. Do your crowing to and get your
back-patting from your colleagues—they'll probably be more appre-
ciative of the nuances anyway.

6. *Prompt positive feedback.* Nothing reinforces like having
someone appreciate your efforts—and the sooner the better. It
increases the chance that the behavior you exhibit gets repeated.
If they make a call, write the memo, or execute a needed change,
then let them know you appreciate it—it may need to be done
again. One note of thanks buys a lot more than ten gripes.

7. *Some people want you to take all the risks.* It may not seem
reasonable, but it is reality. Only you can decide if it's worth it.
Remember that ownership in some action tends to encourage
working toward a successful outcome. If at all possible, get people
to "buy in" and commit themselves. Realistically, the politics may
make it impossible, but try—all they can say is "no"!

8. *Relay sincere compliments publicly.* No one can ever get
enough honest praise. Usually only mistakes are noted, which tends
to reduce attempts at sensible risk taking. Liberal use of kudos
earns you a reputation of being able to share credit when it's
due—and the chance that the person being praised will perform
to your liking again.

9. *Observing protocol—"yes" and "no."* You must be the judge
of how formal the system is. Some people demand strict attention
to the pecking order. Others really don't care whom you consult
for information when it is necessary. But learn the system. It may
be weeks before you learn that the reason Mr. X won't see you
is because you asked Mr. Y instead of Ms. Z to set up an appointment.

10. *Implied power.* Even though you know that the chief administrative officer may never put his job on the line to back you,
it's nice if people think so. Being seen at lunch together, or in
a private conference, won't hurt the illusion that some of the top
man's clout is also yours. Don't ever be foolish enough to say it
does, and don't delude yourself into believing it's true when it's
not. In a political world, few know for sure and generally act
accordingly.

11. *Whose signature appears?* A corollary to #10 is to think
about who carries the most weight. Would they be willing to lend
their name—especially if it doesn't add to their workload or

responsibilities? Choose carefully. The grapevine knows who really is important and who isn't. It's probably better to choose someone who has staying power—the temporary appointee generally has less clout.

12. *Copies to . . . .* The person you send a copy to may not know or even care about a particular outcome. If they do care, so much the better. But if you need action, let people know that others with potential interest also know. It's a good motivator to action (and reaction), so choose your mailing list carefully.

13. *Win–win vs. win–lose.* Nobody wants to be a loser. Manage the situation so that everyone comes out with something positive. It buys you cooperation and has long-range benefits if you have to go back again for further assistance. The expectation is that you're all on the same side—not opponents, but a team working together.

14. *Share ownership.* It's amazing how tough it is for people to sabotage a project if they feel they are responsible for its being done in the first place. It has to do with resolving cognitive dissonance—If you've griped for years about doing things a better way, and someone finally gets around to saying, "OK, do it better, and I'll help you," then it becomes hard to refuse. Commitment, buying in, sharing ownership, whatever you call it, means taking responsibility for action. Once people accept responsibility, they're more inclined to help things go well.

15. *Working with line people.* Ultimately, the line people are the ones who "make you" or "break you," because they carry your ideas out on a day-to-day basis. Avoid their resentment or distrust by involving them, as soon as possible, in the project. Ask their opinions. Probably more than any other group, line people know the subtleties of their jobs and have information no one else has. Working the job with them is probably a very good idea—you'll gain more acceptance as "one of the guys" than as an expert imposing conditions from on high.

16. *Information sharing before taking action steps.* Surprises are not always fun. In fact, some are downright inconvenient. Be assured that people will let you know their displeasure with the latter kind. Give people a chance to voice objections and resolve issues early. It helps them take some "ownership" in the action to follow. Information sharing also helps you clarify in your own mind the fine points of the program. It may even bring up a few that eluded you altogether.

17. *Openness to alternative suggestions.* You may know a lot,

but do you really know it all? It's a fairer question than you might like to admit. Remaining objective and really tuning in to information shared by people involved in the system could provide a totally different direction to your efforts. If you can achieve the same results using suggestions from organization personnel, do so. They'll probably give you a freer hand when you really need to press for implementation of your solutions over theirs.

In addition to these suggestions, here are some dos and don'ts that may be of value to you if you are responsible for developing and implementing management systems in public sector organizations:

- Develop long-range and short-range objectives as well as plans for accomplishing them. Get the chief administrative officer to participate in developing them, and then stick to them.
- If your prior experience was in private industry, don't refer constantly to "how business would handle that" with your fellow workers.
- If you are new to the organization, acquaint yourself with the organization and form of government. Look for current joint programs of the city, county, and state governments. They may require technical coordination.
- Familiarize yourself with constraints of state law and county or municipal operations. Instances may arise in which state law expressly prohibits or reserves to another unit of government a particular activity you may recommend.
- Listen closely to department heads and experienced employees. Many have come up through the ranks and are familiar with the "real" world of problems you are attempting to solve. Their experience can be invaluable in arriving at a workable solution for a particular problem.
- Put things back into focus from time to time. In the hurry of everyday activities, it is not hard to lose sight of goals and objectives.
- You are a professional with a job to do. Do not get involved in local politics to the detriment of your basic objective.
- Keep up-to-date documentation on file. It is your best resource for information and your best protection in a crisis.
- Be practical. If you think it cannot be done, say so and why.
- Be quick to identify problems that require management systems approaches and follow them up through memos or phone calls.

- Keep an agenda for all meetings. Don't waste time in unstructured meetings.
- Don't try to give everyone equal attention. Some people will require more than others.
- Don't try to solve all problems yourself. Refer problems to the right people.
- Get help if you can't define the problem precisely.
- Measure your progress and evaluate your performance regularly.
- Develop a feeling for the local environment or atmosphere. Adapt to it. Don't be an outsider.
- You have a challenging job to do and a great deal to learn. Walk before you run. Take well-considered first steps that will help you build momentum.

16

What's Ahead?

THE previous fifteen chapters have introduced public management systems and have described how they can be applied to combat some of the current cost-revenue squeeze. The public management systems approach has been described in broad terms, and several chapters have been devoted to specific management systems.

The cost-revenue squeeze undoubtedly will be a part of the public manager's area of concentration for years to come. It may possibly worsen as costs continue to rise, as revenues become more difficult to obtain, and unless some practical management systems approaches are utilized to narrow the cost-revenue gap.

Many public sector managers are encountering barriers to their being more innovative in using the management systems approach. These barriers include: *

- An inadequate science and technology capability on the staffs of most public sector managers.
- A low level of investment in research and development aimed

---

* Ronald J. Philips, "A Proposal to Establish and Operate an Experimental Urban Technology Extension Service," Submitted to the National Science Foundation by Public Technology, Inc., April 16, 1973.

at meeting state and local needs, both by industry and by the federal government.

- Difficulty in getting state and local government views expressed in the setting of federal research and development priorities.
- An inadequate information exchange mechanism about successful innovations and management systems.
- Little useful knowledge about how innovation takes place in the nonfederal public sector.

In an effort to address these barriers, the federal government, specifically the National Science Foundation, funds several nonfederal public sector capacity-building programs to encourage innovation. Although most of these efforts apply to local governments, many spin-off benefits, particularly in terms of public management systems, are applicable to other elements of the nonfederal public sector.

Some of the ongoing efforts in this regard include the Urban Technology System, the Urban Consortium for Technology Initiatives, the California and Pacific Northwest Innovation Groups, and the Oklahoma State University and Auburn University Technology Transfer Programs. Specific discussions on two of the larger programs follow: the Urban Technology System and the Urban Consoritum for Technology Initiatives.

THE URBAN TECHNOLOGY SYSTEM

The Urban Technology System is a national experiment designed to develop local government's capacity to use modern technology. As mentioned earlier, many of these same benefits may be spun off to other elements of government in the nonfederal public sector. This is particularly true of improved public management systems approaches, especially those that stand alone or can be packaged for other organizations.

The Problem

As we have mentioned several times, public sector organizations are caught in a squeeze between soaring costs and soaring demands for more and better services. One obvious answer is for public sector organizations to apply the new technologies developed over the past several decades by industry and by the federal government. Obvious, perhaps, but this has not generally occurred. In addition to those barriers previously described, few rewards are given for being "first" in the public sector. If you succeed, you are a hero. If you fail, however, the consequences can be disastrous, because public managers operate in an open arena. What, then, can be done?

The Urban Technology System is a nationwide experiment designed to test mechanisms for overcoming those barriers, particularly in the local government segment. In the experiment, conducted by Public Technology, Inc., and funded by the National Science Foundation, a scientist or engineer spends three years on the staffs of 27 local governments across the United States. These technology agents are today's urban counterpart to the county agents who played such important roles in modernizing American agriculture.

Two years of planning took place before the agents were assigned to their posts in mid-1974. The cost of the five-year program, including a $4.3 million contract with the National Science Foundation, will total about $10 million (see Figure 16-1).

Relationship to Other Programs

The relationship of the Urban Technology System program to several other technology transfer efforts is shown in Figure 16-2.

Figure 16-1. Urban Technology System funding.

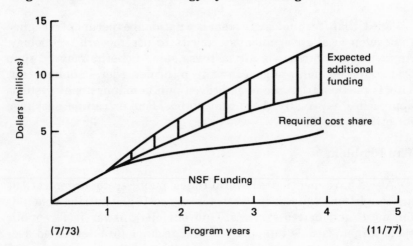

Figure 16-2. Relationship of Urban Technology System to other technology transfer programs.

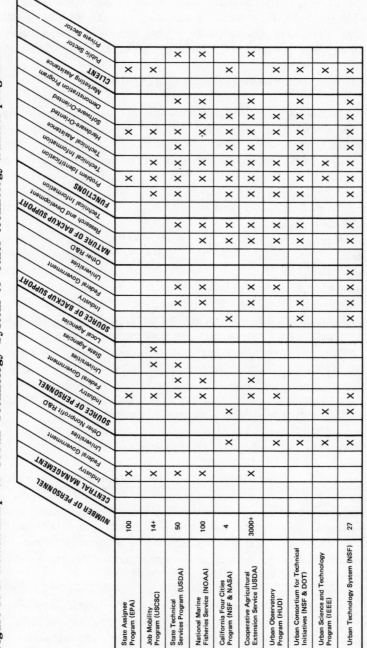

Relationship of urban technology system to other technology transfer programs

In general, the Urban Technology System program possesses attributes that go beyond some of the earlier efforts in technology transfer. Principal among these is the assignment of a full-time technology agent who is not tied to a specific private organization.

How the Urban Technology System Works

The technology agent is responsible to the local government's chief administrator, who gives him his day-to-day assignments. These assignments can cover the full range of local problems. In one case, the agent's first assignment was to investigate alternative fuels for a large fleet of municipal vehicles. In another case, the agent is modernizing the community's solid waste management system. In a third, the agent is installing a computerized financial management system.

In attacking a problem, the agent first identifies and defines the elements that appear to be amenable to technological approaches. Then he turns to a research and development organization that is assigned to help him solve problems.

The research and development organization may have the required technology or the ability to develop it. The problems of local government, however, are so diverse that the solution may only come from other sources. For example, the solution may be adapted from technology developed for other purposes, or it may involve a product already on the market, a product developed by industry to solve a problem, or a product that resulted from applied research in a university or government laboratory.

Participants in the Urban Technology System

The Urban Technology System is composed of a network of 27 participating communities, technology agents, research and development backup organizations, Public Technology, Inc., and the National Science Foundation. The National Science Foundation can use the results of the network to make recommendations about federal policy on research and development incentives to the nonfederal public sector. The participants are:

City and County Governments. The 27 governments were randomly chosen by a computer from a list of all cities and counties (those providing a full range of public services) with a 1970 population of between 50,000 and 500,000. Three factors were considered: location (six in the Northeast and seven each in the

Midwest, South, and West); size (nine each of populations ranging from 50,000 to 100,000, from 100,000 to 250,000, and from 250,000 to 500,000); and level of economic activity, as determined by federal revenue-sharing payments (nine each in the top, middle, and lower third on a per capita basis). Among the local governments participating are West Hartford, Conn.; Independence, Mo.; Atlanta, Ga.; and Pasadena, Calif.

Technology Agents. Selected through a nationwide recruiting campaign, the agents generally have a bachelor's degree in science, engineering, or computer sciences; a master's degree in business or public administration; and an average of ten years' experience involving a technological product or process. For the first two years, the agent is, in most cases, on Public Technology's payroll, with 90 percent of his salary (and all fringe benefits) paid by Public Technology through the National Science Foundation contract and 10 percent paid by the local government he is serving. In most cases, his salary is equivalent to that paid an assistant city manager. In the third year, the agent moves to the local payroll, although Public Technology will continue to pay 20 percent of his salary to permit him to work on matters relating to the experimental aspects of the Urban Technology System.

R&D organizations. The more than 15 organizations chosen to back up the network had to meet a number of requirements, including the ability to identify the technology needed to solve urban problems, a staff of at least 100 professionals, broad skills in science and engineering, an environment conducive to innovation, a primary group committed to spend at least 5 percent of its time on Urban Technology System problems, and a prior interest in solving urban problems. To determine if one type of backup organization might be as effective as another, universities, industrial research and development groups, nonprofit and not-for-profit institutes, and federal laboratories are included. To determine if the location of the backup organization affected an agent's performance, some were located within his metropolitan area, some within his state or region, and some beyond his state or region.

Public Technology, Inc. (See Chapter 13.) Public Technology, the research and development arm of six groups representing local and state governments, planned and developed the system and is responsible for its management and operation. Founded in 1971 as a nonprofit organization with the help of a Ford Foundation grant, Public Technology now relies for funding on dues from the 130 local governments subscribing to its services, as well as on foundation and federal grants and contracts. Its primary purpose is to bridge the gap between the producers of technology and its potential users in local and state governments.

National Science Foundation. Initial support for the Urban Technology System was provided by a contract with the National Science Foundation's Experimental Research and Development Incentives Program, which seeks to increase innovation and productivity in both the public and private sectors.

The objectives of the program are to determine:

1. The effectiveness of the Urban Technology System in increasing technological innovation.
2. Whether the system can aggregate the local government marketplace in order to stimulate private research and development investment.
3. Whether the system can accelerate the diffusion of innovation in local government.
4. Whether the system can assist the federal government in setting research and development priorities.
5. Whether the system can provide information on how innovation takes place in the nonfederal public sector.

Some of the key functions that the technology agent performs in the test site are:

1. Examine local problems and determine which are suitable for applications.
2. Formulate and help implement policies/procedures designed to maximize use of technological resources in solving local problems.
3. Serve as "point of entry" in test site for technical information developed through or utilized within the network.
4. Coordinate local technology transfer efforts.

The role of the technology agent is vital to the success or failure of the Urban Technology System during its very short experimental lifespan.

Experimental Data Collection, Analysis, and Presentation

Because the program is experimental, numerous provisions have been made for collecting, analyzing, and presenting to the National

Science Foundation data that are generated. Considerable data about the innovative climates in test sites and in the 27 control sites will be collected and compared. The 27 control sites have the same characteristics as the test sites, but they do not have the benefit of the Urban Technology System network.

In addition, each technology agent is required to maintain an engineer's log, in which he details attempted and successful innovations at the local level. Such items as increases in productivity resulting from specific actions taken by the technology agent are also recorded in the logs and in various other required reports.

Public Technology provides the National Science Foundation with additional data about test and backup site selection experience and other significant results so that it can determine whether or not the experiment has met its objectives. Because Public Technology is an integral part of the experiment, the National Science Foundation plans to select an outside objective evaluator for the entire experiment.

Problem Definitions and Solutions

Early in the operational phase of the program, all the technology agents worked with various city personnel to develop technological need or problem statements. Many of these needs were in the area of new or improved public management systems. The problem statements were presented to the technical backup sites to determine if the backup site could provide a solution within ten man-days or less (off-the-shelf solution) or if the solution would require greater resources. Some examples of "quick-response" solutions have included:

Noise measurement system.
Drainage planning.
Incinerator feed fouling corrective action.
Bus system cost analysis.
Computer system purchases.
Solid waste disposal system.
Vandalism prevention techniques.
System to remove roots from sewers.

The solutions to each of the above problems and others have been written up in Urban Technology System technical briefs and disseminated to other interested technology agents. At this writing,

115 briefs on a broad range of topics have been produced and distributed.

The technology agents developed and ranked some 250 high-priority problems that required more than a quick response from their backup sites. These problems or needs were submitted to the Urban Technology System's program office for aggregation. Definitive statements were developed for 36 of these high-priority needs, and federal agencies and private industries are funding some proposed solutions. An example of a funded, long-term solution that is currently operating in the network is described next.

Urban Planning Program

One high-priority problem involved the need for improved urban planning techniques. A multiphase program was presented to the Goddard Space Flight Center that called for the use of the LAND-SAT* spacecraft to assist some of the test sites in their planning activities. Recognizing the value of using the specialized skills of the technology agents and the replication potential of the network, the National Aeronautics and Space Administration contracted Public Technology to develop generalized solutions using LANDSAT data for land use decision making. Five test sites are taking an active part in this program, with one considered as the lead site. To demonstrate the system, a simple analysis was performed for each of the jurisdictions on a "real-time" basis. The project was completed in 1976. A final report will be issued by NASA to document the project and to comment on the applicability of LANDSAT data to urban planning problems.

Little Rock, Arkansas—Modernized Refuse Collection

For several years, Little Rock, Arkansas, had been plagued by labor unrest in its sanitation department. The unrest culminated in a strike in the summer of 1974, just as the technology agent started his three-year assignment with the city manager's office.

The two key issues in the strike were, first, the employees' right to receive and understand work information and to have some input into the decision-making process and, second, management's right to introduce new and more efficient technology, both

---

*LANDSAT (land satellite) is a NASA-developed spacecraft used to collect environmental data. Its precursor was called ERTS (earth resources technology satellite).

machines and methods. For several months, five new side-loading trucks sat idle, because the union balked at their one-man crews. At the time, Little Rock's 32 residential routes were served by rear-loading trucks with four-man crews.

New on the scene and not identified with either side of the long-standing dispute, the technology agent was able to serve as a mediator. He convinced the sanitation men that the new trucks made their work easier and that their jobs would be safe until they retired. Moreover, he impressed management with the need to improve communications to avoid future confrontations.

By late summer, the strike was settled, and the sanitation department was reorganized. One important element of the modernized approach was the city manager's decision to move from backyard to curbside refuse collection. To improve communications, management starts each day with a briefing and gripe session. The new trucks are in operation, resulting in better refuse collection, at a savings of more than $350,000 annually (see Table 16-1). The biggest savings is from reduced manpower costs, which result largely from the institution of curbside pickup service and from the new trucks. No workers have lost their jobs. However, a half dozen were placed in other city departments. The other reductions came from attrition—in the past, the department had had a high turnover rate. Savings in manpower will increase still more when Little Rock completes converting 18 of 32 street routes to side loaders. (Side loaders are not suitable for alley pickup, so rear loaders will have to continue to be used on the city's 14 alley routes.)

A route-rebalancing project currently being implemented will also mean reduced manpower costs. Little Rock uses the route completion incentive method, which permits crews to stop work when they have completed their routes, so it is important that routes be standardized, which will also provide substantial savings.

Table 16-1. Projected annual savings in operation of sanitation department in Little Rock, Arkansas.

Workforce and Maintenance	1974	1975 Budget	Cost Savings or Increase ($)
Sanitation drivers	38	40	+ 16,800
Sanitation laborers	131	76	−361,680
Truck maintenance costs	$53,600	$31,800	− 21,800
Total projected 1975 net savings			$ 366,680

Any workers displaced by the new procedures will be assigned to other city departments.

After one year of the reorganization, Little Rock could count more than just savings in dollars. It could also point to these impressive statistics:

Employee grievances. Down from ten a month to zero.
Absenteesim. Down from more than 20 percent to less than 5 percent.
Citizen complaints. Down from an average of 75 to 100 a day, to 5 to 7 a day.

Nashville, Tennessee, and Jersey City, New Jersey—Energy Conservation

The Nashville effort started in September 1974, when the Tennessee Valley Authority appealed to its customers to reduce voluntarily their electrical energy consumption by 20 percent. Threatened by steadily dwindling stockpiles of recoverable coal, the authority hoped that the voluntary program would avoid mandatory cutbacks and rolling blackouts, which could have a catastropic effect on Metropolitan Nashville, because almost two-thirds of the residential units are totally electric.

Metropolitan Nashville government's response was instituted by the mayor and was spearheaded by the technology agent and the Energy Crisis Advisory Committee chaired by a representative of the mayor's office. The technology agent tabulated the monthly electricity usage of all departments for the previous year. The reports were presented to department heads at a general meeting, and follow-up sessions helped each work out his conservation plan. Department heads were urged to examine work patterns and alter them to develop workable conservation programs that would not cut services. The technology agent and the committee did not dictate how electricity use should be cut. Monthly usage reports informed all departments of progress and so were an inherent incentive to reduce consumption. Weekly reports were required of each department listing specific actions taken, as well as long-term measures still in preliminary stages. In addition, the health, hospitals, social services, water and sewage, police, and fire departments evaluated their emergency backup capabilities and what effects rolling blackouts or mandatory cutbacks would have on their needs.

The Metro Nashville program used some of the methods that

have been used in other energy conservation efforts, including turning off lights when not in use; reducing illumination levels; disconnecting unused or unnecessary machinery, pumps, heaters, fans, and so forth; lowering thermostats to 65 and 68 degrees; changing janitorial work hours and habits; and eliminating decorative and outdoor flood lighting. In the first eight months of the program, these changes saved $175,000 over the same period of the previous year. In addition, highway and sign lights were cut off on controlled access interstate highways and expressways, and lights on main arteries were reduced by 50 percent. These changes meant a savings of $41,415 in the first eight months of the program.

Recognizing that Metro consumes less than 5 percent of Nashville's electrical energy, the Energy Crisis Advisory Committee encouraged a broad range of related activities in the community. The Chamber of Commerce implemented a countywide program for retailers. The local power company carried out a vigorous program to help customers reduce consumption, and new street lighting uses more efficient sodium vapor. Finally, Metro worked with civic groups and the news media to promote greater awareness of the need to conserve electrical energy.

The Nashville program revealed a number of points that may be of interest to other public sector organizations:

1. State and local laws are often not adequate to deal with energy shortages.
2. Electric distribution systems do not permit maintaining service to critical areas without providing equal service to surrounding customers with lower priority.
3. Many buildings have inadequate circuit control over individual areas, because it was cheaper to use more electricity than to provide individual switch controls.
4. Emergency generators and support equipment have not necessarily kept pace with new load demands.
5. Water and sewage services use 25 percent of the total Metro consumption but cannot reduce consumption, because pumps and motors are primarily demand systems.

Jersey City had a comprehensive energy conservation program that focused on three major areas: building operations, street lighting, and transportation. The technology agent reviewed systems to find ways to modify them and to save energy. Vehicle preventive maintenance programs, vehicle routing, and gasoline allocations are other areas of investigation.

In one phase of the program, the technology agent worked with one of the research and development organizations participating in the Urban Technology System to furnish technical backup. Together they used a boiler in a housing project to demonstrate that efficiency can be increased when a boiler is modified and properly adjusted. The improvements they recommended included automated breaching dampers, turbulator installation, modified secondary air dampers, and changes in operating procedures. The hardware items cost about $3,000 and, at current fuel prices, produce savings of $17,000 annually. Jersey City already had a full-time boiler repairman who was able to install the hardware, so installation costs were negligible.

Both the Nashville and the Jersey City experiences indicate that public sector organizations can reduce energy consumption without sacrificing service or incurring inconveniences to employees and citizens.

What Has Been the Overall Impact of the Urban Technology System?

To date, there is documented evidence that the Urban Technology System can be termed successful. Although the criteria for success may, at times, be quite subjective, and not broadly applicable to all the local governments involved in the program, the experiment has thus far provided aggregated cost savings and future cost avoidance well in excess of the total investment in it (federal, local, and other).

It is important to note that these savings have been calculated in terms of constant dollars and only for those jurisdictions in which innovations have been developed and implemented. Diffusion and adoption of the same or similar innovations throughout the entire Urban Technology System network would be expected to result in still larger savings to investment ratios.

One of the objectives of the experiment is to determine whether or not the Urban Technology System can accelerate the diffusion of innovation among local governments. A significant contribution toward this objective can be made through the replication of significant early innovations from one test site to another. Ongoing efforts in this area include communications among technology agents and by network telephone, extensive network reporting and other written communications, coordination meetings, dissemination of data about one test site's innovations to other test sites both on a routine and on a special-request basis, and technology agents' assistance to other test sites in implementing innovations. A grant recently approved by the National Science Foundation could further increase the replication of successful innovations.*

Unquestionably, the program has already made significant, positive improvements in the way local governments operate. Additional quantitative savings and qualitative benefits are expected to result as the program continues.

What the Urban Technology System Can Mean

Since the end of World War II, the technological output of U.S. research and development laboratories—both private and public—has been gargantuan. For the most part, however, this output has had little impact on local governments, despite the fact than an increasing number of local problems require technical knowledge if they are to be solved. The Urban Technology System program is an experimental approach to enhance the services of local governments. It is an approach that uses the advances of modern research, development, technology, and marketing; that uses scientists and engineers who recognize the technological aspects of problem areas; and that uses the participation of originators or developers of technological solutions to address both common and unique problems. The repertoire of usable management systems can certainly be strengthened through programs such as the Urban Technology System. Because participating local governments were randomly selected from a universe of some 378 medium-size, full-service jurisdictions, many of their successful efforts should be directly replicable in the remaining 351 jurisdictions, as well as in public sector organizations generally.

THE URBAN CONSORTIUM FOR TECHNOLOGY INITIATIVES†

While the Urban Technology System program addresses the needs of medium-size local governments, the Urban Consortium for Technology Initiatives is a capacity-building effort to serve

*James L. Mercer, "Proposed Research Program on Replication and Evaluation of Selected Innovations Developed within the Urban Technology System," Submitted to the National Science Foundation by Battelle Southern Operations, April 1977.

†Robert J. Havlick, "Urban Consortium for Technology Initiatives First Annual Report," Public Technology, Inc., Washington, D.C., 1976.

the technological needs of the nation's largest local governments. The participating jurisdictions are: Atlanta, GA; Baltimore, MD; Boston, MA; Chicago, IL; Cleveland, OH; Columbus, OH; Dade County, FL; Dallas, TX; Denver, CO; Detroit, MI; Hennepin County, MN; Houston, TX; Indianapolis, IN; Jacksonville, FL; Jefferson County, KY; Kansas City, MO; King County, WA; Los Angeles, CA; Maricopa County, AZ; Memphis, TN; Milwaukee, WI; New Orleans, LA; New York, NY; Philadelphia, PA; Phoenix, AZ; Pittsburgh, PA; St. Louis, MO; San Antonio, TX; San Diego, CA; San Diego County, CA; San Francisco, CA; San Jose, CA; Seattle, WA; and Washington, DC.

The concept of a consortium that would provide a mechanism for technology transfer to major urban jurisdictions originated in 1973 and 1974 during discussions between Public Technology and the elected and appointed representatives of several of the nation's largest cities and counties.

The discussions led to the creation of the Urban Consortium for Technology Initiatives. Each jurisdiction agreed to delegate an official to serve as its permanent representative. Delegates report directly to either the chief executive officer or to the chief elected official of their jurisdictions. The professional backgrounds of those selected vary widely, resulting in a broad spectrum of expertise and opinions.

Public Technology acts as secretariat to the Urban Consortium, which is comprised of 34 urban cities and counties that have populations of more than 500,000. According to 1970–71 Census Bureau figures, about 20 percent of the nation's population lives in the member jurisdictions, which have a combined annual purchasing power of more than $25 billion.

The Urban Consortium is designed to solve urban problems with existing technology and to encourage additional research for developing technologies specifically required by the participating jurisdictions. Many such technologies are in the areas of new or improved public management systems. Developing new technologies and applying existing technologies to urban problems require clearly identified needs and an awareness of the urgency involved in meeting each need. The Urban Consortium focuses on:

1. Formalizing the commitment of large urban governments to cooperative research and development efforts.
2. Mobilizing member jurisdictions to build a common urban-oriented research and development agenda.

3. Developing a consensus on research and priorities based on the deliberations and demands of the member jurisdictions.
4. Developing solutions to priority problems through the organization of broadly representative User Design Committees charged with the responsibility of seeing that the product or service being produced or transferred conforms to user requirements or specifications.
5. Encouraging federal and private investment in developing solutions to priority issues.
6. Developing a program for an information exchange system specifically designed to facilitate the transfer of technologies among member jurisdictions.

During 1975, the first year of operation, the Urban Consortium created a process whereby specific needs could be identified and prioritized by elected officials, senior public administrators, and supervisory officials from line and operating departments. The Urban Consortium developed a list of needs that later were categorized under general subjects such as transportation, energy, public safety, health, housing, economic development, and the environment. To accomplish this, member jurisdictions participated in several full membership and committee meetings throughout the year and cooperated in an extensive process of identifying needs.

The Urban Consortium was initially funded by the National Science Foundation, Research Applied to National Needs, and by the Office of the Assistant Secretary for Systems Development and Technology, Department of Transportation. Continuation funding has been expanded to include support from the Department of Housing and Urban Development and from the Environmental Protection Agency.

Organization of the Urban Consortium

Throughout the first year, the Urban Consortium developed its structure in such a way that flexibility for future tasks was ensured. While the full 34-member consortium is responsible for general policy, day-to-day operations are assigned to the Public Technology secretariat.

The Urban Consortium's first act was to choose an 11-member Steering Committee from among the member jurisdictions. This committee is responsible for organizing and appointing all consortium committees and subcommittees, reviewing all agenda items prior to submittal to the full consortium, and developing interim policy between meetings of the full consortium.

At the first meeting of the full consortium in October 1974, a seven-member Needs Committee was appointed to oversee the development of a needs survey of member jurisdictions. This survey became the major focus of the first year's effort. Task Forces, one for each major need category identified in the survey, were created on the basis of recommendations by the Needs Committee. During the second year, the Task Forces recommended which projects to pursue, each of which is to be organized by a User Design Committee. These committees establish detailed technical specifications for the product or method to be developed.

Task Forces and User Design Committees

The Task Forces, one for each of the needs categories, are structured to encourage interaction among private industry, the federal government, and the member jurisdictions. Each Task Force is composed of city–county and industry representatives. Member jurisdictions select those Task Forces on which they prefer to be represented.

The Task Forces initially focused on selecting highest-priority needs for research and development projects. Selections included projects that require new research as well as those that involve transferring technology from existing applications.

For each project selected by the Task Forces, a User Design Committee was appointed to determine the detailed technical specifications of the proposed methodologies or technologies. These technical groups are composed of specialists from both the private and the public sectors. A small staff has been assigned to each committee to prepare comprehensive working papers and resource surveys on each potential project. In those cases where further research and development are necessary, the committee's specifications outline a proposal and funding strategy.

In each situation where the research and development exists, the Public Technology secretariat staff, under the supervision of the User Design Committee, is responsible for developing transfer packages specifically tailored to each technology and its proposed applications. The packages essentially are how-to-do-it guides for local officials, which emphasize resources in the private sector, previous urban applications, and the cost and time involved in prospective projects.

Problem Identification

In order to develop a consensus on a research and development agenda, consortium members focused on defining problems and needs during the first program year. This process began with alternative methods of identifying and prioritizing needs being considered. The Needs Committee decided to use an open-ended process, allowing each member jurisdiction to describe its own needs rather than respond to a prepared list.

The Public Technology secretariat staff prepared a briefing package on the process to be followed when member jurisdictions submitted needs statements. An important element in the process was the participation of department heads and often of chief executive officers. More than 1,100 needs were submitted, with each jurisdiction ranking its needs. From these returns, 14 needs categories emerged. To ensure that the priority ratings were legitimate, the chief executive officer in each participating jurisdiction was required to attest to the fact that the first three priorities in each category were indicative of that jurisdiction's needs.

Later, the original 14 categories were synthesized into the following, each of which is being addressed by one of the Task Forces:

Community and Economic Development.
Environmental Services.
Energy.
Management, Finance, and Personnel.
Public Safety.
Urban Transportation.
Human Resources.
Health.
Public Works and Public Utilities.

The Urban Consortium's problem-identification process is significant, because it represents the first systematic statement of and approach to meeting the technological needs of large urban local governments.

Second-Year Efforts

Having achieved the major objectives of organization and needs identification established for its first year, the Urban Consortium then focused on responding to members' priorities through the Task Forces. Other specific second-year efforts included the following.

Identification of priority problems. Each Task Force identified 10 to 20 highest-priority needs for intensive analysis and data collection. Resource surveys on each need included a comprehensive search of the literature, contacts with key individuals and national organizations, identification of users and developers of effective technologies, and investigation of potential funding sources.

Development of technical specifications. The User Design Committees for selected projects completed the specification process on several projects. For some projects, preparation of transfer packages began.

Increased federal participation. The User Design Committees had a broad mix of institutional representation, thus assuring that specifications met not only the requirements of consortium members but also those of various concerned federal agencies. Among the consortium's long-range objectives is the extension of its relationship with the federal government to include a variety of agencies. These contacts could be the first steps in expanding the process of technology transfer to all federal research and development programs.

The Future Impact of the Urban Consortium

During the first year, the Urban Consortium for Technology Initiatives identified what the nation's largest cities and counties perceive as their most urgent needs and developed both a process and a structure for systematically addressing them.

The Urban Consortium has focused on bringing together federal policy makers, leaders of private industry, and the chief executives of the 34 participating jurisdictions to redirect the nation's considerable technological expertise to the shared needs of metropolitan areas.

In achieving its early objectives, the Urban Consortium emphasized the need for innovative problem identification. To benefit from expertise in every relevant field, the consortium is establishing contacts through the private and public sectors, including universities, research institutions, and manufacturing/business associations. By bringing together the previously compartmentalized groups of users, vendors, and researchers, the consortium creates the opportunity for maximizing the nation's technological potential and for solving many problems faced by the largest cities and counties.

Mayor Henry W. Maier of Milwaukee emphasized this theme at a consortium-sponsored meeting in Washington, D.C., for members of Congress, federal agency heads, and leaders of private industry. As cited by Havlick, Maier noted that urban cities and counties have been "captives of what has been a closed research and development system. We can only choose from what's on the market."*

In order to change the jurisdictions' role in shaping the technologies they can use from passive to active, the continued support of such federal agencies as the National Science Foundation and the Department of Transportation and the growing interest of a broad spectrum of private industry were required.

The Urban Consortium has provided the forum that has made the redirection possible and has stimulated the unity of the participating local governments. For the first time, Mayor Maier said, ". . . we are together. Although we come from the North and the South, the East and West, from older cities and newer cities, we are bound by a common need and a common goal."

The Urban Technology System and the Urban Consortium are two examples of nationwide efforts to bring the benefits of technology and management systems to bear on the cost-revenue squeeze that faces many public sector organizations. Other such mechanisms are being tested and applied on a state or regional basis. If they prove successful, it is possible that the federal government could sponsor a nationwide mechanism, similar to the Cooperative Agricultural Extension Service, to assist public administrators. The Energy Research and Development Administration is developing such an approach in the area of energy conservation.

THE MANAGEMENT SYSTEMS APPROACH: ITS FUTURE in the PUBLIC SECTOR

Simon Ramo, a leading U.S. scientist and industrialist, stated several years ago that "the public is ready for systems analysis." Dr. Ramo was apparently echoing what is being increasingly voiced in city halls, county courthouses, state capitols, and in Washington.

*Robert J. Havlick, ibid.

The concerned, voting general public is demanding more efficiency and economy from its governments. If the management systems approach that has worked so well in the private sector and in the federal government can be used to meet public needs, then it should be utilized and will probably be politically accepted.*

> It is doubtful if [management systems and] systems analysis can be successful in municipalities [and other public sector organizations] unless the policy makers and management of the . . . government remain involved in the process, lending the project their full support at all times. Perhaps, more than any other place, this strength of support and leadership will be tested when it comes time to accept and implement the recommendations of the systems analysis project. Systems analysis may lead to significant changes in the manner in which certain . . . government operations are administered. In governmental organizations— particularly on a state and local level—change presents problems. For those involved politically or professionally in local affairs, it is particularly difficult to withstand the pressures that will be brought to bear by those who oppose implementation of the change. Only by maintaining a continuous and close involvement in systems analysis from initiation to completion will management and policy boards be able to fully understand the significance and benefits of systems analysis project recommendations.†

> As an organic approach to a total problem, systems analysis is a natural evolvement in our efforts to cope with a rapidly changing, technological environment. "We now live in a global village . . . a simultaneous happening. . . . We must now know in advance the consequences of any policy or action, since the results are experienced without delay. Because of electric speed, we can no longer wait and see.‡

> While many municipalities [and other public sector organizations] may be reluctant to undertake major systems analysis at this time, as the management of urban/suburban America continues to grow in complexity, and local resources continue to become more clear, it is quite possible that public demand for more

*Anthony James Catanese, "The Systems Approach," *Municipal South*, June 1970, pp. 7–10.
†Myron E. Weiner, "Systems Analysis and Municipal Government," Institute of Public Service, The University of Connecticut, Storrs, Connecticut, 1969, pp. 27–28.
‡Marshall McLuhan and Quentin Fiore, *The Medium Is the Message* (New York: Bantam Books, 1968), p. 68.

effective, optimum delivery of municipal services will force local governments to take more serious consideration of this modern concept and its techniques.

If approached carefully, municipalities can begin to introduce the use of [management systems and] systems analysis on an incremental basis. Most of the talents necessary for utilizing this new technology reside in . . . governments either in the . . . government organization or in the community at large. Technical expertise can be acquired on a temporary basis if and when necessary. The initial prerequisites are the recognition that [management systems and] systems analysis can benefit the municipality [or other government]; the willingness to proceed to introduce it into . . . government. The initial step to be taken is educational in nature: educating municipal [and public] personnel on the concepts and techniques of systems analysis and learning to perceive problems that would be best solved by means of systems analysis. As talents, awareness and resources for systems analysis begin to accumulate . . ., it can be undertaken on a more significant basis and the benefits can then begin to be realized." *

There is little question that the management systems approach can be of real value to public sector managers. A problem that exists with many managers, however, is that their educational backgrounds did not prepare them to utilize this approach effectively. In this regard, a recent effort is underway in many schools and colleges of public administration which, among other things, should help strengthen this area with new students. It is hoped that texts such as this one will help bridge a portion of the gap with practicing public sector managers.

Work by Dr. Rensis Likert at the University of Michigan has suggested that before positive change or innovation can occur, the organizational climate must be receptive to it. Undoubtedly the key to this is how the manager handles the "people" aspect of a new or revised management systems approach. Dr. Edgar G. Williams, Graduate School of Business, Indiana University has said, "People can make any change work if they want it to work. The key to successful, orderly, planned change lies in the systems manager's understanding of human behavior—individually or collectively." †

*Myron E. Weiner, pp. 27–28.
†Edgar G., Williams, "Changing Systems and Behavior: People's Perspective on Prospective Changes," *Business Horizons,* August 1969, pp. 53–57.

Experience in the aerospace industry relative to innovation incorporates the need for motivation to innovate:

> Motivation to innovate, to adopt a new management concept or technique, may result from a change in leadership, with an accompanying injection of new energy or ambition. Or it may come from a newly perceived opportunity to accomplish personal or organizational ambitions—political advantage or public service, profit or cost saving, personal advancement or recognition.*

Whatever the reason for innovation or adoption of better management systems, it is clear that public sector managers should pursue this approach in the future in an effort to alleviate the impact of the cost-revenue squeeze on their public sector organizations.

*Gordon Milliken and Edward J. Morrison, "Aerospace Management Techniques: Commercial and Governmental Applications," A report prepared for the National Aeronautics and Space Administration by Denver Research Institute, November 1971, p. 192.

INDEX